W9-CDK-992

"Especially useful . . . to help students . . . in actual human decision-making."—Harvey Cox, professor of divinity, Harvard University, author of *Many Mansions* and *The Secular City*

"An important book for advertising and marketing professionals."—Bruce Crawford, president and CEO, Omnicon, Inc.

"Move over, Garp! This is the world according to Hunter Lewis. . . . He dares to make common sense of our era's intellectual and moral confusion. Audacious yet user-friendly." —Robert K. Emerson, executive editor, *Manhattan, Inc.*

"A highly stimulating guide to . . . the complex, slippery, shifting value sets of real people. This book is the product of a spritely and integrative mind; the distillation of a lifetime of careful reading and thought."—John B. Stephenson, president, Berea College, Berea, Kentucky

"For Hunter Lewis, this book has obviously been a life-long journey of discovery. His lucid writing lets the reader share his insights on an intimate, one-to-one basis."—Samuel L. Hayes III, Jacob Schiff Professor of Investment Banking, Harvard Business School

"With remarkable perspicacity and skill, Hunter Lewis provides a convincing framework of values. . . . His analysis is objective, non-partisan, wide-ranging, current, concrete, and lucid. For general readers this work will prove lively and illuminating; for undergraduates it will be a godsend and an ideal introduction to this vital subject."—Edgar F. Shannon, president emeritus and professor of English emeritus, University of Virginia

"Lewis provides a sweeping perspective on ethical systems in plain language and with a sparkling style. This book can make a real difference in how one approaches ethical problems." —William F. Massy, vice president for finance and professor of education and business administration, Stanford University

A Question of Values

A Question of Values

SIX WAYS WE MAKE THE PERSONAL
CHOICES THAT SHAPE OUR LIVES

Hunter Lewis

HarperSanFrancisco

A Division of HarperCollins*Publishers*

A QUESTION OF VALUES: *Six Ways We Make the Personal Choices That Shape Our Lives.* Copyright © 1990 by Hunter Lewis. All rights reserved. Printed in the United States of America. No part of this book may be used or reproduced in any manner whatsoever without written permission except in the case of brief quotations embodied in critical articles and reviews. For information address HarperCollins Publishers, 10 East 53rd Street, New York, NY 10022.

FIRST HARPERCOLLINS PAPERBACK EDITION PUBLISHED IN 1991.

Library of Congress Cataloging-in-Publication Data

Lewis, Hunter.
    A question of values : six ways we make the personal choices that shape our lives / Hunter Lewis — 1st HarperCollins pbk. ed.
        p.   cm.
    Includes bibliographical references and index.
    ISBN 0-06-250532-7 (alk. paper)
    1. Values. 2. Decision-making. I. Title.
[BD232.L48   1991]
170—dc20   90-56471
                                                                CIP

91 92 93 94 95 MAL 10 9 8 7 6 5 4 3 2

This book is dedicated to the memory of Walter Lippmann, who assisted me when I was a young journalist still in school and whose own work (especially *A Preface to Morals*) is so central to the study of twentieth-century values.

Contents

Foreword by M. Scott Peck   ix

Acknowledgments   xiii

Part One: A Question of Values: An Introduction   1

1. The Initial Question   3

2. Sorting It Out: Six Ways We Choose Values   6

Part Two: Six Basic Types of Value Systems   21

3. Value Systems Based on Authority   23

4. Value Systems Based on Logic   38

5. Value Systems Based on Sense Experience   53

6. Value Systems Based on Emotion   86

7. Value Systems Based on Intuition   98

8. Value Systems Based on "Science"   109

Part Three: Variations on a Theme   133

9. The Cross-Fertilization of Values   135

10. Four Examples: Karl Barth, Albert Einstein, Mohandas Gandhi, Golda Meir   142

11. Why Values Get So Complicated   158

Part Four: Using the Framework 165

12. A Moral Detective Story   167

13. Values in the Classroom   175

14. A Personal Note   185

Epilogue: Values in the Classroom Continued   189

How to Read This Book   257

Sources   265

Index   269

Foreword

A century ago, the greatest dangers we faced arose from agents outside ourselves: microbes, flood and famine, wolves in the forest at night. Today the greatest dangers—war, pollution, starvation—have their source in our own motives and sentiments: greed and hostility, carelessness and arrogance, narcissism and nationalism. The study of values might once have been a matter of primarily individual concern and deliberation as to how best to lead the "good life." Today it is a matter of collective human survival. If we identify the study of values as a branch of philosophy, then the time has arrived for all women and men to become philosophers—or else.

What do theologians mean when they say that we human beings are "created in the image of God"? My own understanding of this is that we human creatures have been given free will, the extraordinary power of choice. But the power to choose is the power to choose the bad or the good; to be loving *or* unscrupulously self-centered. What is the nature of this power? What motivates our choices?

There is mystery here. But there is also some clarity. It is clear, for instance, that a great many humans of many different races, cultures, and nationalities are very strongly motivated by money. Indeed, it is so clear I think it would be quite safe to refer to the human species as *Homo economicus*. But economically motivated acts are not necessarily good acts. Often they are obviously malicious and sometimes downright murderous. If we cannot routinely learn to submit the personal profit motive, when appropriate, to higher principles, then we are in all likelihood—and probably quite quickly—going to murder ourselves off. Such higher principles are matters of values or, as philosophers say, matters of ethics. For our species to be truly *Homo sapiens*, that is, wise enough to figure out how to survive, then it will not be enough for us to remain merely *Homo economicus*; we must somehow become *Homo ethicus*.

So this is hardly an arcane subject; it is a life-and-death matter. And not one that admits a quick and easy, simplistic solution. I mentioned that there is mystery here. Were there not, philosophers would long ago have closed the book on the subject. Indeed, the subject is so grand that no one book, no one author, could possibly address it exhaustively.

But that doesn't mean the frontiers of our understanding cannot be expanded. To the contrary, I hope I have made it clear that we desperately need to do so. Nor does it mean that any one probe into the mystery is going to be as worthy as any other. The subject deserves all that can possibly be brought to it in the way of clarity of thought and language, brilliance of insight, and rigor of discipline.

Although it cannot cover everything, this is a groundbreaking book. It is also an enlightening, thought-provoking, and remarkably well-written book. In it the author compellingly makes the case, through a breadth of erudition that is to all intents and purposes a kind of tour de force, that we human beings have at least six profoundly different cognitive lenses through which we view the world, and hence profoundly different styles of thinking by which we make our value judgments, our ethical decisions.

Why should such an elucidation be of groundbreaking significance? Just this: Ethical behavior is, of necessity, conscious behavior. If we are unconscious of our motives, it is unlikely that we will behave in a consistently ethical manner. If we are not *aware* of the particular lens through which we are looking at the world, then we do not have any true choice about what we are going to see and how we are going to respond.

In this work, Hunter Lewis makes us aware—conscious—not only of our own lenses, but also of a range of different lenses. There are two results. One is to make it possible for us to question the validity of our perceptions and values. The capacity for ethical behavior is dependent on the capacity for such self-questioning. Virtually all of the evil in this world is committed by people who are absolutely certain they know what they are doing.

The other result is that it enables us to make multidimensional rather than one-dimensional simplistic decisions. If we think just logically or just emotionally or just intuitively, then our decisions will be only logical or only intuitive or only emotional. But if we become aware of the variety of different cognitive styles, it opens up the possibility for us to make decisions that are emotional *and* logical *and* intuitive. In other words, such consciousness makes it possible for us to *integrate* different ways of knowing; to think, so to speak, with both our right brain and our left brain.

I believe such integration to be essential to our collective salvation. The noun *integrity* is derived from the verb *to integrate*. If we are going to think and behave with full integrity, then we must learn how to integrate our different ways of perceiving the world so as to develop a multidimensional, integrated world view. To behave ethically is to behave with integrity. In raising our consciousness of the different styles by which we make our value judgments, this important book points us toward greater wholeness and integrity.

—M. Scott Peck

Acknowledgments

I am much indebted to the following individuals: Henry Rosovsky, who designed Harvard's current core curriculum, an important new direction for American higher education that, among other things, requires undergraduates to take courses on values, and that directly inspired this book; Joe Kanon and Bill McPherson, who read the manuscript and generously offered their ideas; Kathleen Chabra, who was unstinting in providing ideas and assistance at every turn; and Tom Grady, my editor at Harper & Row, whose quietly thoughtful and penetrating observations were simply invaluable.

Part One

A QUESTION
OF VALUES:
AN INTRODUCTION

1. The Initial Question

An objective observer, a proverbial Martian visiting this country for the first time, would be struck, not by the unity, but by the unexpectedness, the almost madcap diversity, and the quarrelsomeness of American values. To illustrate this point, one need only pick up a newspaper or switch on a television set. The unexpectedness, for example:

• A wealthy young society hostess in Greenwich, Connecticut, tells a reporter that the dinner parties she is organizing, hosted by the most socially prominent families at their opulent private estates as a benefit for the local Boys' Club, will undoubtedly be a success, because God is "cochairing" the event with her.

• A television series teaches English grammar by using music videos (lyrics flashed on the screen as subtitles contain the instruction). The program devoted to pronouns shows a hot young man, cut to a variety of longing girlfriends, cut back to the young man singing vehemently against the "self-denial we've been sold," cut to a sultry young woman singing "Baby, take me home," cut to more young couples eyeing each other seductively. The series is designed for children and run on public television stations.

• A New Jersey businessman opens a pizza parlor called "Pie in the Sky" with a pink neon sign flashing a verse from Exodus and delivery boxes emblazoned with other biblical messages. The proprietor prays daily with his corporate prayer "consultant": "[In addition to asking for insight] I pray for cash, I ask [the consultant] to pray for cash, and it comes in."

In addition to the unexpectedness, the diversity:

• Country singer Willie Nelson is described by friends as a "Baptist Buddhist."

• A pseudononymous member of a Catholic order describes herself to a reporter as a "practicing Zen, Catholic, lesbian, feminist nun."

• A very different kind of nun, Anne Brooks, is cured of the rheumatoid arthritis that kept her on crutches or in a wheel-chair for seventeen years, studies medicine, and then moves to an isolated county of rural Mississippi to provide the only local health care for the (mostly poor and black) families there. She lives in a dilapidated rented cottage, her bed is a board and mattress perched on cinder blocks, and her chief form of relaxation is listening to a few Mozart tapes before retiring after a twelve-or-more-hour work day.

In addition to the unexpectedness and diversity, the sheer quarrelsomeness:

• Howard Phillips, chairman of the Conservative Caucus, Inc., thinks that the American social and political system is the hope of the world. Yet another "conservative," Saul Bellow, the Nobel laureate novelist from Chicago, indirectly responds by stating on national television that "the [excess of liberty] in American culture is as serious as the deprivation of liberty in the Soviet Union."

• Richard Cohen, a *Washington Post* columnist, argues that President Reagan's decision not to appoint an acknowledged homosexual to the federal government's AIDS commission (a decision later reversed) is "akin to denying Jews a place on the Holocaust commission." Howard Phillips replies that it is "blasphemous" to suggest that the practice of homosexuality is analogous to adherence to Judaism.

Cohen and Phillips battle again on the increasing role of religion in politics. Cohen: "[Politicians seem] now to attend church with a vengeance . . . [but] when it comes to safeguarding civil liberties and ensuring progressive and fair social policies, I would rather take my chances with your average atheist."

• A *Village Voice* reporter in New York blasts the producers of a sex education film because the featured testimony of a former teenage mother ("Let me just say, sex wasn't that great, it really wasn't. I mean, I thought, oh my God, this is what they've been trying to keep me away from?") represents an evil attempt to "preempt" the "sexuality" of ten-year-olds.

Confronted with the unexpectedness, diversity, and quarrelsomeness of American values, with the apparent lack of any real agreement or uniformity in our personal beliefs, the beliefs that guide our everyday speech and conduct and make us what we are, how should we respond? Should we dismiss values as a muddle, a chaos, a Babel that is impossible to make sense of? It would be easy to draw this conclusion, but it would be wrong. Values are *not* the muddle they sometimes seem. There *are* some basic choices, some uniform options that we are all faced with. Our challenge as Americans and as human beings is to identify these options and then to choose among them, not blindly but with a discerning, understanding eye, and thus to answer the recurring biblical question: "What manner of men shall we be?"

2. Sorting It Out: Six Ways We Choose Values

How do we construct a framework in which our most basic value choices can be defined, compared, contrasted, and evaluated? One way to begin is to ask people directly about their values. Assuming that confidentiality is guaranteed and people tell us what they truly believe, we can then go about sorting and categorizing those beliefs. Of course, individual A may think like B in one respect, like C in another, like D in another. In other ways B may be more like D, C like A, and otherwise all four may be quite different.

If we give up on the idea of simply asking people to talk about their values, we might instead try a "scientific" poll. Assuming that we avoid the obvious pitfall of oversimplified, vague, or subjective questions, a "scientific" poll of several thousand people, all given the same questions in exactly the same way, should give us what we need: "hard, factual" information on which to build. On the other hand, poll responses depend very much on the specific questions asked (slight variations in phrasing a question elicit entirely different answers), and how can we possibly know what questions to ask? It's the old riddle "which came first—the chicken or the egg?" We cannot know the right questions to ask without some kind of framework, but we are asking the questions in the first place in order to develop a framework!*

Fortunately, there are other ways to proceed. We might, for example, try to stand back, get some detachment from the hurly-burly of what people say and do, focus instead on some of the simplest, most basic questions about values, beginning with what values are, and see where these questions and answers lead us:

What are values?

The term *values* is a relatively recent one and is sometimes dismissed (for example, by philosopher Allan Bloom) as a piece of barbarous jargon. But everyone uses it—people in everyday life, journalists, politicians. Presidential candidates now campaign by telling crowds, "I share your values," and the general secretary of the Soviet Communist party tells an American president, "We do not need anybody else's values." Although the term values is often used loosely, it should be synonymous with personal beliefs, especially personal beliefs about the "good," the "just," and the "beautiful," personal beliefs that propel us to action, to a particular kind of behavior and life. If one "values" the message of Christ, one will try to "love one's neighbor as oneself."

But do values, in the sense of freely chosen values, truly exist? Aren't human beings driven by inherited instincts, instincts that we like to dress up with the fancy term *values*, so that we can pretend there is a measure of choice in the process, when it's really all programmed into our genes?

---

* The limitations of polling techniques for determining people's values can be seen in a famous study by the Stanford Research Institute of 2,713 demographically representative Americans, each of whom was led through a gargantuan 800-part questionnaire by a professional staff. The resulting nine "value" categories in which Americans were deemed to fall proved to be suspiciously subjective ("Integrateds: have a kind of inner completeness") and judgmental ("Emulators: seem in some sense to lead hollow lives").

This is a complicated subject, but there is plenty of evidence that human beings are not primarily driven by genetically determined instincts but are rather free to make their own choices. For example, self-preservation and sexual drives are often cited as among the most gripping human "instincts." Yet in medieval and even modern Japan, among other cultures, personal beliefs about correct behavior commonly lead to ritual suicide, and in Tibet before the Chinese invasion a substantial percentage of the population chose to live celibately in monasteries. Given these rather large-scale exceptions, self-preservation and sex cannot be instincts in the same sense of the word that we apply to animals. Even if one defines the term *instinct* loosely, it is unarguable that freely chosen values supplement (if they do not completely supplant) instinct as the driving force within human beings, and that without values human behavior is directionless, chaotic, and ultimately self-destructive.

Assuming that human beings are not directly controlled by hereditary instincts, aren't our values nevertheless determined by our personalities, which are in turn largely shaped by our genes?

Whether our personalities are largely shaped by genes, by our childhood experiences, or by a varying combination of the two factors is highly uncertain. For our purposes it hardly matters, because personal beliefs and personality traits are inherently different, not the same thing at all. It may be interesting and useful, following in the footsteps of the great psychologist Carl Jung, to speak of "introverts" versus "extroverts," but it will not tell you whether your highly extroverted spouse is more or less likely to become a born-again Christian. Personal values are beliefs, not personality traits, and no matter how interconnected beliefs and personality traits may be, an effort to analyze the former solely in terms of the latter is certain to fail.*

---

* The relationship between values and personality is one of the many interesting questions that this book will not attempt to address, except to reiterate that values are beliefs and that values and personality are both distinct and interrelated.

Perhaps we are not simply the sum of our inherited urges, whether inherited instincts or personality traits. But aren't we still controlled by peer pressure, by the relentless demands of the society in which we happen to live?

The proposition that individual human beings are programmed into their values, not by their genes but by social pressures, can neither be proven nor refuted. It all depends on how one defines words like *control* and *freedom*, and many semanticists argue that such words are indefinable.* Because this debate is irresolvable, and because most Americans feel entirely "free" to form and express their personal beliefs, even if they do not always feel free to act on those beliefs, it seems reasonable to make a simplifying assumption in favor of individual human choice and freedom.

If values are freely chosen personal beliefs, how do we arrive at these beliefs?

This is the key question. Let's first ask ourselves how we come to believe anything. Think of something that you believe to be true: Your eyes are brown; the earth is round; Jesus was resurrected from the dead. Make a list of such beliefs and then ask yourself: Why do I believe this? How do I know it? If you reflect carefully, you will see that there are only a very few ways that we "know" anything. For Jesus' resurrection, we rely on authority—the authority of Church and Bible—or we refuse to rely on this authority. For the flatness of the earth, we also rely on authority, the authority of scientists, although we could duplicate their experiments, in which case we would be relying on science. For the color of our eyes, we rely on observation (direct sense experience), and so on. What eventually becomes clear is that there are only six ways that we "believe" or "know" anything, and these may be summarized as follows:

---

* It is possible, of course, to define *freedom* in a specific, and especially in a relative, context—"I need more freedom than this job, marriage, or country allows"—but it is difficult if not impossible in a broader, more abstract and absolute context.

SIX WAYS WE CHOOSE VALUES

Mode by which we arrive at knowledge	Explanation	Summary
1. Authority	Taking someone else's word, having faith in an external authority. For example, having faith in church or Bible.	I have faith in the authority of . . .
2. Deductive logic	Subjecting beliefs to the variety of consistency tests that underlie deductive reasoning.	Since A is true, B must be true, because B follows from A.
3. Sense experience	Gaining direct knowledge through our own five senses.	I know it's true because I saw it, I heard it, I tasted it, I smelled it, or I touched it myself.
4. Emotion	Feeling that something is right: Although we do not usually associate feeling with thinking or judging, we actually "think" and "judge" through our emotions all the time.	I feel that this is true.
5. Intuition	Unconscious thinking that is not emotional. Think of the mind as if it were in three parts: the conscious mind; the emotions (hypothalamus or primitive brain); and the unconscious-but-not-emotive intuitive mind. Both the	After struggling with this problem all day, I went to bed confused and exhausted. The next morning, as I awakened, the solution came to me in a flash and I just knew it was true.

conscious mind and the unconscious-intuitive mind are highly sophisticated, but the unconscious-intuitive mind is much more powerful than the conscious mind, just as a supercomputer is more powerful than a microcomputer. Hence most creative discoveries are intuitively derived, and only later "dressed up" by logic, observation, or some other conscious technique.

6. "Science"

A synthetic technique that relies on sense experience to collect the observable facts; intuition to develop a testable hypothesis about the facts; logic to develop the test (experiment); and sense experience again to complete the test.

I tested the hypothesis experimentally and found that it was true.

These six modes not only describe how we think about things in general, they also describe how we develop and choose values. Some value systems are based on authority; others are based on deductive logic, sense experience, emotion, intuition, or science. Over the centuries, for example, Christianity has often been associated with authority, although it makes a strong emotional, intuitive, and logical appeal as well. Political candidates' frequently professed values of "family and neighborhood" are mostly emotional, and so on. All values and value systems may be defined in these terms, as the remainder of this book will attempt to demonstrate. This may not be the only way to organize and categorize what is otherwise a chaotic maelstrom of unrelated personal beliefs but, in contrast to previous frameworks, it does represent the beginning of a workable approach, one that can be used to distinguish, separate, compare, and contrast so that people better understand the choices they face.

Where did these six modes or techniques of moral reasoning come from? Did the author just dream them up?

Authority, deductive logic, sense experience, emotion, intuition, and science are all familiar concepts, familiar tools, part of everyone's world. Although we may not consciously focus on these six modes of reasoning, perhaps because they are so familiar, we use them constantly.*

Are these six modes of moral reasoning truly complete? Aren't there others?

---

* There is admittedly a paradox here. We have already stated that *all* human knowledge — moral or otherwise — derives from one or more of the six modes of reasoning. Therefore, if we have knowledge of the six modes, it must come from one or more of the modes themselves. Assuming that this is true, through which mode did we learn about the *existence* of the six modes? The answer is sense experience; it is through our most basic human senses — seeing and hearing especially — that we become aware of the six modes operating in everyday human life.

Possibly, but not likely. People endlessly dispute this kind of thing, but if they reflect carefully they will discover that most of the argument is over words, not the underlying concepts the words are supposed to represent. What is called intuition here may be given a different name elsewhere—indeed, it may have a dozen or a hundred other names, each with a different linguistic nuance, and the same goes for the other five modes as well.

The problem of terminology, with all the endless confusion that it engenders, may be illustrated in the following way. One reader of this book—in an early draft—objected that the six modes were indeed incomplete because they omitted divine revelation. To this reader, a charismatic Christian, divine revelation was not only a seventh mode; it was the most important mode of all, one that she had discovered at a crucial point in her life and that had transformed her life. After some discussion, however, the reader agreed that revelation could be viewed as a special case of authority, sense experience, intuition, or a combination of these ways of gaining moral knowledge. If the Lord directly appears to an individual, as Jesus appears to Thomas in the gospel, that event certainly involves sense experience: seeing, hearing, and in Thomas's case even touching. In addition, because it is the Lord, any message received has the stamp of authority, of demanding and being worthy of immediate and total acceptance. On the other hand, if the Lord's presence is not physical, if it comes in the form of an interior message, then it is like intuition, which always takes the form of a quiet voice within. Not every reader, to be sure, will accept this explanation. Atheists will dismiss the whole discussion because they dismiss the possibility of divine revelation. Some believers will still prefer to make divine revelation a separate (seventh) mode, because thinking of divine revelation in this way is more helpful or meaningful to them. The lesson here is not that everyone must agree, but rather that everyone should define their terms carefully and thus avoid, as much as possible, unnecessary battles amidst the briars and thickets of the English (or any other) language.

Even if the six modes of moral reasoning are correct and complete, doesn't this framework put too much emphasis on how we arrive at our values? Surely what matters most is the values themselves, not the way we arrive at them.

This is an arguable point. But the larger point is this: Human beings cannot separate the way they arrive at values from the values themselves. Authority, deductive logic, sense experience, emotion, intuition, and science are modes or techniques of moral reasoning, but by adopting and emphasizing one over the other we turn them into dominant personal values. When Sir Alec Guinness, playing the heroic old Obie Wan Kenobie in the film *Star Wars*, repeats to his young protegé Luke Skywalker, "Luke, trust your feelings, Luke, trust your feelings," he is certainly recommending a particular mode of moral reasoning, the mode of emotion. But he is also saying that the testimony of the emotions is more *valuable* than the testimony of an authority such as Scripture, more *valuable* than the conclusions of deductive logic, more *valuable* than the evidence of sense experience, and so on. In other words, he is making a *value judgment*, a value judgment of such importance that it will dominate and color all other value choices, as per the following diagram:

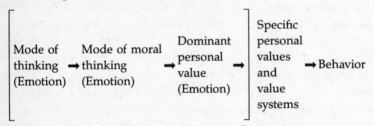

If, like Obie Wan Kenobie, we emphasize emotion over other ways of thinking, will that lead us directly to certain specific beliefs and actions?

Not directly. The choice of emotion as a primary mode of moral thinking—and thus a dominant personal value—means that we are predisposed to certain specific values, as other sections of this book will show. But even if you know what a person's dominant value is, you will not be able to forecast his or her specific values and actions with precision. In *Star Wars*, both Obie Wan Kenobie and the archvillain, Darth Vader, are telling Luke to trust and follow his emotions—in the first instance, an emotional love of humanity and hope for its betterment; in the second instance, an emotional love for one's parent. Part of the drama of the film is seeing where this conflict between related but opposing emotional values will eventually lead.

Characters in *Star Wars* are obviously not real people. Do real people actually choose emotion or deductive logic or sense experience as a primary mode of personal moral reasoning and, concurrently, as a dominant personal value?

Yes and no. It is true that real people in real life do not tend to follow Obie Wan Kenobie's heroic but somewhat simplistic advice, do not rely on a single mode of moral reasoning, but rather rely on a combination of modes, with sharply different emphases. One person may emphasize emotion very strongly but still rely to a degree on the other five modes. Another person may emphasize sense experience and loathe emotional thinking without ever completely escaping it. This is what makes human values so subtle, complex, and infinitely diverse, at least to the casual eye. And when human privacy (we may not want to disclose to others what we believe), deception (we may lie about what we believe), and changeability (we may change our mind about what we believe) are factored in, potential variations on the six primary modes of moral reasoning (six dominant personal values) become literally uncountable.

How can I identify my own primary mode(s) of moral reasoning/dominant personal value(s)?

As a kind of shorthand, imagine that you have a serious personal issue on your mind, such as the choice of a career. Whom would you choose to confide in and seek counsel from?

1. A friendly, compassionate and wise Catholic priest, offering . . .

    or

    A traditional Protestant minister,

    or

    An Orthodox Jewish rabbi, offering . . .

    faith in the higher *authority* of the Catholic church

    faith in the higher *authority* of the Bible

2. A professor of philosophy who befriended you in college and seemed immensely learned and wise, offering . . .

    an ability to think through the problem in a structured and highly *logical* way

3. Another professor from college, this time a professor of history and literature, also a good friend and mentor, also immensely learned and wise, offering . . .

    his own personal sense *experience*, plus the accumulated *experience* of Western culture, as contained in its greatest works of history and literature

4. A family member or very close friend, offering . . .

    strong *emotional* empathy from a member of your most immediate group or "tribe"

5. A Hindu, Buddhist, or "New Age" guru, a person of immense calm, poise, equilibrium, and unspoken wisdom, offering . . .

meditation and other tools designed to unlock your own inner powers of *intuition*, your own inner voice, your own inner guru

6. A widely respected psychiatrist, offering . . .

a systematic appraisal based on *social science* methods and principles

You might reasonably reply that your choice would depend on the issue: one person for career counseling, another for marriage counseling, and so on. But if you could choose only one advisor for *all* personal issues, which one would you choose? Can you rank the six from A (most likely to consult) to F (least likely to consult)? What if you are the kind of person who will never seek advice from anyone? Then you probably fall into category 3 (in effect, you are drawing from your own accumulated sense experience rather than relying on the favorite teacher of history and literature to open up the accumulated sense experience of Western culture).

The preceding question seems to imply that priests, psychiatrists, philosophers, and others to whom we habitually turn for moral guidance are all offering —in some cases, perhaps even "selling"—a particular approach to personal values. Is this true? If so, where can we turn for a broader overview of moral options, presented as fairly, impartially, and objectively as possible?

One of the advantages of a framework based, at least initially, on modes of believing and knowing, rather than on beliefs per se, is that it underscores how bias and subjectivity necessarily creep into any discussion of values, even when an attempt is made to keep the discussion as fair and objective as possible. For example, most books about personal values are written by priests, ministers, rabbis, psychiatrists, academic philosophers, and so on. Such professionals may possess the highest credentials (a lifetime of study and work in their field, a strong professional reputation), but they are by definition specialists, sometimes specialist-advocates, and one should not expect an objective, unbiased account of conflicting value systems from this source. The priest will naturally look at things from one point of view (usually faith in authority); the philosopher from another (usually deductive logic); the psychiatrist or social psychologist from still another (usually science, especially social science). There is an irony here: Neither the philosopher nor the psychiatrist wants to be an advocate; within their own disciplines, they try very hard to minimize bias. Even so, techniques of philosophy or psychiatry are not merely tools; they involve important value choices; they stake out a particular position. To many Christians, any discipline that rejects faith in an authority is biased; to many deductive philosophers, any discipline that accepts faith in an authority is biased; and within their own contexts, each is right. In today's society, a lay person (someone without "professional" credentials in the realm of values) may stand as good a chance as anyone else of producing a truly objective account of the entire spectrum of personal beliefs and systems. Ideally we would have a new academic specialty, one devoted solely to an overall account of values, but such a specialty does not yet exist.

Even if I accept the preceding argument (that a broad and objective look at values would be useful but is not likely to come from priests, ministers, rabbis, philosophers, or psychiatrists, insofar as they are acting as specialists), I wonder whether anybody, specialist or not, can ever be objective.

Ultimately, of course, the answer is that nobody can ever be objective. The author of this book may not be a specialist, he may not be committed in a professional sense to any of the six primary modes of moral reasoning (dominant personal values), but he is a human being: He has personal beliefs of his own, and these will inevitably color what he writes. Not only is the very desire to be objective a "value" or bias, so is the desire to define, categorize, compare, and contrast the different ways that we choose values. Consider the following dialogue between the author and a friend:

AUTHOR: This book is about the six ways we choose values.

FRIEND: Anybody who tries to count the ways we choose values doesn't know what values are.

AUTHOR: People who object to defining and categorizing the way we choose values fall into value system 3.

This dialogue is a variation on the old saying: There are two kinds of people, those who divide the world into two kinds of people and those who don't. In other words, this book is necessarily and unavoidably loaded with personal biases. The only difference is that it tries to provide an overview of the entire realm of values and is not written from the specific point of view of a priest, minister, rabbi, academic philosopher, psychiatrist, or other professional.

If we can establish a framework for thinking about values, and keep it as objective as possible, will it help us in our lives?

Contemporary Americans are not only barraged by an informational overload of conflicting and ill-defined value systems; they seem increasingly unsure about how to respond. The fortunate among us have strong values, however difficult it may be to articulate or defend those values. The unfortunate suffer chronic anxiety, as described by Walter Lippmann in *A Preface to Morals*: "He may be very busy with many things, but he discovers one day that he is no longer sure they are worth doing. . . . He has become involved in an elaborate routine of pleasures; and they do not seem to amuse him very much. He finds it hard to believe that doing any one thing is better than doing any other thing, or, in fact, that it is better than doing nothing at all. It occurs to him that it is a great deal of trouble to live, and that even in the best of lives the thrills are few and far between."

Personal values really do matter. Without functioning values, we can hardly live at all, much less lead a purposeful and satisfying life. Sorting through available value choices in a systematic way is more important than staying slim through diet or exercise, making millions through real estate, extending "peak" sexual performance into old age, or any of the other subjects that seem to preoccupy us. There was a time, seventy or more years ago, when politics, economics, and personal values were all studied together in the same university department, usually called the department of moral philosophy. These subjects were thought to be inextricably linked as well as intensely practical, of immediate use in the lives of students. Today we have mostly forgotten about these natural linkages, have forgotten that finance, economics, politics, and personal values are all related subjects, and while we have continued to devote tremendous intellectual resources to finance, economics, and politics, we have mostly given up the attempt to define, organize, categorize, and study the personal value choices that face us.

This book is above all an attempt to redress this situation, to help restore the study of values in general (as opposed to the propagation of a particular "religion") to its rightful place in our intellectual pantheon, to clarify the choices, and hopefully to spark a more meaningful dialogue between opposing viewpoints. Twenty-five centuries ago in Athens, Plato faced a moment in history at least slightly analogous to ours, in that Athenian values had ceased to be homogenous and a thousand moral "schools" clamored to be heard. The early Platonic dialogues responded by defining, comparing, contrasting—elucidating choices. This is a useful method for our time as well, one that has been followed as faithfully as possible in the chapters that follow.

Part Two

SIX TYPES OF VALUE SYSTEMS

3. Value Systems Based on Authority

In our efforts to learn about the world, we do not just occasionally rely on an external authority to tell us what to believe. This is actually the most common way that we form our beliefs, and not merely as children, when we treat as gospel truth anything that our parents or teachers tell us, but even as adults, when we rely on "experts" of all kinds.

Of course, there is an important difference between the faith of a small child in what a parent says and the faith of an adult in what the experts tell us about a host of everyday matters. In the first instance, the faith is unconditional; in the second instance, it is conditional, even skeptical. If a researcher tells us that a disease is caused by a particular bacterium or virus, we accept that person's authority in the matter on faith, but only as a matter of convenience. We are impressed by the researcher's educational degrees and credentials and acknowledge the authority those credentials confer. Beneath this attitude of respect, however, we are as ready to disbelieve as believe, would not be too surprised to hear from another researcher that the first researcher's account of the disease is wrong, and comfort ourselves that, if we cared enough, we could perform the necessary experiments ourselves, form our own judgments, and thereby dispense with this particular authority entirely.

On this mundane, everyday, secular level, most Americans agree that authorities should be treated provisionally, without excessive respect, especially when authorities start telling other people what to do. Ever since we threw out the King of England, we have bowed our heads to no mere mortal and continue to identify with the frontiersman's boast that "men like me and

Gineral Jackson and Colonel Davy Crockett always demand our rights, and if we don't git 'em, somebody else is might liable to git hell." On another, deeper level, however, Americans are sharply divided about authorities. A very large number, perhaps a majority, think that a skeptical, conditional stance is fine for everyday affairs, but no way to approach God's throne. For these people, Jesus' injunction, "Except a man be born again, he cannot see the Kingdom of God," should be followed as literally as possible. The first step is to open one's heart in the manner of a small child. The second, equally crucial, step is to find an earthly spiritual advisor of unimpeachable authority, one that is truly worthy of an unconditional faith and that can absolutely be counted on to lead an unburdened and childlike soul in the right direction.

In actual life, of course, people who seek an unconditional earthly authority do not necessarily agree on the identity of that authority. A very few Americans choose another living person, an in-the-flesh leader for their spiritual quest; a vastly larger number (especially Orthodox Jews and Protestant fundamentalists) choose a sacred text, the Bible, as a direct source of God's word undefiled by the interpretation of any mortal; and an equally large number of Roman Catholics place their faith in the guidance of an institution, the institution of the Catholic church as it has come down through millennia of time.

The Johannine Daist Communion: An example of unconditional faith in the higher authority of another, living human being

Although most Americans find the idea of pledging absolute obedience to another human being to be foreign, strange, or downright abhorrent, dismissing groups formed for this purpose as "cults," there have always been a wide variety of such "cult" groups to choose from. To offer only one, albeit distinctive, example, there is the Johannine Daist Communion of Northern California, founded by the "God-Realized Spiritual Adept" Da Free John (formerly Franklin Jones), who says of himself: "That one enjoys this Unconditional Awakening . . . is a great opportunity for all others. . . . The Power of it is available for the Transformation of others, if people will enter into right relationship with me. . . . both men and women must make the great feminine gesture of self-transcending surrender."

With shaved head, full face, and rather portly frame, Da Free John makes an incongruous savior, although his followers readily compare him to Jesus and the Buddha. An issue of *Laughing Man* magazine, the Johannine Daist house organ, reports that the Communion has finally purchased the Master's beachfront retreat in the Fiji Islands, where he lives "undisturbed by the troubled activities of secular society and free of the demands of beginning practitioners. . . . However, a God-Realized Spiritual Master is not only Transcendentally Free, he is also free of the conventions of human behavior, including the conventions he creates. To everyone's surprise . . . Master Da announced that he would come to the Communion's northern California Sanctuary, The Mountain of Attention . . . and that he would be arriving in four days!

"During [Master Da's] ten-day stay, many students were Graced by his Initiatory Regard. . . . He . . . would walk among the gathering, touching or hugging a few familiar people, talking to one or two others." At this time, John also gave a somewhat admonitory talk about the governance of the California Sanctuary: "You do not consult one another about the spiritual process. You consult me. . . . Ultimately, everyone is involved in some sense in this cooperative activity, but you could not call it a democracy in the sense that you are on your own, left to think independently about what to do."

Protestant fundamentalism: A (very different) example of an unconditional faith in the higher authority of biblical Scripture

The Johannine Daist Communion (like any other close-knit community lead by a single, living spiritual "master" of unchallengeable authority) lies at the farther fringes of American life. By contrast, Protestant fundamentalism (which condemns the enthronement of any living human being, no matter how wise or spiritually "advanced") is in the mainstream of American life, yet is no less controversial for being so. For example, the *Washington Post* or *Newsweek* reporters have referred to or quoted others referring to Protestant fundamentalists as "bigoted, often illiterate Bible-thumpers," "religious red-necks," "hate-filled anti-intellectuals," "apostles of ignorance" who "pervert faith by using it to smother the mind," "fanatical cultists who prey on the isolated, the inexperienced, and the uneducated," pathological addicts who should be guided into appropriate "therapies" such as Fundamentalists Anonymous, or guileful hypocrites who use "the name of Jesus to defend . . . perceived [economic or political] interests [and] unload onto all of us . . . the values of a particular subculture."

What exactly is Protestant fundamentalism, and why is it so threatening to many people? On one level, the name derives from a group of pamphlets, the *Fundamentals*, published between 1910 and 1915, which tried to define the irreducible core of Christian doctrine. On a deeper level, however, the movement is the true heir of the Reformation of Luther and Calvin and Knox and the Pilgrim Fathers, and as such it reflects central tenets little changed for over four hundred years: first, that God is a completely personal God ("The God of Genesis who walked in the garden in the cool of the evening and called to Adam and his wife who had hidden themselves behind a tree"); second, that human beings participate in an immense historical drama, one beginning with the creation of the world, swiftly descending into human treachery, failure, suffering, and death, reaching its pivotal point in Palestine just under two thousand years ago, and concluding with the "Rapture"—the prophesied ascent of true Christians, living and dead, directly into the "New Jerusalem" of heaven. For those who accept the factual basis of these events, who wholeheartedly accept Christ as their savior, all doubt, uncertainty, weakness, and loneliness are removed. For those who reject this drama, or even for those who reject parts of this drama, heaven will be replaced by an eternity of torment in hell. As Billy Graham has said on television during a crusade in Southern California: "Is Christ the only way? The only way? That is what He says. I don't understand it all. There are many things that I don't understand. But I don't have to understand. All I have to do is believe. Anybody can believe. The old, the young, the deaf, the blind, anybody can and must believe."

For some of Graham's much more strongly fundamentalist colleagues, the imperatives are stricter. Acceptance of Jesus as savior may not be enough—the Christian must be "born again" in a "bible-believing" church to be redeemed. Accordingly, a prominent television evangelist has remarked, "None of the things that [Roman Catholic nun and ministrant to the dying] Mother Teresa does will add one thing to her salvation"; she is in danger of going to hell. In response to Jewish complaints about an alleged attack on their faith, the same evangelist explained that whenever an individual "does not accept Jesus Christ, he takes himself away from God's protection . . . [and] places himself under Satan's domain." Few fundamentalist pastors would endorse these extreme positions. But the doctrine of exclusive salvation, first enunciated by the early church and later reaffirmed by the founders of the Reformation, still means exactly what it says: People who reject Jesus as their savior will be forever condemned to hell.

The third tenet of the fundamentalist faith—the absolute inerrancy of the Bible, the literal truth of each and every event found therein—is most suprising to outsiders and most clearly distinguishes fundamentalist from non-fundamentalist forms of Christianity. Yet it is only in this century that fundamentalists felt the need to articulate this doctrine. It is true that Luther had warned, "If . . . you wish by your own thoughts to know your relation to God, you will break your neck," and had criticized efforts to allegorize scripture as a "beautiful harlot," but neither he nor his immediate successors faced the "historical-critical" method of biblical exegesis or the wholesale attempt to reinterpret scripture.

By the 1920s, however, the president of the World Christian Fundamentalist Association felt compelled to warn against taking some of the Bible and leaving the rest, presenting the Bible in one light for the devout masses and another light for the educated "elite," and especially against "that weasel method of sucking the meaning out of words, and then presenting the empty shells in an attempt to palm them off as giving the Christian faith a new and another interpretation."

Sixty years later, the battle lines were drawn even more firmly. In 1985, a candidate for president of the Southern Baptist church stated that he not only believed that a whale had swallowed Jonah, he would believe that Jonah had swallowed the whale if the Bible said so—and he was then rejected by his convention for being too "liberal." Although factors other than biblical inerrancy contributed to the vote, supporters of the winning candidate stressed, "If there are errors in the Bible, then we cannot know anything for sure."

On these three pillars—an all-powerful personal God, exclusive redemption through Christ, and especially the absolute and unconditional authority of an unerring Bible—the Protestant fundamentalist faith rests. At the same time, faith in a purely passive sense is not enough. Faith must be actively defended. The fundamentalist appraisal of a human, even a reborn human, is cool and dark. People in their original state are weak and depraved, not much better than Adolph Hitler or other villains of history. There is no atrocity, however horrible, that they have not committed or would not commit again in the future. Their souls harbor raging torrents of desire for health and survival, money and power, recognition and fame, sex and love; each emotion conflicts with others and is moderated, if at all, by the passivity of laziness and escapism. Such wayward impulses will never be controlled except through the experience of Christ as Lord and Master. Even after this experience, this cleansing and rebirth, Christians must continually discipline themselves and zealously guard against temptation.

To the always practical fundamentalist, self-discipline is not to be confused with the asceticism of Simeon Stylites, the fifth-century Christian who lived for twenty years atop a pillar, or of one of the other athletes of mystical religion. Ordinary comforts —good food, a nice home or car, worldly success—need not be feared. If earned honestly by hard work and avoiding the sin of idleness, they should be welcomed as a sign of God's grace and favor. Pleasure, on the other hand, whether in the form of alcohol, drugs, sensational entertainments, or sex, but especially sex, must be relentlessly reined in.

Maintaining right beliefs and avoiding the pitfalls of pleasure carry us most of the way toward salvation, but not the whole way. We also need Christian institutions to guide and bolster us and pick us up when we fall. Families and family surrogates such as neighbors and schools are especially important. In America, however, these most basic Christian institutions are further buttressed by larger and even more pervasive institutions: the economy and the national government. Entrepreneurial capitalism, the essence of the American economic system, is really an expression of the religious spirit, "a recognition," in conservative social commentator George Gilder's words, "that beyond the . . . opacity of our material entrapment is a realm of redemptive spirit." Our national government is a divinely ordained instrument for combating the forces of darkness throughout the world. In effect, all American institutions have assumed a special destiny. As Jerry Falwell has said, "I believe that God's role for America is as catalyst, that he wants to set the spiritual time bomb off right here."

The problem with America's special destiny, of course, is that it brings special obligations. One of these is an unrelenting spiritual vigilance. As fundamentalist theologian Francis Schaeffer has explained, America's original Protestant Reformation heritage, the foundation of our greatness, has been under continual attack, first by waves of non-Protestant immigrants in the second half of the nineteenth century and then by secular humanists and atheists in the twentieth. In recent years, he goes on to say, this attack has increased in intensity and made unprecedented headway in the courts: prayer in school has been banned, pornography and abortion have been legalized. Congress has interfered with and threatened to cut off funding for Christian schools, weakened our national defenses, discouraged the work ethic, and subsidized permissiveness. Other governmental bodies have passed women's rights and homosexuals' rights legislation and have allowed drugs to proliferate. The national news and entertainment media have fouled the movies and television with violence and sex and sensationalism, always ardently competing with one another to reach a lower level of taste. Faced with all these trends, the Protestant fundamentalist sees himself, in Falwell's words, "as one to stand in the gap and, under God, with the help of millions of others, to bring the nation back to a moral standard."

Roman Catholicism: An example of faith in the higher authority of an institution

Although it is not widely recognized, Protestant fundamentalism is only one of two great Christian fundamentalisms in America. The other is the Catholic church, which also believes that traditional Christianity is under attack by the modern world and must be strenuously defended; that basic beliefs such as the personhood of God, the immanence of the supernatural in everyday life, and exclusive salvation through Christ must be restored; that discipline must be reestablished in morals; that the artificial separation of church and state must be bridged so that government may be reclaimed as a moral agent. But even when we acknowledge all these important affinities between Protestant fundamentalism and the Catholic church, it must be emphasized that the Catholic version of Christian fundamentalism is different; it is older and deeper. Indeed, to Catholic eyes, Protestant fundamentalism is hardly fundamentalism at all. Although it pretends to espouse the old-time religion, it has actually sold out to the modern world by embracing the three heresies of modernism, capitalism, and nationalism.

Heresy 1: Modernism

On the face of it, the Catholic charge that Protestant fundamentalism is just a disguised form of modernism—where modernism is defined as the abandonment or "reinterpretation" of the most anciently revered Christian principles—might seem preposterous. Protestant fundamentalists consider themselves to be the most inveterate foes of Christian modernism on earth. The Catholic position, however, is that the beginning of Christian modernism must be dated to Martin Luther's attack on the mother church and on what Trappist monk and author Thomas Merton called the "powerful unanimity of Catholic Tradition from the First Apostles, from the first Popes and the early Fathers, on down . . . to our own day." According to this view, any doctrine that upholds the Protestant Reformation and rejects the authority of the Catholic church is modernist to the core. As Merton states the case: "When it comes to accepting God's own authority about things that cannot possibly be known in any other way except as revealed by His [Church], people [refuse] to incline their ears and listen. Things that cannot be known in any other way, they will not accept from this source. [But as Christians we must always] check the inspirations that come to us in the depths of our own conscience against the [truth] that is given to us with divinely certain guarantees by [a Church which has] inherited in our midst the place of Christ's apostles—[which] speak[s] to us in the Name of Christ and as it were in His own Person." Walter Lippmann then summarizes the argument: "From the point of view, then, of the [older] fundamentalism [the Catholic church] . . . the error of the modernists is that they deny the facts on which religious faith reposes; the error of the orthodox Protestants is that although they affirm the facts, they reject all authority which can verify them; the virtue of the Catholic system is that along with a dogmatic affirmation of the central facts, it provides a living authority in the Church which can ascertain and demonstrate and verify these facts."

Mixed in with the denial of church authority is a lesser but related problem: the introduction of democracy into church affairs. About political democracy, the Catholic hierarchy no longer harbors dark suspicions. Toward church democracy, it remains implacably opposed. As Cardinal Malula of Kinshasa, cohead of the Catholic Bishops' Synod, has said: "[We are] a mystery of communion. You cannot introduce democracy [into a mystery]." To which Cardinal Ratzinger, head of the Sacred Congregation for the Doctrine of the Faith, formerly the Holy Office of the Inquisition, adds: "There is one truth . . . this truth is definable and expressible in a precise way . . . and this truth is not reached by voting."

Schism and church democracy should be quite enough to hurl at Jerry Falwell's head, but there are other charges as well. In the area of faith, Protestant fundamentalists are criticized for deemphasizing Mary, the saints, ceremony, liturgy, mysteries—all excised in the name of reform, but actually accommodating "skepticism" and the "scientific mind." In the area of morals, even the strictest Protestant churches are judged to be insufficiently strict. There is the matter of remarriage after divorce, for example, which Jesus appears to forbid (Mt 5:32) but which Protestant churches allow. There is priestly celibacy (for which there is no clear biblical basis), and there is the prohibition against artificial birth control. The latter perhaps typifies the difference between Protestant and Catholic fundamentalism. A Protestant might challenge the Catholic church to consider the plight of a Philippine prostitute who refuses to use birth control because "it is a mortal sin," or at least to take pity on all the homeless, malnourished children picking their way through the refuse heaps of the world. Catholicism responds that God's commandments cannot be bent—not even to save humanity from the consequences of its own wicked indiscipline and folly.

Heresy 2: Capitalism

Protestant fundamentalism has always regarded capitalism as God's instrument on earth. It diverts human energies from military conquest; it rewards honest hard work; it creates wealth for all, not just the rich; as wealth permeates a society, individual human rights, worth, and dignity become more respected. The Catholic church, from its perspective of two thousand years and almost every imaginable economic system, gazes searchingly at this happy vision and pronounces it a fraud. In its view, capitalism is based on the love of money, self-interest, greed, disregard for the poor, and economic inequality—all explicitly or implicitly condemned by Jesus. The task for Christians is not to extol capitalism, but to redeem it.

Catholic economic theology begins with Jesus' injunction to the rich young man to "go your way, sell whatever you have, and give to the poor" (Mk 10:21). Faith, as Pope John Paul II has said, "leads us to see earthly life as a preparation for spiritual life, like gold purified by fire." Money and "consumerism" are obstacles and the desire for ever more money is a "sin." To find Jesus, you must look for him in a homeless schizophrenic, in an old woman huddled over an urban steam vent to protect herself from the bitterest winter cold, in a fatherless family struggling to feed and clothe itself in a roach and rat infested slum.

In one version of this argument, capitalism fails because it teaches selfishness rather than sharing. A society built on these values tolerates in the words of the pope "scandalous" poverty and unemployment in the midst of plenty, a "disproportionate distribution of goods," a "horrifying abyss between the richest and poorest." In another even darker version favored by some Catholic bishops, capitalism actually causes poverty by allowing the few to "amass . . . an imperialistic monopoly of economic and political supremacy at the expense of the many" by "institutionalizing starvation . . . all over the world" and by "dehumanizing" human beings in order to "enslave them to machines."

Whatever version of the indictment is offered by Catholic bishops, the proposed solution is the same: political action. For example, the first draft of the *Pastoral Letter on Catholic Social Teaching and the U.S. Economy*, issued in 1984 by the National Conference of Catholic Bishops, urged the American government to:

- Set wages on the basis of "comparable reward" for "comparable contributions";
- Increase the minimum wage by 33 percent;
- Provide public service or publicly subsidized jobs for all who want them;
- Provide generous federally mandated welfare assistance without "workfare";
- Tax away all income over a predetermined level and;
- Tax away all wealth over a predetermined level.

Most American commentators were critical of the bishops' letter. One ridiculed the very idea of Catholic bishops pouring over volumes of Adam Smith, Keynes, and Galbraith and consulting 156 other economic "experts" in order to provide "the correct Christian position on soybean subsidies." Another argued that "socialist remedies" like those proposed by the bishops created dependency, not justice, and had been tried and failed before, especially in Europe. Another cited the parable of the servant who invested his master's money (Mt 25:14–30) as evidence that Jesus understood and approved of the essential capitalistic method of compounding one's assets. Another objected that although Archbishop Weakland of Milwaukee, the primary author of the letter, had spoken of an "appeal to the generosity, good will and concern of all U.S. citizens," the bishops had said nothing about individual acts of private Christian charity but had instead proposed to rely on crude political power: "Jesus preached the renunciation of wealth, not the expropriation of it." Another noted caustically that "the bishops do not argue that A may reach into B's pocket in order to help needy C, for the commandment does not read, 'Thou shalt not steal except for a good cause.' Rather, they argue that A and D and E and so forth, using the political process, may reach into B's pocket."

What all these outraged pundits, many of whom were Catholic, seemed to miss was the utter fidelity of the bishops to millennia of Catholic tradition. The Catholic church throughout its history has regarded capitalism with suspicion; has sought to work out problems through community rather than individual action; has adopted paternalistic and sometimes coercive methods; and has treated government either as a useful ally or, preferably, a useful subordinate in its struggle to maintain God's law on earth.

Heresy 3: Nationalism

Just as Protestant fundamentalism has always been comfortable with capitalism, it has also been comfortable with nationalism. Protestant denominations have often been identified with a specific country. In America today, fundamentalist preachers often speak of the United States as a second "chosen people" with a special God-given destiny. The Catholic church, however, remains resolutely internationalist and continually warns Americans against sins of pride, arrogance, militarism, and lack of charity toward poorer nations. Through varying means, including papal homilies, the 1982 *Pastoral Letter on War and Peace*, and the later *Pastoral Letter on the U.S. Economy*, the church has asked for the following:

- A concerted effort to close the "widening gap between rich and poor countries" by increasing foreign aid, forgiving Third World debts, reducing trade barriers to Third World goods, and investing overseas in ways that neither "create nor perpetuate dependency"
- An end to American military involvement in Central America and the Caribbean
- An end to American arms sales abroad
- A nuclear freeze that would halt the testing, producing, and deploying of all nuclear weapons
- A termination of space weapons programs

Although Catholicism has never been a "peace church" in the sense of the Quakers (war may be "just" under certain circumstances), its current leanings are increasingly pacifist. Bishop Leroy Matthiesen of Amarillo, Texas, has suggested that Catholic defense workers should think about seeking other employment. Thousands of Catholic parochial schools all over the country use social justice and religion classes to warn students of the temptations of American power, the tendency of imperialism to hide behind a mask of patriotism, and the horrors of nuclear war.

In all these many ways, Catholic fundamentalism is different from its Protestant counterpart. It is not just older or even more uncompromising; its entire world outlook is made of different stuff. Against overt external enemies, the bulwarks of an ancient faith, an immemorial tradition, an unimpeachable authority in the church itself, provide an invincible shield. Confronted with hostility or persecution, whether from Southern Baptists in the old South or from Communist authorities in post-war Eastern Europe, it grows steadily stronger. Like all fundamentalism, it thrives on challenge and struggle. But within its own ranks, a different reality—utter confusion—perpetually reigns.

In Africa, black prelates complain to John Paul II that the "Christian style of [monogamous] marriage does not work." In France, a nation honored as "the eldest daughter of the Church," only about 6 percent of a largely Catholic population attend mass. In South America, some priests espouse violent revolution and have been admonished by the secretary general of their Bishops' Conference, Bishop Hoyos Dario Castrillón of Columbia, "If I see a church with a machine gun, then I can't see the crucified Christ in that church." In the United States, many Catholics are liberals who support the ordination of women and are appalled by the pope's response that "no women were present at the Last Supper." Others are Pentecostals who speak in tongues and practice faith healing. Almost all American Catholics are a little disoriented by the demand to work with right-wing political groups against abortion and then with left-wing political groups for affirmative action and nuclear freeze or by the church's encouragement to question every authority except its own. An assistant to the archbishop of Washington, D.C., keeps a memento in his office from his social protest and activist days—a sign reading "Question Authority" in bold letters—yet serves one of the most authoritarian institutions on earth.

If we listen to all these cacophonous voices within the Catholic church, we might conclude that the hour of dissolution has arrived, that the vast superstructure that survived the demise of the classical and feudal worlds as well as all the depredations of science is finally about to come crashing down. Nothing would be further from the truth. One is reminded of a story about an Alsatian Benedictine monastery during World War I. The choirmaster "was chanting the Magnificat with his confreres, when suddenly a French shell crashed through the roof and exploded in the nave of the church. . . . The smoke thinned and the Magnificat continued." This is the quintessential Catholic attitude, impossible for others to grasp or completely emulate. Despite all the turbulence, despite all the incessant chaos of sinful men, the church remains rooted in one spot. As Bishop John May of St. Louis, vice president of the U.S. Bishops' Conference, has said: "The church is not free to accommodate itself . . . to the modern world. It is not free to change." And precisely because it cannot change, its critics should not expect its extinction but rather, in the words of Catholic essayist G. K. Chesterton, "look first for the coming of the comet or the freezing of the star."

4. Value Systems Based on Logic

As we have seen, having faith in an authority, either an authority of convenience like the many "experts" we consult in daily life or a higher authority such as the Bible or the Catholic church, is a way of thinking, of forming beliefs, of acquiring knowledge. The same is true of deductive logic. Deductive logic is first of all a way of thinking, believing, and knowing; second, a way of thinking, believing, and knowing about values; third, a dominant value in itself (when we place more emphasis on logic than on authority or some other mode of reasoning, we are making a crucial *value* judgment), one that precedes and colors all the other value judgments that we make.

But what exactly is deductive logic? When we speak of having faith in a higher authority such as the Bible, the meaning of the phrase is immediately clear. After all, we have all put our faith in an authority of some kind at some point in our lives, and most of us are familiar with the Bible. Logic is different. Although we all use and rely on logic to some extent, we are often unaware of doing so. The term *deductive logic* is particularly slippery; although it is a technical term, it is commonly misused, or just used differently by different people. If we are going to talk about deductive logic, we are certainly going to have to define our terms, and it may help to begin with a specific example of how deductive logic can be used to solve a difficult moral problem.

Example of logic as a moral reasoning technique:
Religion class at Gonzaga High, as reported by the
Washington Post

On a gloomy day in mid-winter, Dick Christensen, a teacher at Gonzaga High, a Catholic parochial school in Washington, D.C., asked his religion class to consider the following hypothetical moral dilemma:

Russian missiles are headed toward ten American cities and there is not enough time to stop them. About ten million Americans will die including the president. The president must first decide whether to launch a retaliatory attack that would kill at least 150 million Soviet citizens.

If you were president, Christensen asked the students, would you order the strike?

Ten hands went up signifying yes. Who would not? Four hands crept upward. Two boys were undecided.

Christensen then told the boys who would kill 150 million people to sit on the right side of the room for the next several weeks and those who wouldn't, to sit on the left. The undecided went to the middle.

On the second day [of the six-week lesson unit], David Costabile and Pat Ryan jumped from the undecided to the "no-nukers."

"I felt like having revenge . . ." Costabile, a Chevy Chase resident and star of the school play, explained nervously to the class that day. "But I went home and I thought about it, and I realized that it was absurd to think you could ever morally justify doing something like this."

The students had eight days to prepare their final presentations, a five-minute speech defending their positions as if they were the president of the United States. . . . The final tally was ten "nukers" and seven "no-nukers."

Although the students failed to realize it, their teacher, presenting this particular moral dilemma, committed a logical fallacy. The question is: what is the fallacy? Can you, the reader of this book, spot it?

At the simplest level, there are four tools of deductive logic that might be used to catch the teacher in his error. These are Socratic questioning, dialectic, syllogism, and cataloguing of common fallacies. Let's try each in turn:

Socratic questioning

When asked who was the wisest man in Greece, the Delphic oracle replied that it was Socrates. Pressed about this judgment,

Socrates agreed that the oracle was right: He was the wisest because he alone knew that he knew nothing. Continuing in this arrogantly modest vein, Socrates wandered about Athens refusing to take positions but always asking sharp questions. Using the same technique, which has come to be called the *Socratic method*, the students could at least have forced the teacher to convert his moral dilemma into an assertion, that indiscriminate killing is wrong, and that if you accept this moral principle, then it is inconsistent to accept the idea of nuclear retaliation. Working with an assertion rather than a hypothetical situation should make it easier to find the fallacy.

Dialectic

Dialectic operates under the principle that heat produces light. One group is assigned to defend a proposition; another is assigned to oppose it. The spirit of competition supposedly ensures that all arguments are marshaled and weighed in the balance. In this case, the teacher encouraged a dialectical free-for-all between the "nukers" and the "no-nukers." Each side worked strenuously to maneuver the other into a logical trap—a self-evidently false or inconsistent assertion (*reductio ad absurdum*) like talking about a round square—that would end the game with a single knockout blow. Nobody succeeded. Nobody was persuaded by anyone else's argument. And, of course, the teacher's fallacy remained undetected.

Syllogism

Although the ancient Greeks are supposed to have invented the syllogism, a better case can be made for the ancient Indians. Consider, for example, the first three Noble Truths presented by the Buddha:

1. Human life is full of suffering.

2. Suffering is caused by desire.

3. Suffering can be eliminated by eliminating desire.

These three statements, formulated over twenty-five hundred years ago, comprise a classic *syllogism*, that is, a conclusion logically deduced from two premises. For purposes of syllogistic reasoning, it does not matter if the first and second premises are correct. What is being tested is whether the conclusion logically follows from the two premises or whether it is actually inconsistent with the premises. If the conclusion is inconsistent with the premises, then either the conclusion or the premises must (according to logic) be false.

Most human statements do not fall into syllogistic form, but they can sometimes be adapted to fit. Fortunately, the teacher's implied assertion about nuclear retaliation can easily be reinterpreted as a syllogism:

1. Indiscriminate killing is wrong.

2. Massive nuclear retaliation involves indiscriminate killing.

3. Massive nuclear retaliation is wrong.

Restated in this way, the teacher's assertion can be tested according to a variety of rules established by logicians beginning with Aristotle. For example, a syllogism is always false if a positive conclusion follows from two negative premises or if a negative conclusion follows from two positive premises. None of these rules, alas, seems to apply here. Having thoroughly tested the teacher's syllogism, we find that nothing appears to be wrong with it. If a fallacy is buried deep within, we will have to use another technique to dig it out.

Cataloguing common fallacies

Not surprisingly, human beings tend to repeat the same logical errors over and over again. A few brave souls who have tried to count the most common errors have generally arrived at a very high figure. Philosopher, mathematician, and classicist Robert Gula, for example, author of *Nonsense: How to Overcome It*, counted 167 possible fallacies, including such examples as fustianism (impenetrable language like "definition predicates cognizance of intrinsic quiddity," loosely translated as meaning that you have to know what something is before you can define it); the fallacy of the worse evil (thinking, like Pollyanna, that something is really not so bad because there could always be something worse); and the fallacy of the beard (because it is hard to say exactly when a few whiskers become a beard, the qualitative difference between a few whiskers and a beard is denied). After studying the 167 fallacies, however, we find that all the possibilities really boil down to just three: lack of clarity, irrelevance, or incompleteness.

With these new tests in mind, we can now return to the teacher's central assertion:

1. Indiscriminate killing is wrong.

2. Massive nuclear retaliation involves indiscriminate killing.

3. Students who oppose indiscriminate killing but support massive nuclear retaliation are morally inconsistent.

Is this assertion clear, relevant, and complete? On closer inspection, the answer appears to be no. Although the teacher's position is relevant to the problem of nuclear weapons, it is neither clear nor complete. The major problem lies in the third sentence of the teacher's syllogism (the conclusion). The words *massive nuclear retaliation* mask an all-important distinction between *actual* nuclear retaliation and the *threat* of nuclear retaliation. Although it would be inconsistent to oppose indiscriminate killing and still engage in nuclear retaliation, it would be equally inconsistent to renounce in advance the use of nuclear weapons, if such a unilateral renunciation encouraged the other side to start a nuclear war. Expressed as a countersyllogism, this point of view might read:

1. Indiscriminate killing is wrong.

2. Nuclear deterrence prevents indiscriminate killing.

3. Unilateral renunciation of nuclear deterrence is wrong.

Or as Thelma Levine, a philosophy professor at George Washington University, has stated the case: "The arguments against [nuclear weapons] are very nice arguments on behalf of peace and the dangers of nuclear war. But the rationality within the so-called madness of nuclear weapons is the deterrence value."

The point of this story is not, of course, about nuclear weapons or whether the teacher is *ultimately* right or wrong in his position. It is about the detection of logical fallacies, in this instance, Gula fallacy 136, also known as the "false dilemma." Like other difficult-to-catch fallacies, the false dilemma may be impossible to beat on its own terms. Sometimes the only way to overcome it is by presenting a counterdilemma (i.e., the morality of deterrence) in order to broaden the discussion and ensure that all the relevant issues are considered.

Logic as a dominant personal value

As the story of Gonzaga High's religion class illustrates, deductive logic is a technique for clarifying thought and speech, a technique that employs Socratic method, dialectic, syllogism, cataloguing of fallacies, and other more advanced mathematical tools that are beyond the capacities of the average person. At the same time, deductive logic is much more than a technique, if we think of a technique as essentially value free. The technique of logic turns out, on closer inspection, to incorporate a whole series of underlying assumptions and values. One of these, obviously, is that ultimate truth is not to be found in church or Bible but rather in deductive reasoning. Another is that order and consistency are all important in human affairs (moral inconsistency was the charge that the teacher leveled against the "nukers" among his students). A third is that what appears ordered and consistent may not be, and must be continually tested by drawing finer and finer distinctions (it was just such a fine distinction between *actual* nuclear retaliation and the *threat* of nuclear retaliation that revealed that the teacher himself was guilty of inconsistency—or at least oversimplification—in failing to acknowledge the deterrence issue associated with nuclear weapons).

All these assumptions and values are controversial, even the emphasis on order and consistency. Although the desire for order and consistency may appear to be an inbred preference among human beings, it is often matched by an equal preference for disorder and inconsistency. In part, this is a cultural matter. Westerners have generally felt comfortable about defining, distinguishing, labeling (all the intellectual heavy labor that is required to create order and consistency in an often chaotic universe) because the Bible teaches—indeed, requires—this kind of mental attitude. God must be distinguished from the Devil, good from evil, believers from unbelievers. Once this categorizing and structuring habit of mind has been formed, it can easily be transferred from the old religion of Judaism or Christianity to the new deductive logic. Among educated Japanese, by contrast, it was traditional to follow a variety of creeds—Shinto, Confucianism, Buddhism, Taoism, sometimes Christianity—without the slightest effort to distinguish one from the other or to reconcile the differences. Only after the Meiji Revolution of 1868 and the decision to compete with the West did the practice of drawing careful, logical distinctions and seeking strict consistency of belief begin to confer a certain prestige. In India, the very birthplace of formal logic, the logical mind is often thought to be an obstacle rather than a road to illumination. As yoga teacher and author Richard Hittleman has said: "The . . . [logical] mind, being a machine, has but one function: it creates and then goes about attempting to solve problems! It enjoys this game and will continue to play it as long as you allow it to do so, throughout your entire life if it can."

The traditional Japanese objection to logic is mostly practical: Why make such a fuss over all these distinctions? The Indian objection is more mystical: Philosophical logic chopping is thought to obscure the underlying unity of the world and of all creatures. Other criticisms are harsher: that deductive logic is just a series of meaningless puzzles, as in philosopher Bertrand Russell's famous antinomy:

In a certain town there is a barber who shaves all those, and only those, who do not shave themselves. Does he shave himself? [If he does, he doesn't; and if he doesn't, he does.]

Or a series of circular word games, like the following exchange:

PHILOSOPHER 1: All men seek pleasure as their primary goal.

PHILOSOPHER 2: What about men who seek money, fame, power, or success?

PHILOSOPHER 1: These are just means to pleasure.

PHILOSOPHER 2: What about a miser? He clearly seeks money as an end in itself since he never spends any.

PHILOSOPHER 1: Yes, but for the miser, just having money is pleasure.

Or a series of endlessly spun-out conclusions precariously balanced on a single premise that may have little or nothing to do with the real world of common sense or of careful, factual observation. Hitler could be said to have been "logical" about the Jews, in the sense that his views and actions were consistent with his grotesquely warped initial premise. A terrorist who killed a twelve-year-old girl at the Rome airport in 1985 justified himself with a crude syllogism:

It [the El Al ticket counter) is Israel.
Israel is our enemy.
We kill Israel.

Given these important objections, the supporters of deductive logic as a royal road toward moral truth might be forgiven a degree of timidity. Yet, on the contrary, they remain entirely confident. Most of the criticism they regard as the purest nonsense—the very devil they are committed to destroy. In their view, the logical mind is humanity's salvation, and it is only by giving this mind the freedom to explore, to note critical distinctions, and to follow these distinctions wherever they lead, through a hundred or even a thousand deductive steps, always guided by the beacon lights of order and consistency, that humans may eventually find happiness. As a contemporary American logician has put it: "We like to imagine ourselves as paladins, riding the earth, always searching for error, confusion, mendacity, always ready to fight it to the death."

Creating a positive religion of pure logic

In its earliest days, deductive logic was generally negative in its method. Socrates had sought truth, but only indirectly, by finding and eliminating error, just as we searched for error in the teacher's moral dilemma at Gonzaga High. In theory, the patient elimination of error should eventually lead you to the truth (with all the error removed, whatever remains must by definition be true). In this way, logicians could eventually evolve from being critics, usually devastating critics, of other people's values, toward being a source, a life-giving source, of proven values. To make this transition from critic to creator of values was not only inherently desirable (people like to hear suggestions, not just criticisms); it was in some sense necessary. Otherwise, if logic remained forever negative, it could itself be criticized for inconsistency! After all, logic in its purely negative form, continually questioning everyone's most established and cherished beliefs in the manner of a Socrates or an Abelard or any of the other famous practitioners of the craft, inevitably sowed the seeds of social anarchy and relativism. And how could logic, which trumpeted the supreme value of order and consistency, justify its contributing to disorder and social anarchy?

To transform logic from a purely negative to a negative *and* positive force was certainly a worthy goal, but the obvious approach of eliminating all the bad thinking and seeing what is left is arduous, slow work. It is not only that there is so much logical error in the world. Worse, as soon as one error is refuted, a new one springs up to take its place. What is needed, therefore, is a short-cut, a way of developing good values from logic without relying on the laborious process of eliminating all the bad values first.

At least initially, logicians did not see this as a very daunting problem. They agreed that if they could find an initial premise that was self-evidently true, they would be home free, because they could deduce the rest (deduction means that each successive premise must flow out of and be consistent with its predecessors). One by one, philosophers stepped forth like Penelope's suitors to state a self-evident and therefore completely irrefutable initial premise and thus win the glittering prize. In retrospect, the supreme, certainly the most inspiring, attempt was made by Baruch de Spinoza over three hundred years ago in Holland, the attempt against which all others have subsequently been judged, though, as we shall see, similar efforts continue today among contemporary American philosophers such as Mortimer Adler.

Spinoza (1632–1677)

Spinoza's life, as well as his doctrines, reflects the possibilities of a pure religion of deductive logic, where religion is defined as a set of personal beliefs and actions inspired by those beliefs, not just a socially organized religion like Judaism or Christianity. A solitary bachelor, Spinoza moved from town to town to escape the time-consuming attentions of his devoted friends; an imperturbable boarder, he sometimes remained in his room for three months at a time, to the fond amazement of whatever family he was staying with; an expert lens grinder, he always paid his own way and gently declined the financial patronage of princes.

As Spinoza explained the motive behind this unconventional existence, which some of his contemporaries viewed as a kind of extreme secular monasticism:

[From the beginning] I . . . [observed that] . . . the ordinary surroundings of life which are esteemed by men (as their actions testify) to be the highest good, may be classed under the three heads—Riches, Fame, and the Pleasures of Sense: with these three the mind is so absorbed that it has little power to reflect on any different good. By sensual pleasure the mind is enthralled . . . so that it is quite incapable of thinking of any other object; when such pleasure has been gratified it is followed by extreme melancholy. . . . The pursuit of honors and riches is likewise very absorbing, especially if such objects be sought simply for their own sake. . . . In the case of fame the mind is still more absorbed, for fame is conceived as always good for its own sake, and as the ultimate end to which all actions are directed. Further the attainment of riches and fame is not followed as in the case of sensual pleasure by repentance, but, the more we acquire, the greater is our delight, and consequently, the more we are incited to increase both the one and the other; on the other hand, if our hopes happen to be frustrated we are plunged into the deepest sadness. Fame has the further drawback that it compels its votaries to order their lives according to the opinions of their fellow men, shunning what they usually shun, and seeking what they usually seek.

When I saw that all these ordinary objects of desire would be obstacles in the way of a search for something different and new—no, that they were so opposed thereto that either they or it would have to be abandoned, I was forced to inquire which would prove the most useful to me. . . . But further reflection convinced me that . . . evils . . . arise from the love of what is perishable, such as the objects already mentioned [while] love toward a thing eternal and infinite feeds the mind wholly with joy, and is itself unmingled with any sadness, wherefore it is greatly to be desired and sought for with all our strength.

[Even then] . . . I could not forthwith lay aside all love of riches, sensual enjoyment, and fame. [But] . . . while my mind was employed with [deductive logic], it turned away from its former objects of desire. . . . Although these intervals were at first rare, and of very short duration, yet afterwards, . . . they became more frequent and more lasting.

After persevering in this highly disciplined existence for many years, Spinoza concluded that the all-important initial premise, the logical key that would unlock a complete system of values, could be found in the concept of perfection. For perfection to be truly perfect, it must be absolute; and to be absolute, it must exist. From this *a priori* argument (*a priori* because it is thought to be self-evidently true), one may infer that God (another name for perfection) must exist, and one may then proceed, step by step, through definitions, axioms, and propositions laid out like Euclid's geometry, to a complete cosmological and ethical system centered on God.

Like Spinoza's modest life of humility and retirement, the Spinozan philosophical system might seem superficially compatible with traditional Jewish or Christian belief: It places God at the beginning of the reasoning chain. But unlike systems based on the cosmological argument for the existence of God (the observable phenomenon of cause and effect in the universe implies God as a First Cause) or the teleological argument (the organization of the universe implies God as an initial Organizer), Spinoza's ontological argument (to be perfect, God must be) does not necessarily assume a God like that of Judaism or Christianity. Indeed, Spinoza concluded that God was more likely to be the universe (pantheism) than the creator of the universe (theism), and this position led to excommunication from his synagogue, near assassination, and dismissal by a Christian acquaintance as a "wretched little man, [a] vile worm of the earth."

Eventually, Spinoza's ontological argument, together with its cosmological and teleological counterparts, was refuted by other philosophers, notably David Hume and Immanuel Kant in the eighteenth century. Thereafter, these logical set pieces lived a kind of half-life, appearing and reappearing, revived, re-refuted, revived again. Even in the 1980s, contemporary American scientists speculated about an "anthropic principle" that bears a close resemblance to the cosmological and teleological arguments, and toward the end of his life Einstein insisted, "I believe in Spinoza's God." Meanwhile Spinoza's attitude, as opposed to his precise logical technique, has never lost its power to move. As Goethe wrote:

After I had looked around the whole world in vain for a means of developing my strange nature, I finally hit upon the *Ethics* of this man. . . . Here I found the serenity to calm my passions; a wide and free view over the material and moral world seemed to open before me.

Above all, I was fascinated by the boundless disinterestedness that emanated from him. That wonderful sentence "he who truly loves God must not desire God to love him in return" with all the propositions on which it rests, with all the consequences that spring from it, filled my whole subsequent thought.

Mortimer Adler

For this best-known living American philosopher, the logical errors of Spinoza can easily be put right, along with the much graver errors of later philosophers. All that is required is to identify an initial ethical principle that, unlike Spinoza's first principle, really is self-evidently true, then combine this first principle with some readily observable facts about the world. For example, it should be self-evident that "we ought to desire what is really good for us and nothing else" or, put differently, that we ought to desire what we really need and not just what we might like to have. Combining this prescriptive statement with a factual statement such as "all human beings naturally desire or need knowledge," it should then be possible to deduce other "oughts," as, for example, "we ought to seek or desire knowledge." Building on this foundation, Adler then proceeds to sketch and defend a specific moral philosophy, one that rejects "faith in an authority" as the basis of our moral life, that rejects the Judaic and Christian ethos, that places the individual first ("the happiness of the individual person is the one and only ultimate goal or final end in this life"), and that charges the government to secure for the individual, at a minimum, personal liberty, freedom from poverty, education, adequate health care, and social support—these being the essential "goods" that each of us must have and should desire in order to be happy.

In presenting all this, Adler has absolutely no doubts. Uncertainty, pessimism, subjectivism, relativity are just "philosophical mistakes, erroneous views, false doctrines." Deductive logic is not only a source of true knowledge; it is "through [such] thought that we are able to understand everything else that we know [and attain] wisdom." Unfortunately, the premises of

Adler's work, like those of the other philosophers he criticizes, are open to dispute. Take the all-important and necessarily self-evident statement, "We ought to desire what is good for us and nothing else." What does this statement really mean? Is it not equivalent to saying, "We ought to desire what we ought to desire"— a version that clarifies its tautological nature. If the word *need* is substituted for the second "ought to desire," does this distinction help? What exactly is a human need, and apart from a few basic examples (food, water, shelter), can it be clearly distinguished from a desire? Finally, is the alleged observation, "All human beings need knowledge," factual in a meaningful way? What kind of knowledge? Are all forms of knowledge a need? Is specific knowledge of pornography or sadism a need? Was the serpent in the biblical garden correct that we should eat freely of the fruit of knowledge without discrimination?

Such questions could be multiplied, but their import is clear: Whether one agrees or disagrees with Professor Adler's personal values, the program of finding an initial moral premise that is self-evidently true and thus completely irrefutable and then parlaying this premise into a complete value system through deduction is still incomplete, still awaiting another and more convincing approach. In the absence of such an approach, deductive logic is not exhausted; it just has more limited, less utopian options. One option is to return to the old process of elimination, of continually searching for and refuting false arguments and values, on the assumption that the avoidance of illogical (bad) values may, after all, be just as important as finding logical (good) ones. Another option is to abandon a program of "pure" logic and instead try to blend logic with one or more of the other five modes of moral reasoning. For example, if you stipulate that your initial premises will come from an external authority such as the Bible, you can indeed deduce an entire moral system. (This is what St. Thomas Aquinas and other Christian logicians have tried to do over the centuries.) Or, if you prefer sense experience or intuition as your starting point, you can deduce other kinds of value systems, as many modern philosophers have done. Or you can be less formal about the whole thing and simply incorporate logical techniques (such as the avoidance of logical fallacies) into value systems primarily based on other modes. The philosophy of cognitive psychology, for example, a psychiatric and counseling movement described in chapter 8, includes logic very prominently among its several dominant values and has had a rapidly growing influence in contemporary American psychiatric and mental health circles. Whichever of these approaches is adopted, it remains true that logic is a powerful and perennial form of moral reasoning, and at least for some Americans, lies at the heart of their personal beliefs.

5. Value Systems Based on Sense Experience

In ordinary language, the word *experience* can refer to almost anything. We can and do speak of experiencing authority, logic, emotion, intuition, science, and so on, as in: "I experienced [the emotion of] falling in love for the first time." But when we speak of sense experience, we are referring to something narrower and more specific: the knowledge that we get directly by seeing, hearing, smelling, tasting, or touching.

Obviously all of us obtain general knowledge, as well as knowledge about values, through this avenue of direct sense experience. Some people, however, seem to place considerably greater emphasis on the testimony of their senses than on other modes of learning, believing, and knowing. They do not want to accept the teachings of the Bible or the church on faith. They do not want to sit in a dark room working through abstruse logical problems. They want to see and hear it themselves, either on the spot in their own communities or traveling in foreign lands, or vicariously through books and films. If a friend or a stranger or the author of a book tells them that something is true, they do not ask themselves: What credentials (authority) or skill in logic does this person possess to back up this statement? They ask instead whether the alleged truth corresponds to their own entirely personal sense experience in this world—and, if it does not, the alleged truth is quietly but decisively put aside.

Seeing and hearing: Eudora Welty

As one might expect, votaries of a religion of sense experience often possess acutely developed powers of seeing and hearing.

For example, contemporary novelist and short story writer Eudora Welty begins a brief memoir of her early life in Jackson, Mississippi, with an account of sounds, especially the sounds of her parents:

I'd listen toward the hall: Daddy upstairs was shaving in the bathroom and Mother downstairs was frying the bacon. They would begin whistling back and forth to each other up and down the stairwell. My father would whistle his phrase, my mother would try to whistle, then hum hers back. It was their duet ... [from] ... "The Merry Widow." ... Their song almost floated with laughter: how different from the [Victrola] record, which growled.

Later, when Eudora was a young woman, her powers of observation lead her to "mak[ing] pictures with a camera." Both in her celebrated photographs of Mississippi during the Depression and in her even more celebrated fiction, Welty's unblinking but warmly compassionate gaze seemed to penetrate into the very "mind, heart, and skin" of her subjects.

But where does such heightened sense experience, heightened hearing and seeing, take us in our personal values? Miss Welty is reluctant to say; indeed, it might be said to be contrary to her values to comment directly. After all, she suggests, the point of hearing and seeing is to hear and see for yourself. If you want to know what a fiction writer and photographer in Mississippi has heard and seen, you should read her fiction or look at her photographs, then make up your own mind about what it means to you. The point of art is to broaden the reader/viewer/listener's sense experience, put people and things in a different, perhaps a more revealing or telling, perspective, not to serve up ready-made answers.

This might seem to be an uncompromising attitude, but it is tempered by Miss Welty's unfailing courtesy and graciousness. If you arrive at her house on the tree-lined street in Jackson, like so many newspaper interviewers and Ph.D. candidates have, you will probably be taken in for a warm chat. And if you are unhurried, listen intently, and enjoy excellent conversation, you will soon recognize that Miss Welty's values, however reluctant she is to express them directly, are of a particular, recognizable type, one that descends from an individual who may be thought of as the progenitor of all such values in modern Western culture, the sixteenth-century French aristocrat, Michel de Montaigne.

High sense experience:
Michel de Montaigne (1533–1592)

As with Welty, you cannot pursue Montaigne's personal beliefs too directly. You will not find them listed conveniently in some tract, or laboriously argued in a philosophical tome. You must be patient and approach his personal beliefs obliquely by first getting to know the man. For example, when we meet Montaigne in his delightful but purposefully wandering *Essays* (Montaigne invented the term *essay*, which originally referred to an attempt to gain knowledge, especially self-knowledge and moral knowledge), he is wearing silk hose and padded doublet covered by a wrap of vulture's skin to protect himself against a piercing cold wind as he paces his library on the top floor of a tower, which is itself attached to a fortified manor house perched high on a hill overlooking the rolling, checkerboarded fields of rural Gascony. As he observes,

I am above the gateway, and can see below me my garden, my farmyard, and most parts of my house. There I turn the pages now of one book, now of another, without order and without plan, reading by snatches. Sometimes I reflect, and sometimes I compose and dictate my reflections, walking up and down, as at present.

On the first [floor of the tower] is my chapel, on the second a bedroom with ante-chambers, where I often lie. . . . My [top-floor] library is circular in shape, with no flat wall except that taken up by my table and chair; and, being rounded, it presents me with all my books at once, arranged about me on five tiers of shelves. From this room I have three open views, and its free space is sixteen paces across. . . . If I were not more afraid of the trouble than the cost—trouble which deters me from every kind of business—I could easily join to each side a gallery a hundred paces long and twelve paces wide on the same level. For . . . every place of retirement requires a room for walking. . . .

Formerly, [the tower] was the most useless part of the house. Now I spend most of the days of my life there, and most of the hours of the day. . . . It is my throne, and I try to rule here absolutely. . . . Miserable, to my mind, is the man who has no place in his house where he can be alone, where he can privately attend to his needs, where he can conceal himself! Ambition fitly requites her servants by keeping them always on show. . . . They can have no privacy even in the privy. . . . I find it rather more bearable always to be alone than never to have the power to be so.

A servant breaks the spell of solitude by announcing that an armed horseman is at the gate. Montaigne recollects that

I knew him by name, and had reason to trust him as a neighbour and distant connexion. I admitted him as I do everyone. There he was, in a terrible fright, with his horse panting and worn out. This is the story he told me: that he had been set upon a mile or so away by an enemy of his, whom I also knew—and I had heard about their feud; that his enemy had made him clap on his spurs to some purpose; that having been caught in disarray and outnumbered, he had fled to my gates for safety; and that he was very anxious about his men, whom he supposed to be either dead or prisoners. In my innocence I tried to comfort, reassure, and hearten him.

Presently there came four or five of his soldiers, with the same appearance of terror, and demanded entrance. They were followed by more, and by still more, well-equipped and well-armed, to the number of twenty-five or thirty, all pretending that the enemy was at their heels. This mystery began to rouse my suspicions. I was not unaware of the times I was living in, or that my house might be an object of great envy. . . . However . . . not being able to get rid of my visitors without a complete breach, I took . . . the simplest course, as I always do, and had them all admitted.

These men remained mounted in my courtyard, while their chief was with me in my hall. He had declined to have his horse stabled, saying that he would have to depart as soon as he had news of his men. He saw that he was master of the situation, and nothing now remained but to carry out his plan. . . . [Yet] . . . he remounted his horse; and his men, whose eyes were constantly fixed on him, to see what signal he would give them, were amazed to see him ride away and abandon his advantage.

In the midst of religious warfare and banditry, plague periodically grips the countryside:

Apprehension ... is especially dangerous in this disease. ... You ... spend forty days worrying ... with your imagination working on you ... all that time, and making even your health into a fever. ... [Among the peasants], each and everyone renounced all concern for life. The grapes, which are the principal wealth of the district, remained hanging on the vines; and all unconcernedly prepared themselves for a death which they expected that night or on the morrow. ... Because they are dying in the same month, children and the young and old, they cease to be appalled, they cease to lament. I saw some who were afraid of being left behind, as in some dreadful solitude, and I generally found them quite unconcerned except about their burial. It distressed them to see bodies scattered about the fields, at the mercy of the wild animals, which immediately infested them. One man, while still healthy, was digging his grave; some others lay down in theirs while they were yet alive; and one of my labourers, as he was dying, shovelled the earth down over himself with his hands and feet.

Montaigne is spared from plague, but suffers excruciating kidney stones, an inherited affliction which had killed his father: "People ... see you sweating with anguish, growing pale, flushing, trembling ... suffering strange contractions and convulsions, and at times dropping great tears from your eyes. You discharge thick, dark, and dreadful urine, or have it stopped by a sharp rough-edged stone that cruelly pricks and tears the neck of your penis; and all the time you are talking to those around you with an ordinary expression, joking in the intervals with your servants, taking your share in ... conversation."

Notwithstanding these obstacles, and despite long absences from the tower, first to visit Rome by way of Switzerland (where Montaigne views, and rejects, the novelty of using knives and forks instead of fingers at supper) and then to serve as mayor of Bordeaux, the *Essays* are eventually completed. The first two unrevised volumes are presented to Henry III, monarch of France, equally famous for his transvestitism, his court *mignons*, his exquisite manners, and his love of learning. A three-volume edition is later presented to the dashing and energetically heterosexual Henry of Navarre (Henry IV), whom the nobleman has helped ascend the throne. Even the papal censor joins in the praise, although his successors will eventually reconsider and place the work on the Index of Forbidden Books.

Essays: General approach

In setting down his *Essays*, Montaigne reveals himself as the kind of man who does not stick to the subject, and who does so brilliantly. As the French philosopher Diderot later described his method: "He cares little where he starts from, how he goes, or where he ends up." Topic is piled on topic (idleness, books, smells, even cannibals)—"I take the first subject that chance offers me, all are . . . equally good"; digression is piled on digression (a discussion on Christian mysticism merges with a crude scatological story, both adorned by abstruse Latin references). The only thread that runs through all these disconnected impressions is the author himself, his mind and life, the former occasionally contradictory, the latter presented without a trace of chronology.

Even in the midst of this melee, however, the reader is not confused or lost. On the contrary, we are carried along by a transparently clear prose; by an easy, relaxed, entertainingly conversational tone; by an absence of artifice or pretension ("I had rather know what [Brutus] did in his study and his chamber than what he did in the Forum and before the Senate"); and above all by a rivetingly honest stream of self-revelation. It is not just that we learn the nobleman's sleeping habits (late to bed and late to rise: "I like to lie hard and alone . . . without my wife"), or bowel habits (early in the morning), or weakness for physical beauty (the chief criterion by which he chooses household servants as well as lady loves), or fondness for animals ("I cannot easily refuse my dog when he . . . asks me to play with him at an inopportune moment"). It is rather that through this one human being, who has chosen to "spy on himself from close up" with complete objectivity, we are able to learn about ourselves.

A man who is now a doctor tells the story of being unable to consummate his first love affair during high school. In a state of near-tearful collapse, he secretly visits a psychiatrist who tries to be reassuring: Impotence in young men is often curable, though the treatment may take years. Talking sessions ensue, but self-doubt and panic are only further magnified. Then the youth chances on a passage from the *Essays*:

I am . . . of the opinion that those comical impediments which so embarrass our society that they talk of nothing else are most likely caused by apprehensions and fears. I have personal knowledge of the case of a man for whom I can answer as for myself, and who could not fall under the least suspicion of impotence. . . . He had heard a comrade of his tell of an extraordinary loss of manhood that had fallen on him at a most inconvenient moment; and, when he was himself in a like situation, the full horror of this story had suddenly struck his imagination so vividly that he suffered a similar loss himself. Afterwards the wretched memory of his misadventure so devoured and tyrannized over him that he became subject to relapses. He found some remedy for this mental trick in another trick; by himself confessing this weakness of his and declaring it in advance, he relieved the strain on his mind and the mishap being expected, the responsibility for it diminished and weighed upon him less. . . . He was then completely . . . cured of his infirmity. For once a man has been capable with a certain woman, he will never be incapacitated with her again unless out of real impotence.

After reading this passage, the young man is instantly cured.

Attack on Christianity and logic

The author would assure us that there is no message at all buried among the charming intimacies and digressions of the *Essays*, that he has reached no "conclusions," that he is not "well enough instructed to instruct others," that his work is "frivolous" and of "little weight." But such aristocratic subterfuges must be set aside. The *Essays* are not at all what they appear. They are at once a bold repudiation of both authority and logic, and the most complete exposition yet offered of a third alternative, an approach to forming values based primarily on personal sense experience.

Montaigne does not directly attack the idea of authority, much less the all-powerful spiritual authority of his day, the Catholic church of France. To do so would bring himself and his family to ruin. As he tells a favorite lady: "I speak the truth, not to the full, but as much as I dare; and as I become older, I become a little more daring." Besides, in his view the right way to deal with imperious spiritual authorities, Catholicism included, is not to contest them; opposition just makes them wax hotter and stronger. The best approach is to ignore them, to show them a tolerant, even an affectionate, respect, and then to do as you please.

Nor does the nobleman want to interfere with anyone else's beliefs. If you think that you need God or the church, or an infallible book, that is all right. Indeed, popular religion is conceded to have two indisputable advantages, at least in the short run: Not only does it provide answers to questions that are otherwise unanswerable; it also helps you discipline yourself and control passions that might otherwise prove uncontrollable. In the long run, however, too many answers, in a world where answers are not really available, may become a sort of drug. Like other drugs, it may lead to a cycle of craven dependence alternating with boundless pride, a deadly combination that virtually guarantees misery for believer and unbeliever alike. What people really need, according to Montaigne, is just the reverse: an independent spirit tempered by humility and modesty. Such a spirit may choose to worship a God, but not a God who "fears . . . is angry . . . loves" or otherwise suffers "agitations and emotions" common to us. Better still is to make no assumptions, to remain "unresolved and undecided," to rest one's head on the "soft and pleasant and healthful . . . pillow [of] ignorance and lack of curiosity" about all worlds beyond our world.

If the misleading certainty of Christianity is to be resisted, so, Montaigne tells us, is the equally suspect hope of logic. The deductive method is all "preambles, definitions, classifications . . . etymologies [and] disputes . . . about words. . . . A stone is a body. But if you press the point: and what is a body?—a substance—and what is a substance? and so on. . . . One [merely] substitutes one word for another, that is . . . less well understood." Such verbal gymnastics are then followed by

scattering and chopping . . . small questions [until] the world teem[s] . . . with uncertainties and disputes. . . . Have you ever seen [someone] trying to divide a mass of quicksilver into a number of parts? The more he presses and squeezes it, and tries to bring it under control, the more [it] keeps breaking and diversifying itself indefinitely. So it is here . . . by the subdivision of these subtleties, we [accomplish little]. . . . Philosophy's object is to calm tempests of the soul, to teach . . . virtue, which does not, as the [logicians] allege, stand on the top of a sheer mountain, rugged and inaccessible. Those who have approached it have found it, on the contrary, dwelling on a fair, fertile plateau, from which it can clearly see all things below it. . . . Anyone who knows the way can get there by shady, grassy, and sweetly flowering paths, pleasantly and up an easy and smooth incline. . . . Through unfamiliarity with this . . . virtue . . . which is the professed and irreconcilable enemy of bitterness, trouble, fear, and constraint; and which has nature for guide, and good-fortune and delight for companions, [logicians] have created in their feeble imaginations this absurd, gloomy, querulous, grim, threatening, and scowling image, and placed it on a rock apart, among brambles, as a bogey to terrify people.

Flight from abstraction

According to Montaigne, what both Christianity and logic share in common is a high level of abstraction, together with a wearisome habit of constantly drawing distinctions and rendering judgments. According to these two great faiths, life is analyzable, generalizable, categorizable, systematizable, simplifiable. Whatever question or problem arises, there is a commandment, a rule, a recipe, a methodology, or a theory to provide guidance. But, protests Montaigne, this is all a pathetic fallacy, a naive confidence in explanations, which on close examination, explain nothing. The truth is that we operate under a veil of ignorance, both in general ("When I play with my cat, who knows whether she is amusing herself with me, or I with her?") and in the world of value judgments. In addition, the world is ambiguous, full of good that is evil and evil that is good, and "our existence is impossible without this mixture." Under these circumstances, moral evidence is concrete and personal, not abstract or organizable. Put differently, the proper course of action depends on the particular circumstances, and the best guide is always one's common sense, defined as the ability to hold in one's mind a variety of considerations all at once and then to arrive at a sound and experienced judgment.

Lessons of sense experience

The idea that there are no infallible teachers or theories, never have been and never will be, that each of us stands alone and must fashion his or her own destiny, might seem depressing to some. To Montaigne, on the contrary, it would be depressing if answers existed, for then life would consist of passively following someone else's blueprint rather than boldly and vigorously setting out on a uniquely personal and never-to-be-repeated adventure.

But how is this adventure to be conducted? Not, it must be emphasized, by falling back into gross sensationalism, or some form of anti-intellectualism. To reject Christianity, the religion of the book, or logic, the religion of deductive reasoning, is not to reject the mind or reason. What is needed is *empirical reasoning*— the patient, steady accumulation of facts drawn from personal sense experience, the constant opening of oneself to the evidence of one's eyes and ears, no matter how unexpected or uncomfortable this evidence may be, the deliberate opening of oneself to alternative ways of living and being. "Never rely on [others'] opinions," but always base your own opinion on as much information as possible, information that has been sifted with a critical, skeptical, and preferably humorous eye.

To get "the facts," ransack your own daily life—your family, friends, the immediate world around you: "The most familiar and commonplace events, could we but see them in [a fresh] light, would furnish us with the most marvelous examples [of how to live or not to live]." Then amplify this experience with books and travel (both are important). Try not to let any of this raw data "pass and slip by. . . . Rather than let [even] sleep . . . escape me, I used once to have myself woken up, in order that I might catch a glimpse of it. . . . [If] I am tickled by some . . . [moment], I do not allow it to be stolen by the senses; I bring my mind to it. . . . I enjoy [life] twice as much as others, for the measure of enjoyment depends on the . . . attention that we give to it."

Finally, and most important, look for heroes, paradigms, models that can be used, not as authorities to be blindly followed, but as options to be explored, imitated, tested, and—always—eventually discarded. As Voltaire said of Montaigne: "He bases his ideas on the ideas of great men. He judges them, he fights them, he talks with them. . . . Always (and I love that!) he knows how to doubt [them]."

Sense experience, especially intense sense experience, may be a great teacher, but to the extent that people open themselves to it they are often swept away by violent currents and end up either as Don Juan, a mindless voluptuary, or as Leporello, his score-keeping, nonparticipating servant, when the bare minimum goal is to participate and observe at the same time. As usual, Montaigne does not offer any systematic advice for coping with this problem. In his oblique fashion, however, he suggests that certain attitudes, character traits, or (to use the old term) virtues are helpful, indeed may be essential, in order to experience life in all its raw power without losing one's footing. At the risk of systematizing the inveterate enemy of system, these particular cardinal virtues—pagan rather than Christian in inspiration and spirit—may be listed as follows:

Openness to pleasure

On this point, Montaigne places himself entirely at odds with Christian fundamentalism. He is a man "over whom the body exercises great sway," who "give[s] in to those appetites that are insistent," who "loathe[s] that inhuman teaching which would

make us despise and dislike the . . . body," who places no particular value on monogamy or marital fidelity, and who states that
"I have never been harmed by doing anything that was a real
pleasure to me," although he admits to "a couple of [adolescent]
touches . . . both slight and transitory" acquired by unwisely
visiting prostitutes. The only real drawback to sexual pleasure —
as opposed to milder pleasures such as conversation, amusements, books, companionable friends, affection — is that it "withers with age" and, for that very reason, youth should pay no
attention to older persons who have been forced into an involuntary repentance. Nor should one try to dress up sex with a spiritual or intellectual fig leaf: "For in the business of love, which is
principally a matter of sight and touch, one can do something
without the charms of the mind, nothing without the charms of
the body."

Tolerance

To be fully open to sense experience, one must give up the
ingrained habit of condemning and criticizing and interfering
with others: "I do not look closely into a footman's chastity [nor
dismiss as] barbarous anything that is contrary to [my] own habits." What is more difficult, one must cultivate a state of mind that
actually welcomes criticism from others: "My mind so frequently
contradicts and condemns itself that it is all one to me if someone
else does so, especially as I only give his criticism such authority
as I choose."

Avoidance of pride, pretense, formality, dishonesty

Such barriers against the world are a particular bane of the middle class, especially the churchgoing middle class. The very rich
and very poor often dispense with them, although for quite
different reasons (in the one case, complete financial security; in
the other, nothing to lose). The middle class is always fearful of
revealing itself too fully, of causing offense, and of losing what it
has so laboriously accumulated; even so, "it is a cowardly and
servile characteristic to go about in disguise, concealed behind a

mask, without the courage to show oneself as one is. . . . It is not [of course] necessary always to say everything, for that would be foolish; but what we say should be what we think." The very worst part of dissimulation and pretense is that it always leads to crippling inner conflict. By being one thing "inwardly" and another "on the surface," we dissipate our energy and purpose, losing our ability to "go forward all of a piece . . . [with an] undivided strength."

Avoidance of rigidity, eccentricity, fastidiousness

Inflexibility is a prison to which many of the most independent minds consign themselves. Montaigne himself is not free of this vice, but

to be tied and bound of necessity to one [habitual approach] is . . . to exist . . . not to live. . . . Our chief talent is the power of suiting ourselves to different ways of life. . . . A young man ought to break his rules in order to stir up his energy, and keep it from getting mouldy and weak, [as] there is no way of life so foolish as one that is carried out by rule and discipline. If he takes my advice, he will often plunge even into excesses; otherwise the slightest over-indulgence will upset him, and he will become difficult and disagreeable in company. The most perverse quality in a well-bred man is fastidiousness . . . delicacy of humor . . . [or too much concern about] health. . . . I thought I was honoring a certain nobleman . . . when I asked him, in good company, how many times in his life he had got drunk in Germany in the interest of the king's business. Taking this in the right spirit, he answered "three times" and told us the circumstances.

Avoidance of obsessions, ambition, hard work, too much seriousness of purpose

Obsessions are "evil" and an "enemy of life" because they blind a man to all the rich detail and texture of the surrounding world ("When I am walking by myself in a beautiful orchard . . . my thoughts [may] dwell for part of the time on distant events, [but] I bring them back . . . to the walk, the orchard, the charm of this solitude"). Ambition is particularly to be avoided, partly because it requires perjuring or obligating or even enslaving oneself to others to gain their support; partly because it is so frequently futile ("The highest places are usually seized by the least capable men. . . . If you do succeed . . . you leave the world and—'that is that!'"); partly because even the most idealistic projects are rarely justified ("Statilius replied in just that strain when Brutus invited him to join the conspiracy against Caesar; he considered the enterprise a just one, but did not think that men were worth taking any trouble about"); above all, because it is based on a misapprehension of success:

"He has spent his life [on nothing]," we say, and "I have done nothing. . . . " What! have you not lived? . . . Our great and glorious masterpiece is to live properly. . . . The man who knows how to enjoy his existence as he ought has [already] attained to an absolute perfection. . . . We [only] seek other conditions . . . to reign, to lay up treasure, to build . . . because we do not understand the proper use of our own, and go out of ourselves because we do not know what is within us. [But] it is no good our mounting on stilts, for even on stilts we have to walk with our own legs; and upon the most exalted throne in the world it is still our own bottom that we sit on.

The case against hard work is similar, and just as vehement: "As for biting my nails over the study of Aristotle [or putting my] mind . . . on the rack, toiling for fourteen or fifteen hours a day, or stoutly pursuing any knowledge . . . that I have never done." Although pure idleness is burdensome and not to be desired, "I am a sworn foe to constraint, assiduity, and perseverance." Moreover, the most dangerous hard work is specialized hard work because "our object is not to make a grammarian, or a logician, [or any other professional], but a gentleman."

The worst feature of all these worldly obsessions is the way they persist, first in one shape, then in another, always adopting some new and clever disguise. When faced with their blandishments, the only remedy is to check one's seriousness at the door, to reorder one's priorities, to sup at table with "the amusing rather than the wise," to remember to "prefer beauty to goodness . . . in bed," and "for serious conversation [to seek out] ability . . . combined with dishonesty."

Detachment

Montaigne's first five virtues "open" a person who might otherwise be "confined and pent up" inside. But openness to life is an incomplete virtue; it must be moderated and disciplined in order to prevent a self-destructive orgy of sense experience—of too much sex or other pleasures or a total abandonment of work and ambition—leading to an eventual breakdown. The first and, in some respects, the most important moderating virtue is detachment. More than any other device, it is the ability to watch ourselves from outside, to see ourselves with the same cool impersonal gaze we turn on others, that protects us from an excess of mood or action. Without detachment, we "flush" and "tremble" from alternating reveries of greed and fear. As proof of his own efforts to achieve detachment, Montaigne attempts to refute the idea that sexual pleasure at its orgasmic peak completely obliterates consciousness. He reports that "it may be otherwise, and that one can sometimes, by force of will, successfully direct one's mind at that very instant to other thoughts, but one must prepare and brace it deliberately."

Self-discipline

In addition to detachment, Montaigne approves of old-fashioned self-discipline. This is not unlike Christian self-discipline in some respects, especially in its underlying assumption about human nature. Whereas most Christians believe in a doctrine of "original sin"—that unredeemed human nature is inherently evil and sinful—Montaigne believes that everyone, himself included, "is nothing but a fool," a difference more in tone than in substance.

On the other hand, this self-discipline is different. It does not entail dependence, submission, or conformity before a wrathful or loving God; nor deprivation of the flesh; nor the grave and majestic solemnity of ancient puritanism; nor the prim prudery of a bloodless and attenuated puritanism. It is a combination of personal training (thus resurrecting the Greek root of asceticism, which refers to "practice" and, indirectly, to games and sport), of refined good taste, and of ordinary good sense. A mature mind knows that "the appetite for [worldly goods] is . . . made sharper by their enjoyment than by their scarcity . . . that excess is the bane of pleasure, [that] temperance is not its scourge but its seasoning." The best precaution to observe is a simple one: Whenever desire becomes insistent, even commanding, pull back. Let a little time pass before indulging that particular appetite again. Montaigne even strikes a metal with the words *Que sais-je* (What do I know?) engraved on one side and *Je m'abstiens* (I restrain myself) on the other.

Self-reliance

To strive for self-reliance is yet another way to control oneself. Why? Because self-indulgence, in the form of impatience or too much pleasure or too much ease, invariably involves an imposition on others. When Montaigne faces a variety of worldly dangers, ranging from marauding bandits to court intrigues, he considers seeking help from a more powerful lord. But he quickly realizes "that it [is] safest to rely on myself in my distress . . . see to my own protection, [and so to strengthen myself] that it would take a heavy blow to throw me out of [the] saddle." In this respect, a degree of personal misfortune is a positive good. It hardens us, keeps our passions and weaknesses in check, and helps us to maintain some order and sobriety in the face of limitless temptation.

Eight virtues in one

Can all eight virtues be summarized in one? One might speak of being simultaneously open and closed; of being a lover but also an athlete of sense experience; of never commanding oneself but always relying on detachment, self-knowledge, and an easy, unserious, good-natured self-discipline; of being in harness, but loose in harness; of being successful and effective without any apparent effort. Although each of these formulations reveals something, they are still entirely too stiff to capture Montaigne's designedly paradoxical doctrine. A picture would be better—a picture, for example, of the younger Scipio, "first of the Romans," who in the midst of planning his fateful military campaign against Hannibal in Africa, a campaign that would decide the future of the civilized world, takes time to "stroll . . . along the seashore, gaily engaged in the childish amusement of picking up and selecting shells, and playing ducks-and-drakes; or, in bad weather entertaining himself with the ribald writing of comedies, in which he reproduce[s] the most ordinary and vulgar actions of men."

Objections to Montaigne

If one were sitting with Montaigne in his tower, enjoying the kind of civilized conversation that he loved, it would be interesting to learn what he thought about the following objections to his doctrine of relying on a highly cultivated and disciplined form of personal sense experience.

It is like a library without a catalogue

According to philosopher Bertrand Russell, Montaigne is "content with confusion; discovery is delightful and system is its enemy." On the surface, this approach sounds appealing. Do we not learn more from wonder, search, ambiguity, inconsistency, disorder, paradox, irony, and nuance than from their opposites? Besides, the rest of Montaigne's arguments possess an undeniable nobility: that each of us must find our own way, with only personal sense experience as a guide; that there are no true authorities, that dependency is self-destructive, whether on a God or on another human being; that there are valuable models to be studied and emulated, but only up to a point, and only insofar as they fit one's individual case; that one must immerse oneself in experience, in everyday life, in books, and in travel, all the while remaining aloof and detached and forming one's own unique judgment, taste, and character.

Appealing and noble these doctrines may be, but are they practical? Is a way of life designed by a sixteenth-century gentleman living in a remote corner of France even conceivable today? Since Montaigne's time, many millions of books have been published. The entire world has been opened for travel. Where is one to begin? Should one still regard Horace and Seneca and Plutarch and other ancient Romans as the place to begin in forming and testing one's personal beliefs? What about the ancient Greeks? Merely reading the relatively few surviving works of the ancient world, together with all the books written about them, would consume a lifetime, leaving the moderns and all the limitless vistas of travel untouched.

One is reminded of the novelist Thomas Wolfe's gargantuan appetites, of how he tried as an undergraduate at Harvard to read every volume in Widener Library, beginning at random with one stack, and proceeding book by book from there. It is not recorded where Wolfe abandoned the attempt, which was more symbolic than real. The point is that most library users rely on a catalogue to guide them, and Montaigne not only eliminates the "catalogue"–the direct teaching method of other "religions"–he despises it as an obstacle to our development. Even Montaigne's literary legacy, the essay form that he invented, tends to thwart the modern student of sense experience. For almost four hundred years, the prestige of the essay, with its charmingly unstructured, digressive, and conversational tone, has been immense. We see it everywhere, in newspapers, magazines, books, or, increasingly, transposed to radio and television. Reporters who have tired of recounting the news like to write short pieces on "loneliness" or "the relations of men and women" or similarly airy topics that mostly serve as a point of departure for unrelated observations or discursive autobiography, and whose contents are often immediately forgettable. The convention of the essay is so strong that even scholarly research articles in some fields are expected to follow the form, to convey new information not just simply and directly and precisely and economically, but with art and indirection. Because few researchers are artists, the result may be only squandered time, both the writer's and the reader's.

It lacks a goal or purpose

In this respect, Montaigne's brand of high sense experience completely denies the basic outlook of authority and logic. For example, in Catholicism, the form of authority with which Montaigne was most concerned, even the church, God's representative on earth, is seen as only a means to the ultimate goal of God. In logic, deduction is the means to the goal of an irrefutable argument, a Q.E.D. (*quod erat demonstrandum*) proof. In high sense experience, sense experience is both the means *and* the goal. In other words, truth is not something that we find at the end of a quest, it *is* the quest. This is a revolutionary idea in a purely theoretical sense and in a practical sense as well. Westerners have always been work- and goal-oriented. Yet here is a rather admirable man, Montaigne, who says that the work ethic is misguided; that goals are not important; that one goal, so long as it is disciplined and not an imposition on other people, is about as good as any other; that how you live is more important than what you accomplish.

It is selfish

To the observant Christian eye, something else is odd about this ethic of high sense experience. Although it strongly disavows the standard egoistic longings—to reign as a monarch, to win military triumphs, to gain immense riches—it nevertheless glorifies and cultivates the self. *Personal* sense experience, *self*-knowledge, and *self*-control are emphasized to the exclusion of all else, even to the exclusion of unselfish and altruistic acts. Montaigne himself is so likable, so calm, so comfortable, so intimate, that it is easy to overlook this aspect of his doctrine. But it is there all the same, and freely admitted: "It pleases me not to be interested in the affairs of others, and to be free from responsibility for them." Toward his close friends, the noble seigneur is both protective and loving. Toward his wife and children and servants, he is protective if not particularly loving. Beyond this narrow circle of benevolence there appears to be only self-absorption and duty. Of course, Montaigne would argue that one must put one's own house in order before attempting to assist others and that assistance all too often creates dependency. If self-reliance and self-knowledge require all one's energies, no harm is done to others, which cannot always be said about more directly altruistic religions.

It is elitist

To say that a way of life assumes an unlimited leisure for its particular activities, that it eschews common purposes and goals, that it ignores the masses in favor of oneself and a select few is to say, in brief, that it is elitist. And this is, indeed, a central feature of what we have called high sense experience. It is a privileged way of life, symbolized not only by Montaigne's hereditary manor house with its famous tower-library, but also by the spires of Oxford and Cambridge universities, by the undergraduates' scouts (servants), by spacious suites and gardens, by a tutorial system that assigns a private tutor to each student.

Such elitist privilege is not to be confused with either snobbery or luxury. High sense experience is "open to all the talents" and likes nothing better than to find protegés among the ranks of the "natural aristocracy," the most gifted students of modest or even impoverished background. Nor is it especially enamored of worldly goods, other than beautiful objects of art, for which it has a decided fondness. But snobbery and luxury aside, Montaigne is concerned with the elect, not with the masses, and he does not share the idea that a doctrine must be suitable for the masses in order that it be suitable for the elect. When he endorses sexual adventure or leisurely reading at a fine university or foreign travel as an essential part of education, it does not occur to him that the masses might want or expect these things, or that his methods might eventually collapse under the sheer weight of numbers. It would indeed have been remarkable if he had foreseen any of this: high sense experience steadily gained in prestige for nearly four centuries, and only reached a kind of peak in the United States in the early 1960s. Shortly thereafter, the evidence of collapse became increasingly apparent: in Ph.D.s who hoped to retire to their own tower but who could not support themselves and ended up as insurance brokers; in the students who expected to find something of the Oxford and Cambridge experience at their state university but were unable to get close enough to a professor to engage him in conversation; in the hordes of would-be travelers who had to settle for being "tourists"; in the disappointed pioneers of free love and the sexual revolution—in other words, in all those people who naively trusted that high sense experience could be a mass phenomenon but who learned that in its purest form it was for the few, and the very few.

It is a status symbol

For much of the 1960s and 1970s, high sense experience was anything but a status symbol. The effort to transform it into a mass phenomenon had failed; the Ph.D. glut was a joke; students abandoned art, history, and literature in droves for economics and business courses; art museums and rare book libraries languished. Then, during the 1980s, something rather unexpected happened. The newly rich, of whom there was an unprecedented supply during the Reagan presidency, especially in New York and Los Angeles, began to covet the domestic style and artistic furnishings long associated with people of Montaigne's ilk. The reasons for this phenomenon were complex, but at least one factor was clear. If you had just made millions in a world awash with newly made millions, money alone would not guarantee social standing or personal prestige. On the other hand, if you owned rare and irreplaceable objects, the kind of objects that Montaigne and others like him had always taken for granted in their households, some of the objects' value and uniqueness might rub off on you.

This transmogrification of high sense experience into high status was at once broadly and narrowly based. It was broadly based in that the newly affluent, often represented by young professional couples, not just the newly rich or newly super-rich, ardently competed as "collectors" or for places on museum committees. Yet it was also narrowly based in that favored objects and institutions had to be suitable for public display, not just private connoisseurship. For example, as recently as the turn of the century, truly rare books often sold for more than even the rarest paintings. By the 1980s, however, rare paintings sold for vastly greater sums, at least partly because they could be displayed on a wall, either in a private residence or in a museum.

A library without a catalogue, aimlessness, selfishness, elitism, status seeking: These are harsh charges, and at least partially warranted. It is only fair, however, to listen to a rebuttal, a rebuttal implicitly offered by Joseph Alsop, a contemporary American who closely resembled Montaigne in his distinguished lineage, his immense learning and culture, his participation in the public life of his day (as a leading newspaper columnist covering Washington during the post–World War II years of American paramountcy), in his enjoyment of all the civilized and uncivilized pleasures that life has to offer, and not least in the size and frequent use of his library.

Alsop in effect argued that what we call high sense experience in this book has become misunderstood and debased. High sense experience, he said, is simply what the English philosopher and statesman Lord Bolingbroke called "philosophy teaching by examples." The goal of life is to find and follow the example that is right for you; the goal of education is to inculcate a variety of worthy examples from which to choose. Inculcation can be both extensive and luxurious, drawing on huge libraries, comfortable university reading rooms, fine collections and museums, and a long canon of exemplary works; or it can be plain and rough, as plain and rough and nonelitist as Abraham Lincoln educating himself with five or six dog-eared volumes. As Alsop pointed out in the *Washington Post*:

Lincoln's texts . . . were first of all the Bible and Shakespeare. . . . He not infrequently recited the [Bible] or the great soliloquies, sometimes in the course of important policy discussions, and on a five-hour boat trip to City Point, after Appomattox . . . passed the time for his companions with Shakespeare readings. It is interesting trying to imagine a similar journey by water with one of our last three presidents. After the Bible and Shakespeare, history was his main study. As a young man in New Salem, he read the whole of Gibbon and all of Rollin's history of the world . . . with . . . much space devoted to . . . Greek and Roman history. . . .

The first point that strikes you about the foregoing [list] of books [is that what] Lincoln read and learned is neither read, nor learned, nor even taught in any normal American school or university today. . . . I do not suppose as many as one university student in a thousand has ever read so much as a chapter of the Bible in the . . . noble . . . King James version, and I fear the same ratio of ignorance prevails among American university professors . . . Lincoln, *per contra*, went through life without the slightest acquaintance with the social sciences, in happy ignorance of the brand of English favored by the Modern Language Association. . . . If all of us learned to [think and] express ourselves as Lincoln did—by all but getting by heart the King James version—we might even have the cure of the gummy tide of jargon and pseudoscientific pretentiousness which is spreading . . . today.

The prodigal alternative to high sense experience

High sense experience is composed of one part license and one part discipline, with a garnish of grace and refinement to render the discipline effortless, or at least invisible. Gradually lighten the discipline, eliminate it entirely, or take both license and discipline to fantastic extremes, and you have a very different approach to sense experience, an approach that in Walter Pater's famous phrase seeks "to burn always in [a] hard, gem-like flame, to maintain [an] ecstasy" of experience. Such an approach is no longer the way of Montaigne but rather the way of a prodigal son of Montaigne's, a son who has rebelled against the gentle restraint of the father just as the father rebelled against the severe restraint of Catholic Christianity.

This basic intergenerational quarrel between two related but very different doctrines, each based on sense experience but drawing quite different conclusions, may be illustrated by an episode from Thomas Merton's memoirs, *The Seven Storey Mountain*. Both of Merton's parents had died, and while he was studying at an English secondary school his godfather, a fashionable English doctor and an old friend of his father's, offered his London flat to Merton as a refuge during school holidays. The flat was luxurious, with beautiful antiques, a French maid, and every comfort, including breakfast in bed. Conversation at the dinner table or later over coffee in the drawing room was sophisticated, witty, worldly, derisory of Christianity and middle-class morals, preoccupied with new art, films, books, or the latest word on which English aristocrat was "thought to take dope." Tom breathed in this atmosphere like the purest oxygen and began to imitate his godfather's every taste and mannerism. Yet when he began to squander his allowance and got a girlfriend pregnant, this led to an irreparable breach: It was one thing to be free in conversation, quite another to be free in conduct. For as Montaigne had said, a gentleman might be "disordered," "unrestrained," even "depraved" in his "opinions," but not "imprudent" in his "appetites."

Merton did not long remain a prodigal son. By embracing the Roman Catholic church and becoming a Trappist monk in Kentucky, he repudiated a religion of sense experience entirely, both his godfather's high version and his own wilder version. In any case, it is doubtful whether Merton was ever a complete prodigal because, although he was always attracted to rebellion, escapism, and fantasy, he never completely gave himself up to a biblical "wasting of substance." To be a complete prodigal, one must be determined to affront the comfortable; to defy the respectable; to abjure "maturity" and "responsibility"; to repudiate seriousness, caution, decency, normalcy, and wholesomeness; to avoid a "normal" career, raising children, or participating in politics; to be rebellious and insolent, yet playful and light hearted; full of brilliance, wit, extravagance and surprise; capable of shocking, dazzling, and charming all at once—in short, to retain all the superficial ease and polish and verve of the high religion of sense experience without any of the character building that is supposed to take place beneath the surface.

Although the traits just enumerated describe a similar approach to sense experience, there is no single, uniform way of life among prodigals. Even more than with high sense experience, which already abhors systematization or generalization, prodigality must be approached through specific individuals, all of whom are rebels, escapists, and fantasists, but who differ sharply in interpretation and degree. Only by separately scrutinizing their lives, beginning with the romantic escapism of the contemporary novelist Lawrence Durrell and ending with the profligacy of the playwright Tennessee Williams, is it possible to build up a collective portrait, to define the faith in concrete terms, to decide what prodigality really means, both for those who adopt it and for those who must live with those who adopt it.

The romantic escapist

At age twenty-three, poet and novelist Lawrence Durrell abandons industrial society "as serene and bland as suet . . . which dispossessed me of myself and tried to destroy in me all that was singular and unique." With one completed novel, a new wife, and a $20 per week allowance from his mother, he sets out for the Greek island of Corfu, a verdant gem set in the blue Ionian Sea ("Somewhere between Calabria and Corfu the blue really begins") and discovers a world of sun, land and seascape, friends, work, love, physical pleasure, tastes, sounds, sights, smells, touch; a world of pure happiness, protectively bracketed against the intrusion of past or future. The description that follows is taken from a diary, kept between April 1937 and September 1938, later incorporated into *Prospero's Cell*:

29.4.37

It is April and we have taken an old fisherman's house in the extreme north of the island—Kalamai. Ten sea-miles from the town, and some thirty kilometres by road. . . . The hill runs clear up into the sky behind it, so that the cypresses and olives overhang this room in which I sit and write.

5.5.37

The books have arrived by water. Confusion, adjectives, smoke, and the deafening pumping of the wheezy Diesel engine . . .

7.5.37

The cape opposite is bald; a wilderness of rock-thistle and melancholy asphodel—the drear sea-squill. It was on a ringing spring day that we discovered the house. The sky lay in a heroic blue arc as we came down the stone ladder. I remember N. saying distinctly to Theodore: "But the quietness alone makes it another country." We looked through the hanging screen of olive-branches on to the white sea wall with fishing-tackle drying on it. A neglected balcony. The floors were cold. Fowls clucked softly in the gloom where the great olive-press lay, waiting its season.

4.7.37

We breakfast at sunrise after a bathe. Grapes and Hymettos honey, black coffee, eggs, and the light clear-tasting Papastratos cigarette. Unconscious transition from the balcony to the rock outside. . . . Sitting here on this spit we can see the dolphins and the steamers passing within hail almost. We bathe naked, and the sun and water make our skins feel old and rough, like precious lace.

27.10.37

Unlike the majority of recluses [Count D.] is a hospitable man. . . . We dine late by candlelight . . . portraits of Venetian ancestors stare pallidly at us from the walls in their mouldering frames. . . .

After the dinner the Count takes up a branch of candles and leads the way to the vine-covered terrace. . . . Here we sit and talk away the greater part of the night. In the silences between our sentences we can hear the oranges dropping from the trees in the orchard—dull single thuds upon the mossy ground. The marble table is wet with dew. An owl cries, and the watchdogs at the lodge grumble and shake their chains.

. . . And so quietly back to the house, and through the great doorway. The candles have burnt down to their guttering ends. The Count distributes them like blessings. We make our way to our several rooms in silence . . . closing the shutters against the staring moon.

The naif

If an island idyll in the Mediterranean represents one kind of rebellion, escape, and fantasy, another is simple naivete, a child-like refusal to face the realities of adult life, as exemplified by Lawrence Durrell's description of his good friend and mentor, the novelist Henry Miller: "As for Henry, he was never *there*; he was always lost in his dreams. One day he even had the idea of taking a train to Berlin, so as to go and talk to Hitler for five minutes to persuade him to abandon his military ambitions! . . . Miller was confident: "If he could only be made to laugh, it might change everything."*

The aesthete

For the aesthete, rebellion, escapism, and fantasy are closely allied with a larger agenda of beauty and taste. To live well is to surround oneself and devote oneself to *objets d'art* and *objets de luxe*. At its worst, this approach is everything that Montaigne dislikes: a kind of hothouse "ladies-and-gents" mentality, that is, a passive and conspicuous fastidiousness, an elaborately self-conscious ritual of choosing the right wines, clothes, and interior decoration. Yet as the British-American writer Harold Acton demonstrates, estheticism has a positive dimension as well, a dimension of genuine appreciation, style, and erudition. In Acton's case, the style is cosmopolitan and gently nostalgic, reflect-

---

* Eudora Welty offers this account of Miller's visit to her in Jackson, Mississippi (Welty was a largely unknown short story writer at the time): "Henry Miller! I don't think he knew where he was since he didn't know we took him to the Rotisserie for supper three nights in a row. He said, 'Imagine a town like this having three good restaurants.' He had written . . . he'd be coming to Jackson in a glass automobile [although he arrived with no car at all] and wanted to see me. My mother said, 'Not in this house.' She didn't give a hoot what he had written in his books, it was what he had written to me. He had offered, some time earlier, to put me [a young Southern lady] in touch with an unfailing por-nographic market that I could write for if I needed the money."

ing passage through a variety of dying worlds, beginning (and ending) with a Florentine *palazzo*, but encompassing prewar Eton and Oxford, prewar China, southern Italy, and America:

In 1936 I celebrated the twenty-fifth anniversary of the Chinese Republic by moving into a perfect [Peking] mansion, with three successive courtyards and a side garden in Kung Hsien Hutung. . . . The landlord was a decrepit Manchu noble, riddled with debt, who vegetated in an outhouse with his opium paraphernalia.

Here I had ample space to hang all my pictures and arrange the old furniture I had collected. . . . A scroll of . . . Marshal [Wu Pei-fu's] blossoms, inscribed to myself, hung on my study wall. . . . [The Marshall, a former warlord] devoted himself to studying the Buddhist sutras and painting blossoms of the *Prunus mume*.

Thrust out of China by war and the Communist revolution, Acton turns his attention to the fading Bourbon aristocracy of Southern Italy: "The Princess of Trabia held a formal court of abbes who still took snuff, pallid ladies dressed in black, jaded gentlemen with pointed beards, a rubicund private chaplain, a learned librarian, an antiquated English governess of Jane Austenish gentility, and retainers who wore their liveries with a Catalan air. . . . Unfortunately I had no leisure to browse in the library which contained many rare tomes I longed to read."

A few years later, Acton visited his mother's closest friend, Florence Crane, who lived at "Castle Hill" on Boston's North Shore (the Massachusetts coast above Boston). The original structure on the site had been built by Mr. Crane as a surprise for his bride. When he asked how she liked it, she had responded, "I don't like one thing about it," and had then demolished it and built a "more classical residence of pink brick imported from Holland."

[The new mansion] was splendidly furnished in Queen Anne style, seven of the fifty-two rooms with panelling from Hogarth's London house, and ancestral portraits by Lely, Dance and Joseph Wright of Derby adorned the walls. The sporting and marine paintings interested me less, but I coveted Zoffany's portrait of Lunardi the Balloonist at

Windsor. Sumptuous editions of the classics gleamed on the shelves of the library transported from Essex House. From the terrace where exquisite humming-birds sipped the tiger lilies a wide grass mall flanked by high hedges and Venetian statues at regular intervals rolled up and down to the sea.

[Mrs. Crane and her friends] were devoted gardeners. . . . Having sublimated or eliminated what is now generically called sex, they had settled down to cultivate "gracious living." The Garden Club was a perennial resource, and at one of its meetings I was privileged to attend Mrs. Ellery Sedgwick delivered an erudite lecture on the wild flowers and exotic plants which had sprung up among the ruins of the London docks, their seeds wafted from distant lands and continents. Another lady discoursed with emotion on the tea gardens of India and Kashmir.

The decadent

A 1983 photo in *W* (the glossy periodical offshoot of *Women's Wear Daily*) shows a tall, thin, mustachioed man standing beside various Art Deco objects in his house. The caption reads:

It's inappropriate to call Richard Nelson, creative director of Neiman-Marcus advertising, a collector of Art Deco. It's his entire life style, from the vintage Howard Hughes-type printed sportshirts and pleated pants he finds in thrift shops to his 1936 Deco house, complete with a 1949 DeSoto in the garage.

"My favorite moments come when I fill the house with old records of Dick Powell and Fred Astaire, invite a few friends over and forget we're living now. My mother and father were like Ozzie and Harriet; and my name's Nelson, so I grew up with apple pie," he reflects. "Maybe that's why I want to be decadent."

As Nelson implies, decadence involves something more than a combination of rebellion, escapism, and aestheticism. It looks backward, toward an idealized and irrecoverable past. As French couturier Yves Saint Laurent says: "People think decadence is debauched. Decadence is simply something very beautiful that is [dead or] dying." It is also quintessentially passive in its attitudes. Ironically, decadents may be the very reverse of prodigal libertines: They may lead forgotten, hidden, covered-up lives with little travel, a routine job, few friends, few adventures, few beautiful objects. Yet pleasure and experience are still their gods, and the very sparseness of their existence, the unbridgeable distance that separates them from the past that they crave creates a kind of burning emotional intensity. The idea of loss, of love affairs living only in memory, of objects that might have been possessed but that are snatched away by a capricious and ungovernable fate, kindles the imagination and transmutes vanity, corruption, disillusion, cynicism, pretense, depravity, vice, self-deception, paralysis, fear, and irresolution, all the weary weakness of the flesh, into the highest and most esoteric form of art. Constantine Cavafy, one of Lawrence Durrell's favorite poets, the aging Alexandrian waterworks official who lived in a tiny upstairs flat in Alexandria, wrote in "One Night":

> The room was cheap and sordid,
> hidden above the suspect taverna.
> From the window you could see the alley,
> dirty and narrow. From below
> came the voices of workmen
> playing cards, enjoying themselves.
> And there on that ordinary, plain bed
> I had love's body, knew those intoxicating lips,
> red and sensual,
> red lips so intoxicating
> that now as I write, after so many years,
> in my lonely house, I'm drunk with passion again.

The profligate

At the end of the downward spiral, with self-discipline positively scorned,* are the sexual and hallucinatory experiences of the playwright Tennessee Williams, as described in his *Memoirs*:

The other night I was feeling lively, so we took to the streets, here in New Orleans. I whispered to my companion that I was "in heat," so

---

* One thinks of a remark by the French author and film director (and quintessential prodigal) Jean Cocteau: "The tact of audacity consists in knowing how far to go too far."

we went again to that delightfully scandalous night spot on Bourbon Street which features the topless and bottomless. . . . The one I found most attractive . . . had lovely proportions, a clear sweet face and a smooth, nicely curved behind. . . . You can be pretty sure what you're getting. I would recommend, however . . . no intimacy beyond the tactile . . . this restriction is particularly prudent since I am allergic to penicillin . . . and that you have a pubic pesticide such as A-200.

Some time later, Williams describes a television interview in which he berates Richard Nixon for his "lack of . . . a moral sense" and espouses his "devotion . . . to the cause of Senator McGovern." This in turn reminds him of another incident:

On the subject of television shows, I was living, at a point in the sixties, in a high-rise apartment building adjoining the Dakota Apartments on West Seventy-second Street, in New York City. I was at that time under drugs, rather deeply, and did not know, when I got up one morning, that I had previously acquiesced, perhaps involuntarily, to a request by the TV commentator Mike Wallace to interview me in my apartment that morning.

Out I came stumbling in a pair of shorts from my bedroom with the twin beds, one never occupied. I entered the blaze of television cameras in the big front room of the thirty-third-story apartment. A full TV crew had been set up and there was Mike Wallace, an old friend of mine, staring at me with a blend of dismay and chagrin and God knows what else. I fell down flat on my face. I had a habit of doing that in the sixties. They picked me up. Somebody put a robe on me. Then Mike Wallace began asking me things. I don't remember what. I simply remember that I sat there in a blank silence and that after about fifteen minutes Mike turned sadly to the crew and said, "Pack up, we're not going to get anything."

Based on the foregoing, it is obvious that prodigals share much in common. Although some carry both self-discipline *and* license to exaggerated extremes (treks to the North Pole followed by wild bouts of sexual promiscuity) and others are spurred by at least one of the three great conventional disciplines (family, chosen profession, or financial necessity), the general idea is to abandon restraint and constraint, to overcome the massed enemies of stuffiness, convention, and pomposity, to attain a rarity and intensity, not just a quantity or duration, of sense experience.

Especially in their youth, prodigals are often immensely attractive. They may be charming and companionable, full of humor and delight. Rebellion, escapism, rootlessness, narcissism—these are almost necessary elements of youth and only add to the sense of overflowing life, of grabbing everything, seeing everything, investigating everything. Ask an accomplished young prodigal to draft a thousand-word essay on oranges as a literary symbol of California or the Mediterranean, two favorite locales; he will dash it right off the top of his head—and it will probably be good. Take the same golden youth on a romantic trek to the top of a mountain range; he will happily sleep with pack animals in the wilderness—and then complain of the scarcity of fine wines to choose from at a restaurant back in town. Later, by remaining adolescent at heart, by refusing to grow up and adapt to reality, he will find the incomparable sense experiences that he seeks and transmute them into art (objects or works of art or life itself as art) or, more likely, he will not. In most cases, adolescent immaturity and irresponsibility, prolonged too long, prove self-destructive. By the late thirties, the average prodigal discovers that he is not the great actor or artist of his dreams; he is, in fact, a waiter, a cab driver, or a sales clerk. By this stage, youth has become an addiction and reality a torment. Even for the most successful prodigals, middle and old age are often barely endurable.

A few kill themselves, either intentionally, like the German film director Werner Fassbinder, or unintentionally, like Elvis Presley. Others, like the film director Roman Polanski, make the best of a bad situation, but without much joy: "I'm afraid it's inevitable that the more experience you acquire, the more you lose your desires, your dreams, your fantasies. [For example] sex. I just don't enjoy it as much as I used to. It's getting a bit repetitious. . . . [But I] hate to become wiser. . . . Wise people are boring."

Some prodigals, on reaching middle age, recoil in horror from their "misspent" youth, experience a conversion, and set off in a totally new direction. Evelyn Waugh, for one, wrote a brilliant novel exposing the pitfalls of prodigality (*Brideshead Revisited*) after adopting a fervent Catholicism. Only a very few, battered but not bowed, cleave to the original faith. Tennessee Williams again:

It is now time for me to consider the question of whether or not I am a lunatic or a relatively sane person. I suspect that most of you . . . have already come to your own conclusion on the point, and it is probably not in my favor. With those of you, the suspected plurality, I say *non contendere*. You have your own separate world and your own separate standards of sanity to go with it. Most of you belong to something that offers a stabilizing influence: a family unit, a defined social position, employment in an organization, a more secure habit of existence. I live like a gypsy, I am a fugitive. No place seems tenable to me for long anymore, not even my own skin. . . . [But] if you can't be yourself, what's the point of being anything at all?

6. Value Systems Based on Emotion

We devote what might seem to be an inordinate amount of space in chapter 5 to a variety of value systems based on sense experience. This is not because sense experience is more representative of contemporary America than authority or logic (it is not), but because sense experience is a hard-to-pin-down religion—hard-to-pin-down because votaries of sense experience resist being categorized (may even claim, somewhat foolishly, that theirs is a doctrine of holding no values at all) and because votaries of sense experience by definition are individualists who think they are supposed to follow their own personal path and not copy anyone else's too closely. Faced with this somewhat hidden doctrine, it is necessary to draw it out stroke by stroke, shading by shading, example by example.

Turning to value systems based on emotion, we confront a similarly hard-to-pin-down situation. Although tens of millions of Americans would agree that their deepest personal values are based on the Bible (a specific form of authority in contemporary America) and a certain number of Americans would agree that their personal values are based on logic, few, if any, would agree that their personal values are based on emotion. This is primarily because the word *emotion* has acquired a slightly pejorative ring. (We hear, all too often, "You are being too emotional about this," or, "Get control of your emotions.") If we rephrase the question by asking people if they consult their feelings about whether something is right or wrong, they will probably answer yes. At least for the present, the term *feelings* evokes a positive response in people, whereas the term *emotions*, for no good reason, sits under a slight cloud. For example, when the previously mentioned wise man Obie Wan Kenobie in the film *Star Wars* counsels his young protegé Luke to "trust your feelings," we nod sympathetically. Not only do we approve of feelings; in addition, we know that this is not real life, where your feelings can get you into trouble, but rather a fable in which feelings will never lead you astray. In any case, whether we refer to feeling or emoting, there is no question that we commonly arrive at beliefs and judgments in this way, beliefs and judgments about the world in general but also about our personal values.

Once we have acknowledged that we do indeed "think" and "judge" and "believe" through our emotions, the next question is where this tends to lead us. At first glance, it might seem that our emotions are almost infinitely variable, even chaotically so, leading us hither and thither and yon. Like the children of Israel, we may worship the golden calf one minute—the next minute cringe in contrition. And our own preferences and allegiances may have little if anything to do with our neighbors'. But if we look beneath all this superficial change and diversity, we discover something interesting: Value systems based on emotion are actually more constant than changing, more alike than unalike. In particular, they all share three features, corresponding to three basic emotional needs. First, they all focus on a particular group of people, a "chosen" people to use the biblical metaphor. Membership in this group automatically provides emotional security. Second, they all propound a particular way of life or a particular way of organizing society, belief in which provides an emotional identity. For example, most of us identify ourselves not just as Americans (members of a group) but also as defenders of an American "way" of democracy and free enterprise. Third, they all require an emotional stimulus, usually expressed as an enemy, a devil, sometimes an enemy of all mankind such as a disease to be conquered, more often another group of people, frequently those people who oppose the way of life in question and are thus irremediably alienated from the "chosen" group. The combination of these three features defines a tribe, and in this limited sense emotional values, even the most refined, beneficent, and inspiring emotional values, are really tribal values, as illustrated by the following chart:

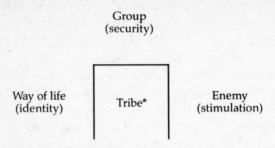

Group
(security)

Way of life
(identity)

Tribe*

Enemy
(stimulation)

At the very simplest level, tribal value systems emphasize the group over the other two dimensions, although all three are always highly interrelated. These simplest emotional value systems, what might be called value systems of blood, may center on any of the following:

- Family

- Work group

- Neighborhood

- Nation

To find examples of a simple emotional value system of blood, all you have to do is listen to the people around you. One day your sister-in-law says over coffee: "You know, your brother lives and dies for his family, for me and the children. That is all he cares about, or deeply cares about. He doesn't care about his job, except as a way to put a roof over the children's head and food on the table; he doesn't have any other friends; he doesn't have other interests; he doesn't go to church. He just loves his family and works day and night for us."

---

* If the term *tribe* strikes the reader's ear as negative or condescending, substitute the term *community*. On the other hand, in *A Different Drum*, Scott Peck persuasively argues that the word *community* should be reserved for a particular kind of tribe, one that has transcended selfishness and has come to express love, both within itself and in its relations with other tribes.

On the other hand, a young single person, working together with a few friends to start a new company, might admit that the group he cares most deeply about, the group that he would personally sacrifice for, that represents the be-all and end-all of his life, at least for the moment, is his coworkers at the office. This phenomenon is more common now in contemporary America than it was in the past, since young workers commonly take jobs thousands of miles from their family or old friends, and it is exemplified by a company like Apple Computer that begins in a garage, quickly develops a distinctive, highly participative corporate culture (no ties, beards OK, creativity over conformity, informality, no or few titles, and so on), and has plenty of enemies (IBM, other computer companies) to provide emotional stimulus along with feelings of group security and identity.

Caring deeply about a neighborhood, in the same way that one might care about a family or work group, is less common today than in the highly ethnic neighborhoods of the American past. But people still identify with and love their neighborhoods, still use neighborhoods to define "our group" versus "other groups," "our way of life," versus "other ways of life," insiders versus outsiders. At its worst, we see this when white neighbors band together to prevent black families from moving in, or when urban geography shapes the identity of competing youth gangs on the streets of Los Angeles (if you're from Irvine Street, I can shoot you on sight; if you're from Jones Street, I have to treat you as a "brother"). But we also see the positive side when residents of a New York City block band together to rid themselves of pimps, prostitutes, and drug dealers, and it is not unheard of for some individuals on the block literally to devote their lives to this communal cause.

From family or neighborhood to the nation is a large leap, but the underlying emotions are similar. Instead of devoting ourselves, heart and soul, to Astoria in Queens (where Greek-Americans keep alive their ethnic heritage as well as the uniqueness of their neighborhood), we devote ourselves, heart and soul, to our country, or we devote ourselves heart and soul for a period of time. A veteran of World War II who fought at Iwo Jima: "I actually miss those times. It was a nightmare to lose so many close friends, but we were fighting the good fight, we were totally united, we were very together, and it gave life meaning. Life has never been as meaningful since."

We are often reminded by commentators that national political campaigns are supposed to be about "issues," issues such as whether we should or should not build a particular kind of expensive weapons system or nuclear power plant. But national politics is also about values, especially emotional (tribal) values. When Geraldine Ferraro, the first woman chosen to run for vice president of the United States, accepted the Democratic party's nomination in 1984, she spoke of the "values that we hold in common—you know what they are—family, neighborhood, community, country"; and Republican George Bush based his successful 1988 presidential campaign on these same "blood" values.

Because political values are largely emotive, especially at the national level, they are almost always suffused with an element of us-against-them thinking. During Ronald Reagan's presidency, it was well understood that the ruler of Iran, the dreaded Ayatollah Khomeni, portrayed the United States as the "Great Satan" in order to unite his people against a common enemy and thus make them forget their internal hatreds. Less well understood was that Reagan himself, to a degree, used the ayatollah for the same purpose, along with other foreign "devils" such as Colonel Khadafi and his terrorist regime in Libya, the Cubans in Grenada, and the Sandinistas in Nicaragua. However justified or unjustified the bombing of Libya or the invasion of Grenada may have been, both events helped to unite a majority of Americans behind Reagan. The only point at which Reagan seemed in danger of losing his majority support, and thus much of his power, came when he was caught not only talking to the foreign devils in Iran, but even sending them weapons.

Mikhail Gorbachev's reforms in Russia illustrate the same

dilemma for politicians and, ultimately, for the human race. In his 1988 speech before the United Nations, Gorbachev argued that the "old thinking," in which nations defined and united themselves emotionally through their opposition to other nations, must cease. Yet in attempting to reorient the Soviet Union away from its longstanding enmity toward the United States, Gorbachev could not dispense entirely with the unifying power of us-against-them. In effect, he simply substituted the previous regime in Russia, the Brezhnev era, the entrenched Communist party hacks, as the devil against which a majority of the Russian people could be united in common struggle, and thereby forget, at least for a moment, their other squabbles and internal divisions. Moreover, as the Gorbachev era unfolded, it remained unclear whether this substitution would work. An external devil, such as another country, is not only a more strongly unifying force than an internal devil; it is also politically safer, so long as enmity does not lead to a shooting war. The question for Soviet Russia, which is not a nation in the modern sense but rather a collection of nations, some with their own language as well as cultural tradition, is whether it can survive at all without an external enemy to unite it.

Obviously, not all value systems based on emotion are as simple and tangible as family, work group, neighborhood, or even nation. Emotive value systems may also be centered on:

- Class (e.g., "family farmers")
- Race (e.g., Ku Klux Klan or black separatists such as Louis Farrakhan)
- Some other defined group cause (e.g., feeding and sheltering the homeless in America's cities)
- Humanity (e.g., the nuclear freeze movement which seeks to halt any further testing or deployment of nuclear weapons)
- History (e.g., mankind projected into the future)

These value systems may be highly abstract: If you love and value and devote your life to the nuclear freeze movement, that is not quite like loving and valuing and devoting your life to a family that you can see and hold and hug. But even the most abstract emotional causes have a way of transforming themselves into a group, a tribe, a band of brothers and sisters who know and love and are committed to each other, who are united by the animosity or sometimes just by the indifference of outsiders.

Consider Mitch Snyder, for example, the advocate for homeless people in Washington, D.C., and leader of the Community for Creative Non-Violence. At age twenty, he was living with a wife and two small children in a small Brighton Beach, New York, apartment, being honored as the Maytag "man of the month" for selling appliances. Then "I just literally woke up one day in a cold sweat and realized it was crazy. I was not going to spend the rest of my life doing what I was doing. That was not what I was supposed to be. . . . [My wife] wanted me to be like other people, and I . . . wasn't like other people."

Shortly thereafter, Snyder abandoned his family, who had to survive as best they could on welfare and family handouts, and came to Washington, D.C., to become part of the antiwar movement. Twelve years later, during the 1984 presidential campaign, he began a fast to protest the federal government's refusal to turn over a dilapidated building for use as a shelter for the homeless. Fifty-one days into the fast and two days before the election, with Snyder's life in jeopardy and *Sixty Minutes* planning a segment for Sunday evening television, the White House agreed to provide the building and to help renovate it. When Snyder later appeared on *Sixty Minutes*, his ex-wife saw him for the first time since he had fled their home. What she saw shocked her: Here was a man with long, unkempt hair wearing a uniform of donated army surplus jacket, faded jeans, and work boots, who had slept on the streets for two winters, otherwise slept on a mattress on the concrete floor of his shelter, who ate discarded food, frequently fasted to try to move the renovation of his building along faster, who took no salary whatsoever and drove to appointments in a decaying old Chevy. By his side was a new companion, Carol Fennelly, who had divorced her husband in California because "he wanted bigger cars and bigger houses and I didn't." The first wife just shook her head and concluded: "[Mitchell] always told me he could love an abstract. It's hard for him to love on a one-to-one basis."

Snyder both agrees and disagrees with this assessment. As much as he regrets what happened in Brighton Beach and enjoys an occasional visit with his sons again after so many years, he feels that he has a new family, one that extends beyond Carol, beyond the other members of the CCNV whose daily struggles he shares, beyond even the homeless of the nation's capital: "All human beings are members of one family . . . and that dictates that we shouldn't allow people to freeze and starve. I believe that a healthy family takes into account more than just a small group of people who share blood. . . . We're essentially tribal creatures anyway." At the same time, Snyder acknowledges that his first wife has a point: "I don't consider myself a good person," he says, "I tend to be very impatient, I tend to be very short, I tend to make heavy demands on people. I don't have time or energy to give much one-on-one, and so I'm very hard on people around me. I take much more than I give. I give to people in the shelter, I give to people on the streets, I give to people who are suffering, but that's got little to do with people who are around me. They pay the price."

To reiterate, the word *emotion* often has a negative connotation, as if it were synonymous with childishness, unpredictability, or violence. In referring to value systems based on emotion, we mean something quite different: the human faculty for knowing by feeling, especially refined feeling; the kind of knowledge that people care deeply about, that they can build a way of life and especially a community on, that they are prepared to defend, even to defend with their lives. In this sense, a religion of emotion—whether it is focused on family, country, an abstract issue such as the nuclear freeze, or a surrogate family like the

Community for Creative Non-Violence in Washington, D.C.—
may be childish or violent, but it is just as likely to be magnetic,
forceful, positive, full of life and action, even larger than life and
action.

Criticisms of a religion of emotion may be launched from a
Christian, logical, or sense experiential perspective. Christians
are occasionally harsh in their attacks because they sense, quite
rightly, that some emotive value systems, especially those
devoted to social activism, are "knockoffs" of Christianity—
imitations that follow the Christian script in all respects save one.
The difference—the all-important difference—is that although
social activists may be as disciplined, as doctrinally committed,
as willing to become childlike and selfless as Christians, their
paradise is on earth and will not be experienced by any but future
generations, whereas the Christian paradise is in heaven and will
be shared by all who take Christ into their hearts. Even on a
purely emotional level, Christianity, which draws upon both
authority and emotion, may have a stronger argument here. How
can any god of this world—whether family or the eradication of
world hunger or anything else—be a true god? How much like
the Tower of Babel are all these secular causes that we pledge our
lives to, only to reconsider and pledge to something else? If there
is some sort of test that we must pass before reaching utopia,
some sort of fiery trial to be overcome, is it not more likely that
the test or trial would be life itself, not some ephemeral devil
such as (for Mitch Snyder) the Reagan White House or the capitalist system? If so, if Christianity is right, devotees of secular
causes who rely on those causes—and solely on those causes—
for meaning in their lives are making a tragic mistake: Their
hearts are not "fixed where true joys are to be found."

The logical critique of a religion of emotion is that it is often—
well—illogical. In the first place, words are often used carelessly.
Two people may spend all day talking about a nuclear freeze
without once talking about the same thing. When words become
confused and corrupted, they can be used interchangeably, as
when communist nations describe themselves as democratic

republics. The worst offense is when political leaders such as Hitler throw all sorts of disparate words into a pot—Jew, nation, history, revolution, socialism, greatness, freedom—to make a particularly noxious stew. The result cannot be confused with knowledge, even emotional knowledge—it is pure mood, nothing more, and the action it begets is almost always barbaric.

It would be nice, say the logicians, if one could combat this "virus" of misdirected emotions with critical analysis, but that is rarely possible. The situation is exactly as described by Dean Acheson, secretary of state under President Truman, who recounted in a speech how a philosopher friend had taken him to task for being too rational:

You are trained in law; I in philosophy. We are in a small minority. Most people associate ideas and hold them together by the strength of their wish to do so. Our colleague knows that the situation in which we [find] ourselves—let's call it point A—is undesirable and possibly dangerous. He looks around and sees a vision of Point B, which seems

> To lie before us like a land of dreams,
> So various, so beautiful, so new.

But you with cold analysis and relentless logic prove that there is no road from A to B, and, that if there were, B is only a mirage which

> Hath really neither joy nor love, nor light
> Nor certitude, nor peace, nor help for pain.

You leave him robbed of hope and have stirred his resentment at you as the robber. You cannot argue him into accepting a sounder and more practicable alternative, just as—to use Justice Holmes's metaphor—"You cannot argue a man into liking a glass of beer." You must associate your alternative with his desires. Your suggestion, let's call it point C, must be pictured with even more charms than point B. In point C the sun is brighter, the girls are prettier, the fountains run with champagne, and even the Russians have good manners and are tractable.

The sense experience dismissal of a religion of emotion is even more condescending and runs as follows. Montaigne taught that life is about living (ontology), not striving after phantom goals (teleology) that will ultimately never be realized. In this regard, a religion of emotion is just as bad as Christianity: It whips men into an obsessive and fixated state of fear and hope that can only be released by some manic burst of violence. Since votaries of emotion generally define themselves and their loved ones in terms of opposition to some imagined hate figure (Manichaeanism), suitable victims for the orgy of bloody activism are not hard to find. If you love your family, it is perfectly all right to make money by exploiting or cheating other families; if you love your country, you must hate other countries; if you want to help the homeless, you must picket and call the president of the United States a murderer. Within the sphere of emotive religion, everything is fight, fight, fight, pure animal spirits, and sheds no light whatever on the underlying question—how we ought to think and live—especially since this question can only be answered through the calm and patient accumulation of personal sense experience. If a religion of emotion seems to help us, it is only in the most twisted way. Consider the Russian fable about the peasant who told his priest that life was unbearable and that he planned to commit suicide. The priest advised him to move all his goats and chickens into his hut for several weeks, then move them out again. At the end of this time, the peasant found life much improved. In this view, Mitch Snyder's fasting and sleeping on sidewalk grates is much the same thing: It makes the organism so miserable that any relief produces happiness.

Even so baldly stated, the various criticisms of a religion of emotion are powerful, very much worth listening to. But, as always, there is another side to the story. Although Hitler offered a value system based on emotion comprised of several parts German nationalism, racism, and street gang thuggery, Churchill was also a nationalist, a kind of chivalric nationalist, one who wanted to fight on the side of the angels, not just glorify and enrich his own people. Is not one Churchill, who helped save the world from barbarism, worth a thousand connoisseurs of a purely personal sense experience? Could even Montaigne see it any other way? Surely for every revolutionary terrorist, willing to slaughter innocents for a tawdrily abstract cause, there is a woman like Mary Breckinridge, who rode on horseback into the wild and remote "hollows" of the Kentucky mountains in the 1920s to bring professional medicine into that part of the world for the first time, or a Peace Corps volunteer, or an African famine volunteer, all of whom are answering an essentially emotional "call." On balance, the religion of emotion cannot so easily be dismissed. The noblest as well as the most lurid human episodes fall within its long and spectacularly colorful history.

7. Value Systems Based on Intuition

What is intuition?

Journalist Robert Updegraff on Dr. Banting:

One night in October 1920, Frederick Grant Banting, a young Canadian surgeon [and teacher], was working over his next day's lecture. His subject was diabetes. Hour after hour he pored over the literature of this dread disease, his head a whirling maze of conflicting theories, case histories, accounts of experiments with dogs. Finally he went wearily to bed. At two in the morning he got up, turned on a light, and wrote three sentences in his notebook: 'Tie off pancreatic duct of dogs. Wait six to eight weeks for degeneration. Remove residue and extract.' Then he went back to bed and slept. It was those three magic sentences which led to the discovery of insulin. Banting's conscious mind had come to grips with one of the most baffling problems in medical science; his subconscious mind finished the job.

Ferris Alger, one of three people with a documented intelligence quotient (IQ) of 197 out of a possible 200 (Stanford-Binet test), on his working method as a weapons researcher and inventor during World War II:

I would take [any] problem, study it carefully, store it all away in my head, and forget it. The following morning, I would go back to work, and the problem would be solved. [I could mentally check the reasoning backward to be sure I had the right answer.] But if I tried to push it along forward, I would get confused.

Philosopher Bertrand Russell on preparing a lecture:

When I was young each fresh piece of serious work used to seem . . . beyond my powers. I would fret myself into a nervous state from fear that it was never going to come right.

The most curious example of this . . . occurred at the beginning of 1914. I had undertaken to give the Lowell Lectures at Boston, and had chosen as my subject "Our Knowledge of the External World." Throughout 1913 I thought about this topic. In term time in my rooms at Cambridge, in vacations in a quiet inn on the upper reaches of the Thames, I concentrated with such intensity that I sometimes forgot to breathe and emerged panting as from trance. But all to no avail. To every theory that I could think of I could perceive fatal objections. At last, in despair, I went off to Rome for Christmas, hoping that a holiday would revive my flagging energy. I got back to Cambridge on the last day of 1913, and although my difficulties were still completely unresolved I arranged, because the remaining time was short, to dictate as best as I could to a stenographer. Next morning, as she came in at the door, I suddenly saw exactly what I had to say, and proceeded to dictate the whole book without a moment's hesitation.

Economist John Maynard Keynes on Sir Isaac Newton:

In the eighteenth century and since, Newton came to be thought of as the . . . greatest . . . rationalist, one who taught us to think on the lines of cold and untinctured reason . . . but [this was] not, I am sure, his *peculiar* gift. His peculiar gift was the power of holding continuously in his mind a purely mental problem until he had seen straight through it. I fancy his pre-eminence is due to his muscles of intuition being the strongest and most enduring with which a man has ever been gifted. Anyone who has ever attempted pure scientific or philosophical thought knows how one can hold a problem momentarily in one's mind and apply all one's powers of concentration to piercing through it, and how it will dissolve and escape and you find that what you are surveying is a blank. I believe that Newton could hold a problem in his mind for hours and days and weeks until it surrendered to him its secret. Then being a supreme mathematical technician he could dress it up, how you will, for purposes of exposition, but it was his intuition which was pre-eminently extraordinary. . . .

There is the story of how he informed Halley of one of his most fundamental discoveries of planetary motion. "Yes," replied Halley, "but how do you know that? Have you proved it?" Newton was taken aback—"Why, I've known it for years," he replied. "If you'll give me a few days, I'll certainly find you a proof of it"—as in due course he did.

Economist A. E. G. Robinson on John Maynard Keynes:

[Keynes's] economic thinking [which seemed so brilliantly logical] was, in reality, intuitive [and] impressionistic.

Mitch Kapor, founder of Lotus, a leading producer of computer software in the U.S., and thus a company specializing in logical applications, on himself:

An intuitive style of decision-making lets the entrepreneur make a creative leap.

All seven of these individuals—Banting, Alger, Russell, Newton, Keynes, and Kapor—are known for their powers of direct observation and logic. Yet they all readily admit their most fundamental and creative way of tackling a problem is intuitive. What exactly, then, is intuition? In our ordinary language we use words like emotion, instinct, and intuition as if they meant the same thing. For example, in *Tropic of Cancer*, novelist Henry Miller writes that "Nichols is a . . . man of feeling, of intuition . . . [a] child-man." Clearly, this is wrong. Emotion and intuition may both be aspects of the unconscious mind, and therefore beyond our conscious control. But emotion *is* childlike, indeed animallike, whereas intuition is a highly developed and powerful mode of purely abstract thinking, one that synthesizes masses of facts and theories with extraordinary speed. We all rely on intuition to form at least some of our beliefs about the world in general; equally, we rely on intuition to form some of our most personal beliefs, our values.

The eight steps

Since intuition is a form of abstract and speculative thought yet still largely an unconscious reflex, the question arises: How can we stimulate what Keynes called our "muscles of intuition," our ability to use all of our mind and not just the small part that controls conscious thought?

At the simplest problem-solving level, the secret seems to lie in not trying too hard. As the German physicist Hermann von

Helmholtz, wrote: "Happy ideas come unexpectedly without effort like an inspiration. They have never come to me when my mind was fatigued or when I was at my working table." To which Robert Updegraff adds: "Any place, it seems, other than at the desk!"

On the other hand, some kind of preparation is definitely required. As Updegraff continues: "One rule always holds good: you must give your problems to your subconscious mind in the form of definite assignments, after assembling all the essential facts, figures, and arguments. The cooking process must first be started by focusing our minds on this material long and intently enough to get it thoroughly heated with our best conscious thinking. [Then] . . . go fishing, golfing or motoring, or if it's night, go peacefully to bed."

So much for the rather simple case of intuitive problem-solving. But what if you want to become a highly intuitive person in general, without reference to any specific problem? The first step seems to be to quiet the emotions. If the subconscious mind is inflamed by strong passions such as fear, anger, ambition, desire, or sexual love or, conversely, drained and exhausted by such passions, there is little chance for the still, quiet stirrings of intuition to be heard. To unblock the intuitive powers, you must make every effort to attain emotional equilibrium, calm, detachment, openness, flexibility. Then, as a final paradoxical step, you must dispense with even the effort to attain these desirable states so that body and mind rest together in an alert but thoroughly relaxed fashion. In other words, to use the jargon of modern psychology, Type B behavior is required, not Type A—where Type A is defined by impatience, anger, turbulence, fear, a chronic state of fight-or-flight readiness. Over millennia, various human cultures have developed a series of specific practices to control this condition, practices that have appeared again and again on different continents and at different times but that have been thoroughly systematized in the eight steps of classical yoga.*

---

* *Yoga* is a Sanskrit word that, like *humanism* or *liberalism* in the West, has been used in so many different ways that it has come to mean almost anything. Translated literally, it means "yoke," which is variously interpreted as discipline

Step	Practice
1. Tolerance	Emphasize non-violence, avoid conflict with people: moral beliefs aside, these disciplines tend to quiet the emotions.
2. Self-restraint	Avoid or limit • alcohol • tobacco • drugs • sweets • meat • overeating • sex • materialism all of which are thought to jeopardize health as well as mental calm. *Extreme* abstinence, "mortification of the flesh" and the like, however, is not recommended.
3. Physical exercise	• Stretch the body. (Hatha yoga exercises are designed to unlock tight muscles and relieve tension). • Relax the muscles. (For example, lying on your back, tense each muscle group in your body in turn, one by one, for 5 seconds,

or union. Uncapitalized, the term *yoga* usually refers to a series of social, physical, and mental exercises that may be used by anybody regardless of religious or philosophical beliefs. The capitalized term *Yoga* traditionally refers to the combination of these exercises with any specific set of religious and philosophical beliefs but especially with Yoga-Samkhya, one of the six orthodox schools of classical Hinduism.

then let them fall limp imagining that you are breathing out through the specific muscle group instead of breathing out through your lungs.)

4. Breathing	Breathe deeply. (*Hatha yoga pranayama*—also designed to relieve tension and fuel the mental faculties*.)
5. Detachment	• Retreat from the world for a few hours, a few days, a few months, however long, either in a monastery or on the proverbial mountaintop (passive detachment). • Observe yourself in the course of everyday affairs from the outside, as if you were another person (active detachment).
6. Concentration	Quell mental noise by concentrating on a thought, a prayer, or an object. Repeat each day.
7. Meditation	Meditate (using any of innumerable techniques), or simply evoke Dr. Herbert Benson's "relaxation response": At a minimum, sit comfortably; close eyes or, if in public,

---

* Frequent running, although not a specifically yogic discipline, potentially combines three of the above stages: self-discipline, physical exercise, and deep breathing. Running, however, tightens muscles unless accompanied by stretching, and may become "violent," "pounding," "competitive," and "agitating," rather than "graceful," "easy," and "calming," especially if the day is hot, the runner is in poor physical condition, or is in competition.

ignore outside stimuli; breath steadily, deeply, and slowly; repeat a word (for example, "One") on each exhalation or count each exhalation up to ten, then repeat (never go over ten); let distracting thoughts pass gently without paying attention to them, and either stop when completely relaxed or when distractions break your concentration, usually after ten or twenty minutes. With daily repetition, induction (falling into meditative state) comes easily.

8. Trance

Meditate deeply (self-hypnosis). While in a state of maximum receptivity, review desirable changes in habits or instruct yourself to suppress physical pain or other unwanted physical symptoms.* Then clear the mind to receive innermost intuitions.

The way of pure intuition

The central problem—or paradox—of intuition is that it is nonverbal. Once intuitive insight is translated into language, it sounds like something else: authority, logic, experience, or emotion. One way to transcend this problem is to say, with the Indian sages Ramakrishna and Vivekenanda, that religious doctrines are equally true and false, because they are just shadows of an underlying, incommunicable truth. Another way is to refuse to verbalize one's insights—to take the position that religion is nonverbal and has nothing to do with beliefs per se.

---

* Even without self-hypnosis, mind and body sometimes respond to autosuggestion. On the physical level, for example, studies indicate that the act of smiling, even if forced, tends to evoke happy emotions, whereas pretending to be angry brings forth the actual emotion of anger.

To see how this latter method works in real life, we may turn to the Sawan Kirpal Ruhani Mission, based in New Delhi, India, with 150,000 followers worldwide and five thousand in the United States. To be a part of the Mission, one need not give up Christianity or Buddhism or any other faith into which one has been born. One need not give up one's job or family or pledge allegiance or donate money—donations in particular are never requested. All that is required is sincerity; abstinence from drugs, alcohol, tobacco, and meat; and a willingness to explore one's "inner space" through daily meditation ("When you slowly withdraw the feeling from feet, and knees, and waist, and so on . . . the soul actually withdraws from your body [and] you go into inner space").

Instruction on meditation (but never on religious beliefs or values per se, which are thought to be entirely inexpressible and personal) is given by a kindly looking white-bearded and white-turbaned Sikh in his late sixties named Darshan Singh (all Sikhs bear the common name Singh, which means "lion"), who characteristically insisted on keeping his job as a deputy secretary in the Indian government even after founding the Mission but who is now widely regarded in India as a "living Master," a person of "oceanic calm" in whose presence one feels neither excitement nor electricity, only total relaxation and openness. Having retired from the civil service, the master is now free to travel, has visited the United States twice, and has been quietly encouraged by the devotion of the people he has met and enrolled in his movement, people such as a professor of international relations at Rhode Island University ("I've studied most of the world's religions and this is a way to bring them together") and a Phi Beta Kappa member of Ohio Senator John Glenn's staff.

Darshan Singh is intensely humble (his followers say that if you rolled out a red carpet for him, he would not walk on it) and refuses to be glorified or to let anyone follow him slavishly: "Masters come and go. All of them have spoken of love. But the 'religions' they found became [full of themselves], and instead of love they preach hatred. . . . So masters have to come again and again. This time let us hope and pray that the message will spread. We are like the lotus blossom, which has its roots in muddy water, yet it blooms into a beautiful flower. We must live in this world, but have the ultimate aim of knowing ourselves."

The Sawan Kirpal Ruhani Mission advises us to live fully and actively in the world, albeit with daily ventures into "inner space." Another viewpoint, however, says that the Mission is right to regard religious truth as totally intuitive, incommunicable, inexpressible, but wrong to remain rooted in the world of maya or illusion. Our real goal should be absolute extrication from this world through the most persistent practice, the deepest, truest, most continual trance, with as little time as possible devoted to the distractions of eating, drinking, and sleeping (mostly eating and drinking since trance largely replaces sleeping). As human beings, we naturally hesitate: It is distasteful or worse to detach ourselves from all that we know. To use Aldous Huxley's metaphor, it is like staring at the surface of the sea, watching its gleaming radiance and wanting to explore the bottom, the divine truth "as it is eternally in itself," yet being afraid of its dark "depths," hidden "to the analytic mind," and refusing to take "the final, necessary plunge."

There are several techniques available to help us anesthetize the conscious mind, and thus end its power to hold us back from attaining salvation, here and now, through the unlocking of our inner powers of intuition. One technique is simply to repeat, over and over: "What am I? Am I my mind? Am I my body? Am I my senses?" This is the self-questioning of the great Indian mystic Ramana Maharshi. It is meant to baffle, to stupefy, and finally to force the mind into submission, into a readiness to abrogate itself, to seek out the truth of deep trance, to fold itself into God. Another similar technique is to reflect on paradoxical statements—for example, the paradox of the Tamil mystic, Manikkar Vasagar: "You are everything that is and you are nothing that is." Or to engage in Mondo, a rapid-fire exchange of questions and answers between two people, so fast that the conscious mind cannot keep up and abdicates. Or to try to answer a koan, a nonsensical question such as: What is the sound of one hand clapping? (These are both Zen Buddhist techniques.) Or to study an argument until, in Thomas Merton's words, you see "that on both sides of every argument there is both right and wrong [which] in the end . . . are reducible to the same thing." This is a Taoist technique, and when "the wise man grasps this pivot . . . of Tao . . . he is in the center of the circle, and there he stands while 'Yes' and 'No' pursue each other around the circumference."

And what exactly lies within the pivot, at the nucleus of the circle, at the point where the conscious mind finally sees everything (in the words of St. Thomas Aquinas), as "straw," gives up its lordly dominance over the soul, and defers entirely to our innermost intuition? Because intuition is nonverbal, no one can say, although the Indian saint Sankara gives us this report from an imaginary spiritual sojourner:

I have been in union with Brahman [God]. All I know is bliss, but not its extent or limits. What I [know] cannot be described. Just as a hailstone falls into the sea, so I am merged into this vast ocean of joy. The world has gone. That which I perceived exists no more. I am indifferent to everything, and only know I am Atman, pure consciousness, pure joy.

I have achieved my object; the goal of all life and existence. I have found the Atman. I am without attachment, and without body. I am sexless and indestructible, calm, infinite and without strain.

I am neither doer nor enjoyer, without change and without action. I am neither this nor that, neither within nor without. Like space I go further than thought. Like a mountain I am immovable. Like the ocean I am boundless. I am the Atman, Self-illumined and infinite.

There are those who regard intuition as a kind of nonsense, although if they consider the matter carefully, they will come to see that important insights are often intuitive at first, before assuming the garb of reasoning. Others respect intuition highly but see it solely as a catalyst for the conscious mind, a precursor of formal observation and logic, whether observation and logic applied to the physical realm or to the moral realm of personal value choices. But is this limited view the correct one? Or will intuition carry us farther, if we give it the right environment of self-discipline and detachment? Will it take us all the way to ultimate truth, albeit an inexpressible and anti-intellectual truth, or are these extremes of intuitive training just so much neurotic masochism? The great mystic masters all agree—no one can provide you with the answer; there is no substitute for self-effort; to find out what awaits you at the end of this particular rainbow—whether dross or gold, vacuity or complete enlightenment about the world, yourself, and the riddle of human values—you must follow the path yourself.

8. Value Systems Based on "Science"

The saga of the jogging pigs

Was the following experiment, reported in *Smithsonian Magazine* during 1986, scientifically valid? If not, can you spot the flaw?

Recently several dozen jogging pigs gave their all for science in an unusual health experiment at Arizona State University. The animals were . . . put on different diets . . . [then] required to run nearly a mile around an oval track every morning. . . . Early on . . . it became apparent that the pigs were no more enthusiastic about running laps than the average person is. Consequently [the researchers] had to prod the bulky creatures around the track. . . . At the end of five months all . . . were slaughtered for laboratory analysis. The results indicated that a well-balanced diet is more important than moderate exercise when it comes to preventing heart disease.

In order to determine the scientific validity of the experiment, we need to define what we mean by the term *science*. At the simplest level, it is an amalgam of three already quite familiar elements: sense experience, intuition, and logic. To solve a scientific problem (such as the effect of diet or exercise on heart disease), you are supposed to:

1. Gather all the available facts (sense experience).
2. Immerse yourself in the facts until a solution flashes in your mind (intuition).
3. Think through all the *logical* implications of the proposed solution (if A is true, B and C must also be true).

4. Devise an experiment to test the validity of B and C against the same facts. For the experiment to be completely successful, it must also satisfy a number of very stringent conditions:

   • The facts must be clearly and objectively stated (no hidden bias).

   • The key research variables (e.g., diet or exercise) must be independent (not all mixed together with other variables).

   • Experimental procedures must be measurable and repeatable (anyone following the same steps should get exactly the same results).

Based on this composite definition of science, it should be evident that the experiment of the jogging pigs was only partly successful. In theory, the researchers had isolated a single research variable—diet—by ensuring that all the pigs had exactly the same exercise, the same housing, the same weather, the same everything except diet. In fact, the reluctance of the pigs to jog, together with the researchers' prodding them around the track, meant that another variable—stress—had unwittingly been introduced. Conceivably, some pigs might have been more adaptive, better able to handle the stress, than others; if so, this factor might have influenced the condition of their hearts and arteries. We can therefore conclude that diet is *probably* more important than moderate exercise in preventing heart disease, but the point is not *proven* for pigs, much less for human beings.

Is there a larger lesson—about the nature of science and the relationship of science and religion—to be learned from the saga of the jogging pigs? Yes, there is. The story of the pigs should help us distinguish between three entirely different modes of truth seeking, modes that are often confused in contemporary America:

Exact science   Meets all the stringent conditions
                                 just outlined.

Inexact science, quasi-science, or "science"	Generally relies on a combination of experience, intuition, and logic but falls short of meeting all the conditions of exact science.
Pseudoscience	Pretends to be scientific but is not even completely factual or logical. Hence a confused or even fraudulent attempt to wrap oneself in the prestige of exact science.

Viewed in these terms, it must be obvious that no religion (whether an organized religion like Christianity or a set of personal values) can ever be scientific in the exact sense. Religious "facts" are rarely clear and never free of bias; neither God nor the good life can be defined in a clear and unbiased way. Nor are religious variables ever independent; the good simply cannot be separated from the beautiful or the just. Above all, religious truths cannot be tested by measurable and repeatable experiments, certainly not by controlled laboratory experiments. The sociologist Max Weber concluded rightly when he said that science cannot be used to discern the "big picture," cannot be used to find "a way to God."

At the same time, religions can be "scientific" in the more limited sense of relying on a synthetic combination of experience, intuition, and logic over other modes of truth seeking. Even if exact science and religion do not mix, we can still approach religious questions—how and for what one ought to live—by trying to gather as many relevant facts as possible, even unclear and biased "facts"; we can still intuit solutions; we can still insist that the intuited solutions be consistent with the facts as stated and internally consistent—that is, not logically self-contradictory. Solutions that pass these two minimum consistency tests will not be definitive in the sense that exact science is sometimes definitive. Two quite opposite solutions for the same problem may both fit the facts and be internally consistent; there may be no obvious basis for claiming that one is superior to the other. But quite a few proposed solutions will fail to pass even these minimum tests. And in this limited, exclusively negative sense, one may speak of a cumulative knowledge of religion, even a "scientific" religion, a religion that must be equally distinguished, on the one hand, from exact science and, on the other, from pseudoscientific nonsense or fraud.

The way of "science"

The single most persistent thread running throughout value systems based on "science" is an emphasis on "hidden knowledge."* Such knowledge is the key to the good life—the problem is to obtain, organize, and manipulate it through a series of disciplines—chiefly psychology, sociology, economics, biology, and medicine. These disciplines do not in themselves represent or define specific faiths. But what they tell us about the nature of the world or of human beings may be subtly transformed into advice about personal beliefs and actions, and thus into a personal religious creed. In this chapter, we will explore a limited number of "scientific" disciplines that have either immediately or gradually, often imperceptively, transmuted into specific value systems, beginning with one of the most dominant "scientific" value systems of the twentieth century, Freudian psychology.

Freudian psychology

On the most popular level, Freudianism has always been a battle cry against the massed conventions and institutions of society: Down with the repressive state! Down with the repressive church! Down with the repressive family! If only sex were free and guiltless for all, humanity would say goodbye to police, courts, prisons, armies, and wars. As psychologist Wilhelm Reich summarized this viewpoint: "[Once] the indispensability of gen-

---

* As Karl Marx wrote: "The final pattern of . . . relationships as seen on the surface . . . is very different from, and indeed quite the reverse of, their inner but concealed essential pattern."

ital gratification" is recognized, the "moral straitjacket drops off . . . and . . . the organism regulates itself." If for some reason the organism does not regulate itself, it is because of easily correctable childhood traumas. For example, a developmental neuropsychologist testified before the Maryland General Assembly that American males' aggressiveness could be curbed if they were given two-and-a-half years of breast-feeding as babies instead of the average three months.

Freud himself, it should be noted, had little in common with this kind of millennarian Freudianism. His characteristic hope was merely to raise people "from the depths of neurotic despair to the level of general unhappiness which is the lot of mankind," although he did believe that at least some sex was necessary, that its absence would produce "illness," and that breast feeding was a good idea. As a medical doctor, Freud's real ambition, indeed his obsession, was to be seen and judged as a research scientist. Yet it is precisely on this technical level that his reputation has suffered the most damage in recent years. A Harvard course description (Philosophy 161), for example, lists psychoanalysis along with astrology as "failed attempts to be factual." A professor at Berkeley calls it "little more than a collective contagious delusional system." A British psychiatrist dismisses it as "metapsychological claptrap" that is "irrelevant where not actually dangerous," a "talking cure industry" that will earn up to $17 billion [in 1986] by "milk[ing] the unhappy of a fast buck." An American colleague adds that psychoanalysts are "phony experts [who] have no meaningful tools to do what we think they can do."

Are these critics right? Yes and no. Although much of Freudianism seems to be pseudoscientific, some of its doctrines, especially the "defense" theory elaborated by Freud's daughter Anna, may be "scientific" in the limited sense of being simultaneously empirical and logical. These doctrines, updated and reformulated by Dartmouth psychiatrist George Vaillant in his book, *Adaptation to Life* (an account of several hundred graduates of a prestigious Eastern college both during and after schooling) are by now quite familiar, at least in pieces, to most of us, and may be summarized as follows: We respond to life's anxieties with unconscious coping mechanisms or defenses, and these defenses tend to follow a recognizable pattern. Freud was only concerned with what he called negative defenses or "repressions"—Vaillant and others use the term "defense" in a broader sense to include positive as well as negative adaptations and habits. Some undesirable defenses are thought to be normal and adaptive at a specific age (for example, infancy or adolescence) but, because of their unconscious nature, are often carried into adulthood. Vaillant's complete scheme, including four levels and eighteen defenses, may be set forth as follows:

Psychotic Defenses (normal for children up to age 5)

Delusional projection	Paranoia, persecution complex: "They are after me."
Denial	"I am not in a mental hospital."
Distortion	"I am Napoleon, or maybe God."

Immature Defenses (normal ages 3–15, conflicts manifested on the outside with others, not inside the self; often referred to as "character disorders" if observable in adults)

Projection	Blaming others; attributing one's own feelings ("I hate myself") to others ("They hate me").
Schizoid fantasy	Incapable of human intimacy. Repellently eccentric.
Hypochondria	Imaginary illnesses (although symptoms may be real).
Passive-aggression	Manipulating others by making them feel guilty or by being

| | inactive, unresponsive, or passive to the point of self-destruction. Stubborn and willful but dependent. |
| Acting out | Always giving in to impulse, no matter how self-destructive. Fighting, drinking, nonstop sex, drugs, and the like. |

Neurotic Defenses (conflict mostly inside self, very exhausting emotionally)

Dissociation	Chronic desire to escape (change cities, change jobs, change lovers).
Reaction formation	Overcompensation. If you have a problem with sex, you become a monk.
Repression	Selective amnesia. Whatever bothers you doesn't exist. Repression combined with dis-sociation (escape) sometimes causes hysteria.
Intellectualization	Hiding; lots of projects to hide in; need to keep control (extreme case: never leave the house); rigidity (everything has to be done one way and one way only!).
Displacement	Substituting, for example, a big house or car (materialism) for what you really want; or books for real life. Combined with intellectualization, can produce

obsessive compulsions ("I must have that car") or phobias (e.g., fear of cats that really masks more basic fears).

Mature Defenses

Humor — Provides detachment, perspective, emotional release.

Altruism — Forgetting your fears by helping others.

Sublimation — Throwing yourself into useful work, being creative, achieving.

Anticipation — Looking ahead, anticipating future problems, taking corrective steps now.

Suppression — Toughness, stoicism. Unlike repression, you don't kid yourself, just accept things as they are.

Vaillant's schema is interesting, but is it truly "scientific" in the minimal sense of being empirical (a factual description of human behavior) and logical (not internally self-contradictory)? Although it does have a familiar ring to it (to choose a farfetched example, the Soviet Union throughout much of the Cold War period appeared to be "character-disordered" in its response to the United States, and the United States, conversely, somewhat neurotic in its response to the Soviet Union), the theory is a little slippery. First, there is a tendency to dress up old ideas in new words. Sublimation, to choose one example, seems to be a fancy term for old-fashioned goal-oriented hard work. Second, the terminology is vague, with the result that everyone defines "defenses" a little differently or feels free to emphasize different aspects. Third, the concepts are endlessly manipulable, sometimes degenerating into a nutty-fruity game: Might Vaillant's analysis of defenses be just an intellectualization on his part?—to which he replies: "Bravo. You are learning."* Fourth, defenses are by definition unconscious (if adopted consciously like Gandhi's or Martin Luther King's passive-aggression, they are no longer defenses), but how can a therapist be certain of what is genuinely unconscious? Fifth, many defenses seem to be similar (repression-suppression; intellectualization-sublimation). Is the only difference here the individual therapist's degree of approval or disapproval? Does the therapist's approval depend on context, on the individual? What are the evaluative rules, how are they derived, how applied? Is it brilliant sublimation to start a business that is highly successful, but fantasy, dissociation, displacement, or intellectualization to start a business that immediately flops? Is it all, in the end, just a question of success? And who or what defines success?

As the foregoing suggests, the theory of psychological defenses is not entirely "scientific" even in the limited sense of being factual and logical. Some elements are both nonempirical and less than perfectly logical (ill-defined words) and other elements are illogical (normative judgments about what constitutes a "good" or "bad" defense are not really logical because, as the philosopher David Hume pointed out, an *ought* cannot be deduced from

---

* In the same spirit, an analyst of defenses might evaluate the "nonscientific" value systems described in this book as follows:

Value systems based on authority	Psychotic, immature, masochistic, fantasy, projection of devil, hypochondria regarding sin, acting out, addiction to Jesus instead of drugs, reaction formation, repression
Value systems based on logic	Intellectualization
Value systems based on experience	Acting out, repression, intellectualization, displacement
Value systems based on emotion	All the same defenses as authority
Value systems based on intuition	Intellectualization, repression, reaction formation, displacement, dissociation, passivity, fantasy

an *is*, whether the *is* describes the physical world or the world of human behavior). Yet despite all these caveats, defense theory does have a bedrock factual basis, which may be expressed as follows:

- We develop and rely on unconscious habits or coping mechanisms.
- There appear to be at least three of these habits, namely:
  Denial*
  Escape†
  Externalization‡ (blaming or helping others)
- These three basic defenses may be expressed either positively or negatively, depending on the situation and one's particular normative values.

Thus stripped to its bare essentials, Vaillant's updated Freudianism is both a "scientific" discipline *and* a value system, a value system that offers survival, adaptation, and maturation (the process by which we adapt and survive) as the highest observable goals of life; that teaches the desirability of reducing conflict with others and within the self as a means of adaptation; and that regards maladaptations, such as immature or neurotic defense mechanisms, simply as problems to be overcome with the right kind of technical knowledge.

Cognitive psychology

Freud observed that his patients' mental disorders appeared to originate deep in the unconscious mind and were therefore exceedingly difficult to diagnose and treat on a conscious level.

---

* Including psychotic denial, hypochondria, passive-aggression, reaction formation, repression, intellectualization, suppression.

† Including distortion, schizoid fantasy, acting out, dissociation, displacement, humor, anticipation, sublimation.

‡ Including delusional projection, projection, altruism.

Working with his own students and patients in the early 1960s at the University of Pennsylvania Medical School, Aaron T. Beck, a psychiatrist who had been trained in traditional Freudian psychoanalytical techniques, observed something quite different: that mental disorders such as depression or a severe inability to get along with others began in the conscious mind, with extremely negative thinking, which then led to emotional disturbance. As Beck's student and colleague David D. Burns has written: "Unpleasant feelings merely indicate that you are thinking something negative and believing it." Moreover, most of the time the negative thinking is not just negative; it is also unfactual and illogical. For example, a person may think, over and over, that he or she is a complete failure as a lawyer, accountant, clerk, husband, wife, parent, and so on. Not surprisingly, the person becomes depressed. Exaggeration, however, is by definition unfactual and illogical (see chapter 4 – "Gula fallacies" – for the major logical fallacy involved), and once the facts and logic are straightened out, the patient is often considerably improved, sometimes even spontaneously cured.

Beck's techniques, which build on earlier work by psychiatrist Karen Horney, are both simple and sophisticated. We all know that the conscious mind incessantly chatters (the internal dialogue); this dialogue very often takes the form of a debate with a severe "internal critic": "I'm not such a bad person"–"Oh, yes you are, you are the worst! You did this, you did that, you failed to do this, etcetera." Or this same internal acidity is silently turned on another person: "My husband/wife never listens to me, ignores my feelings, is not behaving as I have a right to expect, etcetera." To change this unpleasant internal dialogue, which often takes the form of a broken record played obsessively over and over again, one is simply supposed to talk back to oneself: "No, I am not so bad as all that (he/she is not so bad), etcetera."

Cognitive psychology is effective. If you tell depressed persons to stop being negative, they will ignore the advice; after all, their negativism, to them, is just seeing the world in its true colors. But if you tell depressed persons that their negative statements are unfactual and illogical, it makes an impression; and if the thinking changes, the feelings tend to follow. This does not necessarily prove that unconscious feelings are caused by conscious thinking rather than the reverse. It is possible that the conscious and unconscious minds maintain a two-way commerce, and that both Beck and Freud are right. Even so, Beck's therapy works, and often works rapidly, whereas Freudian therapy works slowly, if at all.

Like Freudian psychology, cognitive psychology is supposed to be a technical discipline, not a value system. But there are all sorts of values embedded in the therapy, values that together define a particular approach to life. First, the emphasis on factuality and logic are themselves value choices, as we have already shown in prior chapters. Second, cognitive psychology emphasizes personal stability, which is another value choice, and some of the movement's critics wonder if it does not unduly truncate feelings, thereby robbing life of its color and drama. A depressed person will not, it is true, see the color and drama of life, but if one avoids the valleys by continually monitoring one's inner dialogue for factuality and logic, will one also miss the heights? Finally, cognitive psychology is thought by some to place too great a value on positive thinking. Some cognitive therapists appear to be arguing that negative thoughts are always unfactual and illogical, which is itself an illogical position. For example, in his excellent exposition of basic cognitive techniques, *Feeling Good*, Burns tells a mother who repeatedly refers to herself as a "bad mother" that the term "'bad mother' is an abstraction; there is no such thing as a 'bad mother' in this universe." Although this response is undoubtedly useful in a therapeutic sense (and thus consistent with a scientific emphasis on getting results), many people would question its factuality. The term *bad mother* is an abstraction, also an essentially emotive word, but most people would agree that bad mothers do in fact exist, even evil mothers, and that phenomena such as physical child abuse provide *prima facie* evidence of it.

Psycho-neuro-immunological medicine

The "scientific" research discipline that doctors refer to as *psycho-neuro-immunological* medicine occupies the zone where mind and body interact. Among its relevant research findings:
(1) The body has two *physical* defense systems. The first system, controlled by the most primitive portion of the brain, alerts the body to physical danger (an approaching grizzly bear) and produces the fight-or-flight response by pumping adrenalin (now called noreprinemine) and other chemicals. The second system, the immune system, guards against invading pathogens (viruses, fungi, unwelcome bacteria) or runaway cells (cancers). The key finding is that these two systems are inversely linked: When the full fight-or-flight mechanism is triggered, the immune system is suppressed and vice versa. The body does not seem to be able to mount a full defense on both fronts at the same time. (2) A corollary of this is that chronic fight-or-flight behavior (so-called type A behavior) is potentially injurious to health. If triggered by minor threats and prolonged over days, weeks, and months, it can cause illness, cancer, perhaps heart disease as well (the link with heart disease is more speculative). (3) Type A behavior is not the only problem, however. The opposite of Type A, so-called Type C behavior (passive, depressed, adrenalin in a state of chronic depletion), or a continual alternation between A and C, is just as bad for the immune system. The key to long-term health is therefore supposed to lie in finding the middle way, that is, so-called Type B behavior.*

A good diet, enough vitamins, moderate use of coffee and alcohol, aerobic exercise, meditation, avoidance of drugs, and the like

---

* It is commonplace among therapists that all human emotional states may be viewed as variants of four basic categories: anger, fear, sadness, and happiness. The type A, B, C model argues persuasively that anger and fear are so closely connected that they should be viewed as one syndrome, type A behavior. Type B behavior (which may be equated with happiness) represents the equilibrium position while type C (sadness or depression) represents the other kind of disequilibrium.

are all thought to strengthen one's ability to lead a Type B lifestyle as well as contributing to health in other respects. In general, we seem to have all the tools necessary for a completely positivistic "science" of life. You want to survive and be healthy—right? Then live this way. Mom, your minister, your psychiatrist, *and* your doctor are all saying the same thing.

There is really no doubt that these kind of "tools"—summarized by the impressively "scientific" standardized test in which everyone's life expectancy is statistically derived (smoke heavily: deduct 24 months; happily married: add six months; satisfied with sex life: add nine months)—provide many people with their most cherished personal values. As Gregory Pence, a philosophy teacher at the University of Alabama's School of Medicine, recently wrote in *Newsweek*: "I practice a secular religion of body and health whose orthodoxy decrees that exercise and preventative medicine will help me live." Yet there will always be nagging questions about the underlying rationality, the underlying "science," on display here. As newspaper columnist Ellen Goodman writes:

In California, members of a family cut back on sugar in the decaffeinated coffee they drink in their house—on the San Andreas fault. . . . In Maine, a woman rides to aerobics class—on her motorbike without a helmet. . . . A friend of yours, mine, ours decides that . . . he will fly only in emergencies. He explains this earnestly, while chainsmoking cigarettes. Another friend drinks only bottled water these days, eats only meat untouched by steroids and spends weekends hang-gliding. . . . Watching parents demonstrate against one school and then another for allowing an AIDS victim into their building, I couldn't help wondering how many packed up their picket signs in the back seat, their children in front and drove away without buckling the seat belts.

This kind of irrationality amidst rationality is not the only problem. Another is the way in which psycho-neuro-immunological data is generated. Accept for a moment that Type A behavior really does suppress immune response. Has this behavior been adequately defined in a physiological sense? How do we know that we are dealing with Type A's in these studies? Is the diagnosis made by an observer?—that's not very impartial. By a questionnaire—how precise or impartial is that? To what degree is it all wish fulfillment—the idea that being "better, nicer" people will also make us healthier? What if the "science" changes, and it turns out that aggressiveness-hostility-mistrustfulness-impatience are actually more healthy? Will we then follow this new advice?

That neuromedicine offers a valuable real-life discipline need not be disputed. At the same time, one thinks of the young Thomas Merton's account of being told to eat ice cream (now forbidden because of high fat and cholesterol content) as a palliative for what may or may not have been an ulcer:

The whole result of this diet was to teach me this trivial amusement, this cult of foods. . . . It made me think about myself. It was a game, a hobby, something like psychoanalysis had been. . . . I was reduced to the condition of a silly old woman, worrying about a lot of imaginary rules of health, standards of food-value, and a thousand minute details of conduct that were in themselves completely ridiculous and stupid, and yet which haunted me with vague and terrific sanctions. If I eat this, I may go out of my mind. If I do not eat that, I may die in the night.

Defense theory/neuromedicine

One of the pitfalls of "scientific" discourse is that technical specialists from different areas may not communicate with one another. As a result, the opportunity to integrate particular tools may be missed. For example, some classic Freudian or post-Freudian emotional defenses appear to be manic, assertive, Type A in character; others appear to be depressive, nonassertive, Type C in character; the balance appears to fit well with Type B. The proposed relationships may be schematized as follows:

DENIAL	Type A *(Manic, assertive)*	Psychotic Denial
	Type B *("Normal")*	Suppression
	Type C *(Depressive, nonassertive)*	Hypochondria, Passive-aggression, Reaction Formation, Repression, Intellectualization
ESCAPE	Type A *(Manic, assertive)*	Acting Out, Dissociation, Displacement
	Type B *("Normal")*	Humor, Sublimation, Anticipation
	Type C *(Depressive, nonassertive)*	Distortion, Schizoid Fantasy
EXTERNALIZATION (LIVING THROUGH OTHERS)	Type A *(Manic, assertive)*	Delusional Projection
	Type B *("Normal")*	Altruism
	Type C *(Depressive, nonassertive)*	Projection

The point of this analysis is that a Type B outlook may indeed be necessary to make positive defenses work, and vice versa.

Socio-demo-anthro-eco-enviro-techno model building

Not all "scientific" research disciplines focus directly on the individual or on his personal life. What is called by its practitioners *socio-demo-anthro-eco-enviro-techno model building* (yes, that's what it's called), is concerned with the very big picture, the future of humanity. For example, Jay Forrester, an M.I.T. professor who is a leading computer modeler as well as a creative economist, developed a model of American social and economic behavior that is capable of incorporating 250 years' worth of data and providing population, energy, resources, capital investment, pollution and other forecasts through at least A.D. 2100. Based on his work, Forrester foresees a world of rising population, increasingly constrained growth, correspondingly reduced standards of living, and the possibility of sophisticated new social controls (for example, the right to live in a particular city might be denied, or sold to the highest bidder).

Such predictions may be important for planners or politicians, but what, one wonders, do they have to do with personal values? To answer this question, we need only listen to one of Forrester's eager and devoted students: "I was brought up as a Catholic. . . . This weekend I listened to a priest talk about having hope for the future [and how that was] related to our ability to worship Christ. . . . It may well be. But an even greater hope for the future is our ability to understand the forces and behavior of our system as it is." In other words, models are valuable because they identify the central problems. Once we know the problems, our personal value choices should be easy because good values will contribute to solving the problems whereas bad values will exacerbate them.

The student continues: "Professor Forrester [observes] that [traditional] religion doesn't present us with [a] framework for the kind of value change we're heading into as things become scarce and limited. . . . I have had to re-examine my own beliefs. My church for a long time advocated such things as food relief . . . [or] subsidized low income housing. But in the long run [low income housing] may hurt those it's designed to help." A second student adds that protecting the earth may be more important in the future than protecting human beings, and a third concludes that "altruism may in the last analysis be just another luxury, [an] economic luxury . . . [that] we may not be able to afford."

Does this brave new world of model building actually lead to a positivistic and problem-solving ethic, a path that humanity must follow in order to save itself? Forrester and other pioneers are quick to deflate such immodest expectations. The models that are supposed to give us our values, however indirectly, are hardly value free to begin with: They reflect the biases of their creators. If you look for personal values from this source, you will probably just find the values that you already had, perhaps without ever quite knowing it.*

Sociobiology

Sociobiology as a research discipline

Sociobiology as a scientific research discipline is not controversial. The general idea is to study animal behavior as a means of learning more about human behavior.

Sociobiology as a religion

The specific "religion" that devolves out of the research discipline of sociobiology is another matter. It includes the following beliefs:

---

* Another problem is that the explanatory variables used are not sufficiently independent, nor are conclusions testable by experimental method. In other words, the models are "scientific" (simultaneously empirical and logical) rather than scientific in the exact sense, and as such can be manipulated to defend a wide variety of quite different theories. In effect, the models are a descriptive language, a rigorous method of presenting a theory rather than a prescriptive means of testing alternative theories.

1. *Most* human behavior is biologically determined (built into us, like eating and sleeping, and thus beyond our conscious control).

2. *All* human behavior has a single goal: to help the individual survive and reproduce.

3. People may be viewed as "throwaway survival machines" used by "selfish" genes to perpetuate themselves.

4. Even altruistic actions, unselfishness, heroism, love, devotion to higher ideals, and appreciation of knowledge or art are ultimately explained by genetic evolution, which is guided by natural selection, which in turn has the aim—the sole aim—of gene survival through reproduction. For example, an individual cannot survive and reproduce unless the group on which he or she depends also survives and reproduces—hence the inherited tendency to help others, not just compete.

5. The inescapable urge to spread one's genes as widely as possible spells unending trouble and conflict—thus effectively limiting the potential for altruism in society.

Some otherwise lucid and realistic observers such as journalist and historian Paul Johnson have hailed the religion of sociobiology as "an exact science" that is "testable . . . by empirical data." This is obviously false. Most sociobiologists admit that "in the chaste idiom of scientific discourse, we are permitted to conclude only that the evidence is consistent with the proposal," or in other words that the religion of sociobiology is "scientific" in our sense rather than scientific in the exact sense, that is, simultaneously empirical and logical but not testable. In fact, however, the religion of sociobiology is not even empirical or logical. The assertion that all behavior serves the purpose of survival and reproduction, for example, is, in Harvard biologist Stephen Jay Gould's fairly charitable phrase, "unsupported." Many other sociobiological assertions are clearly illogical:

1. "Only hard-won empirical knowledge of our biological nature will allow us to make optimum choices among the competing criteria of progress."

   QUESTION: If the behavior in question is biologically determined, it is either completely fixed, or at least very hard to change. If so, how are we going to be free to make optimum choices?

2. "If the decision is taken to mold cultures . . . some behaviors can be altered experientially without emotional damage and loss of creativity. Others cannot."

   QUESTION: Is this what is meant by biologically determined behavior—behavior that cannot be altered without "emotional damage and loss of creativity"? If so, the "selfish" genes do not seem to have a very firm grip on us. Who wouldn't be willing to accept some "emotional damage and loss of creativity" in order to avert the possibility of nuclear war?

3. "We are going to need a planned society on a global level. It can't originate from the invisible hand of the laissez-faire activity of billions of humans."

   QUESTION: Why would social planners be less subject to negative biological drives than masses of humans?

The underlying problem with sociobiology (the religion, not the underlying technical research discipline) is not just its apparent lack of fidelity to the facts or its logical deficiencies. Nor is it simply a case of oversimplification, although sociologist Robert Nisbet is right to point out that finding common acquisitive instincts among jackals, gazelles, and people will not necessarily contribute to a study of "the economy, education, international [relations], or the business cycle," and others are right to point out that oversimplified biology has been used to justify Nazism, racism, sexism, or other forms of aggression. The core problem with the religion of sociobiology is that it pretends to be scientific when it is not even "scientific" in the loose sense, and is thus guilty either of intellectual confusion or of pseudoscientific fraud.

Behavioral psychology

Behavioral psychology as a research discipline

Like the research discipline of sociobiology, the research discipline of behavioral psychology is straightforward and uncontroversial. If you have a physical or emotional habit (learned behavior) that is causing distress, you should be able to unlearn it by applying a "conditioning" technique. For example, assume that you have a very strong drive to smoke cigarettes. Since eating is an even stronger drive, you might stipulate that smoking is permissable, but each cigarette must be followed by a 24-hour fast. After you have experienced intense hunger for a few days, an aversion to smoking may be quickly established. If, on the other hand, the undesirable habit takes the form of avoidance rather than indulgence (fear of airplanes or elevators rather than smoking or drinking), desensitization techniques (imagining and then gradually confronting the feared object) may be applied. Although behavioral techniques will not tell us why or how to live, they provide a direct, hopeful, "scientific" way to pursue a given end.

Behavioral psychology as a religion

The "religion" that devolves from behavioral psychology is a mirror image of the religion that devolves out of technical sociobiology: that is, it agrees that human behavior is determined (free choice rarely if ever exists), but the determining factors are environmental or cultural, not biological or genetic. In the view of behaviorists, individuals are born with few predispositions (genes almost never control behavior) and may be guided in almost any direction, for good or evil, by wise or malevolent mentors. If one is conditioned to be criminal, one will be criminal; no one, however, needs to remain criminal as a permanent condition. What has been programmed can be reprogrammed; intractable thugs may be reconditioned into the most exemplary citizens.

The most famous exponent of this kind of behavioral determinism is B. F. Skinner. Skinner thinks that human beings, like rocks or other forms of inanimate matter, are moved by external forces and only by external forces. As he puts it:

Aristotle argued that a falling body accelerated because it grew more jubilant as it found itself nearer home. . . . All this was eventually abandoned, and to good effect [by the physical sciences], but the behavioral sciences still appeal to comparable internal states. . . . Every issue of . . . a daily paper [or] . . . professional journal . . . [supplies] examples. . . . We are told that to control the number of people in the world we need to change *attitudes* . . . overcome *pride* . . . build some sense of *responsibility* . . . that wars begin in the *minds* of men. . . . Almost no one questions . . . this staple fare. Yet there is nothing like it in modern physics . . . and that fact may explain why a science and technology of behavior has been so long delayed.

This is heady stuff, both wildly optimistic in its hopes for the world ("man's genetic endowment can be changed only very slowly, but changes in the environment of the individual have quick and dramatic effects; our culture has produced the science and technology it needs to save itself"), and frightening in its vision of massive social control ("if [society] continues to take freedom or dignity, rather than its own survival, as its principal value, then [it may] find [it]self in hell"). Yet on closer inspection it simply dissolves in vagueness, semantical confusion, and tautological reasoning. What does Skinner mean by "determined" behavior? How does he propose to isolate cultural from genetic influences in the real world? If we state that a Christian is not actually devout but is rather moved by external contingencies, have we really said anything different, anything useful, anything measurable? Or have we just indulged in a form of empty verbal gymnastics? As with the religion of sociobiology, the indictment against the religion of behavioral psychology is a subtle one: It is not primarily that Skinner's philosophical speculations are nonempirical or illogical, although they are. It is rather that Skinnerism pretends to be what it is not—namely, exact science, or at least "science" in our special sense, when it is actually pseudoscience.

A composite religion of "science"

One need not, of course, be solely a Freudian, cognitive psychologist, psycho-neuro-immunologist, socio-eco-enviro model builder, sociobiologist, or behavioral psychologist. One might choose bits and pieces from each of these disciplines, or from many other research disciplines, and combine them into one's own personal religion (value system) based on "science." Whatever particular amalgam is chosen, however, a few underlying assumptions are likely to be present: that life is about *problem solving*; that problem-solving requires good *management* and an effort at *self-improvement*; that management and self-improvement demand *realism*, that is, looking squarely and logically at the facts; that by studying the facts "scientifically," one can penetrate the *secrets of nature* and thereby come to possess a degree of *power and control*; that, as a shortcut to this *hidden knowledge*, it is wise to consult *experts*; that experts must have the right *credentials*; that, even more important, experts must have the right *technique*; that the most powerful techniques are probably new, only *recently discovered*; that powerful techniques are usually *complex*, rarely simple; that to make new techniques work requires an *openness to change*; that *change is healthy*, usually for the best; that with hard work and relevant *technical knowledge* we *can transform the world*, make it a very good place to live.

The list of underlying assumptions could go on and on, but they are already quite familiar, because value systems based on "science," as we have defined it here, are part of the very air that we breathe in late twentieth-century America. All of us, even those who might deny it most strenuously, even the most devout fundamentalist Christians, for example, have absorbed its distinctive and all-pervading essence.

Part Three

VARIATIONS ON
A THEME

9. The Cross-Fertilization of Values

So far, we have looked at six ways of thinking about and choosing values, each of which represents an important value choice in itself, as per the following chart, which illustrates movement from the general to the specific:

1. Authority

    WAY OF THINKING (Having faith in a higher authority)

    ↓

    WAY OF THINKING ABOUT VALUES (Having faith in a higher moral authority)

    ↓

    DOMINANT PERSONAL VALUE ("Having faith in a higher moral authority is very important to me.")

    ↓

    TYPE OF VALUE SYSTEM ("My value system is based on faith in a higher moral authority.")

    ↓

    GENERIC BELIEFS ("The rules for a successful life are known. The difficult part, the challenge, lies in opening up our hearts, putting aside our wayward impulses, not only following the rules that we have been given but making them part of our very being.")

    ↓

    SPECIFIC BELIEFS illustrative of this type of value system (Protestant fundamentalism and Roman Catholicism—the most influential examples in America today)

2. Deductive logic

WAY OF THINKING (Subjecting beliefs to the variety of consistency tests that underlie deductive reasoning. "Since A is true, B must be true, because B follows from A.")

↓

WAY OF THINKING ABOUT VALUES (Subjecting moral beliefs to logical tests)

↓

DOMINANT PERSONAL VALUE ("Logic is very important to me.")

↓

TYPE OF VALUE SYSTEM ("My value system is based on logical thinking.")

↓

GENERIC BELIEFS illustrative of this type of value system ("Order in life is essential. Different people's personal beliefs need not always agree, but at the very least should be organized, follow first principles, and be internally consistent.")

↓

SPECIFIC BELIEFS illustrative of this type of value system (The philosophy of Spinoza . . . or of the leading contemporary American philosopher Mortimer Adler)

3. Sense experience

WAY OF THINKING (Gaining direct knowledge through our own five senses: "I know it's true because I saw it, I heard it, I tasted it, I smelled it, or I touched it myself.")

↓

WAY OF THINKING ABOUT VALUES (Gaining moral knowledge by directly seeing, hearing, etc.)

↓

DOMINANT PERSONAL VALUE ("My own personal [sense] experience is very important to me.")

↓

TYPE OF VALUE SYSTEM ("My value system is based on personal [sense] experience.")

↓

GENERIC BELIEFS illustrative of this type of value system ("You only live once; make the most of it. Don't be too concerned with specific goals; experience is an end in itself, not just a means. Don't accept anyone else's values: develop your own uniquely personal approach through contact with teachers, friends, books, and travel. On the other hand, do pay close attention to the accumulated standards, taste, and wisdom contained in the cultural treasures—great works of literature, great art, etc.—handed down from the past, the common currency of all civilized people." [In one variant—high sense experience—all this education and freedom must be tempered by strong self-discipline; in another variant—prodigal sense experience—the discipline is mostly eliminated.])

↓

SPECIFIC BELIEFS illustrative of this type of value system (High sense experience: the personal beliefs of Eudora Welty . . . or of Montaigne; prodigal sense experience: although no one individual is fully illustrative, Lawrence Durrell, Henry Miller, Harold Acton, Yves St. Laurent, Elvis Presley, Tennessee Williams, and many others suggest the multifaceted possibilities.)

4. Emotion

WAY OF THINKING (Feeling that something is right: although we do not usually associate feeling with thinking or judging, we actually "think" and "judge" through our emotions all the time: "I feel that this is right.")

↓

WAY OF THINKING ABOUT VALUES ("I feel that these values are right.")

↓

DOMINANT PERSONAL VALUE ("Feelings are very important to me.")

$\downarrow$

TYPE OF VALUE SYSTEM ("My value system is based on my feelings.")

$\downarrow$

GENERIC BELIEFS illustrative of this type of value system ("To live fully, one must commit oneself and one's feelings to a cause (a purpose larger than oneself) and a group (cause and group are actually synonymous). What counts are shared objectives, shared way of life, shared struggle against common enemies.")

$\downarrow$

SPECIFIC BELIEFS illustrative of this type of value system (Love of family, of neighborhood, of nation, of mankind, as exemplified by people as disparate as Winston Churchill or Mitch Snyder, social activist and radical advocate for the homeless in Washington, D.C.)

5. Intuition

WAY OF THINKING (Unconscious thinking that is not emotional. Think of the mind as if it were in three parts: the conscious mind; the emotions, that is, the hypothalamus or primitive brain; and the unconscious-but-not-emotive intuitive mind. Both the conscious mind and the unconscious-intuitive mind are highly sophisticated, but the unconscious-intuitive mind is much more powerful than the conscious mind, just as a supercomputer is more powerful than a microcomputer. Hence most creative discoveries are intuitively derived and only later "dressed up" by logic, observation, or some other conscious technique: "After struggling with this problem all day, I went to bed confused and exhausted. The next morning, as I awakened, the solution came to me in a flash, and I just knew it was true.")

$\downarrow$

WAY OF THINKING ABOUT VALUES (Drawing moral knowledge from the inner wellsprings of intuition)

↓

DOMINANT PERSONAL VALUE ("My intuition is very important to me.")

↓

TYPE OF VALUE SYSTEM ("My value system is based on intuition.")

↓

GENERIC BELIEFS illustrative of this type of value system ("The conscious mind, with all its desires and conflicts, is often a snare and an illusion. What counts is not what you accomplish or what you have, but what you are; to know what you are, you must unblock and develop your intuitive powers by learning to be calm, peaceful, immune to the storms of life.")

↓

SPECIFIC BELIEFS illustrative of this type of value system (The personal beliefs of Darshan Singh . . . or of the Indian saint Ramana Maharshi . . . or of Zen Buddhism.)

6. "Science"

WAY OF THINKING (A synthetic technique that relies on sense experience to collect the observable facts; intuition to develop a testable hypothesis about the facts; logic to develop the test [experiment]; and sense experience again to complete the test. "I tested the hypothesis experimentally and found that it was true.")

↓

WAY OF THINKING ABOUT VALUES (Although exact science is value-free, values may nevertheless be said to be "scientific" in a more limited sense if they are based on careful, empirical observation and are internally consistent.)

↓

DOMINANT PERSONAL VALUE ("A 'scientific' approach is very important to me.")

↓

TYPE OF VALUE SYSTEM ("My value system is based on 'science'.")

↓

GENERIC BELIEFS illustrative of this type of value system ("Life is a series of problems to be solved, objectives to be achieved, by developing and applying the right kind of technical knowledge.")

↓

SPECIFIC BELIEFS illustrative of this type of value system (Freudianism, especially the contemporary Freudianism of a George Valliant; cognitive psychology; philosophies of "body and health" based on psycho-neuro-immunology; philosophies based on "socio-anthro-eco" modeling, sociobiology, or behavioral psychology.)

As summarized here, each type of value system stands separate and apart; in real life, however, the various types of value systems invariably blend and interact with one another. We have already had a hint of how this might work in science, which synthesizes experience, intuition, and logic. On the other hand, science combines these three ways of thinking in a highly formal manner, subject to a specific and demanding set of rules. The rules are so specific and demanding that science has, in effect, become a unique mode of perception, not merely a blending together of different elements.

By contrast, in the normal everyday human world, we combine ways of thinking and resulting value systems without any formal rules at all. One person is attracted to logic but also to sense experience, notwithstanding the acute differences between these two approaches and somehow, human beings operating as they do, an unspoken, even unconscious, accommodation is reached. For example, a devout Protestant fundamentalist embraces an emotive nationalism, even though there is nothing in the Gospels to support nationalism and there is even some explicit advice from Jesus about *not* investing temporal institutions like the state with spiritual authority.

To be sure, some combinations are less likely than others. For example, the basic method and attitude of authority is harder to reconcile with "science" than with emotion. On the other hand, there are plenty of people who have tried to reconcile authority (usually in the form of fundamentalist Christianity) with "science," including in recent years theologian-sociologist Harvey Cox (*The Secular City* and *Religion in the Secular City*). An even more surprising combination (much beloved by humanistic psychologists and other New Agers) is "science"-intuition, usually a blend of psychology and Eastern religion (as in Swami Ajaya's *Psychotherapy East and West*, written by an American of Jewish background who became a celibate Hindu monk).

The important point to emphasize, in thinking about these or other complex composite faiths, is that all human beings without exception are multidimensional in their personal beliefs. Everybody is influenced at least to some degree by authority (if not the authority of church or Bible, then some other authority), logic, experience, emotion (emotion especially!), intuition, and "science." Whereas many people weave these strands together in artful and coherent ways, others, like the lesbian nun mentioned in chapter 1, are obviously incoherent.

In the next chapter we will explore some particularly complex, multidimensional value systems in more detail, beginning with the Christianity of Karl Barth, a theologian widely regarded as the most influential Christian thinker of the twentieth century, continuing with the neo-Buddhism of Albert Einstein and the "passive" revolutionism of Mohandas Gandhi, and concluding with the Judaism of Golda Meir, a former American who became prime minister of Israel. The final chapter of this section will take up a host of related issues—human choice, honesty, temporary alliances, and change—under the heading "Why Values Get So Complicated."

10. Four Examples of Cross-Fertilization: Karl Barth, Albert Einstein, Mohandas Gandhi, Golda Meir

The Nonfundamentalist, Nonmodernist Christianity of Karl Barth (An attempt to reconcile a faith based on "authority," that is, fundamentalist Christianity, with values and practices based on sense experience, logic, "science," emotion, and especially intuition)

Working as a young Swiss Reformed Church pastor before World War I, Karl Barth concluded that both "modernist" Christianity (also referred to as "liberal" Christianity) and fundamentalist Christianity were fatally flawed. Modernism had abandoned the supernatural and tried to find heaven on earth. Fundamentalism had pretended that it had a direct pipeline to the Almighty. Both were essentially guilty of impatience, of wanting to find shortcuts and easy answers.

Initially, Barth was much more hostile toward Christian modernism. In his view, it had committed at least five cardinal sins. The first was to make an idol of human reason, to believe that God might be discovered through a syllogism or located in an experiment, to forget that "reason sees the small and the larger but not the large," to forget that Christianity must always be "an embarrassment" and a "grotesque contradiction of the facts," to forget Luther's warning that "I do not know it and do not understand it, but sounding from above and ringing in my ears I hear what is beyond the thought of man." The second was to abandon reason in a fit of disillusion in favor of the "whole melody of anti-intellectualism" and "mysticism." The third was to attempt to pacify the "cultured despisers of religion" by constantly changing doctrine as if "this meant anything more than the turning over of a sick man in his bed." The fourth was to try to find in frenetic good works what could not be found in faith; to put all the emphasis on Jesus' ethics; to "build community houses, push [a] young people's program, organize discussion groups, [erect] donors' tablets, attend committee meetings, [observe] twenty-five year anniversaries, and [take] countless mutual bows." The fifth was to suffer disillusion over good works and to turn to romantic notions of Marxism and violent revolution. What all these various sins shared in common was a "disastrous . . . dim-sighted[ness] in regard to the fact that man as man is not only in need but beyond all hope of saving himself; that the whole of so-called religion, and not least the Christian religion, shares in this need; and that one cannot speak of God simply by speaking of man in a loud voice."

After thus surveying modernism and finding it totally wanting, Barth turned to Christian fundamentalism. The original fundamentalism, the Catholic church, had sinned in his view by putting itself—its "history and . . . traditions, [its] intelligence and [its] capacity for grace—in the place of God." It had failed to see that the church's true role was "as a witness, a quite earthly reflection, of a lost and hidden order—and as such . . . [in]capable of sustaining any special sacredness"; it had forgotten that "in the heavenly Jerusalem of Revelation nothing is more . . . significant than the church's complete absence: 'And I saw no temple therein.'"

On the other hand, Barth said, Protestant fundamentalism may have committed an even greater sin by putting religion itself in the place of God:

Religion forgets that she has a right to exist only when she continually does away with herself. Instead, she takes joy in her existence and considers herself indispensable. [She] makes a veritable uproar with [her] morality. . . . She does not tolerate her own relativity. She has not the patience to wait; she lacks that spirit of the stranger and pilgrim, which alone justifies her coming into the world. She is not satisfied with hinting at the x that is over the world and herself. She acts in her lofty ecclesiastical estate as if she were in possession of a gold mine; and in the so-called "religious values" she actually pretends to give out clinking coins. She takes her place as a competitive power over against other powers in life, as an alleged superior world over against the world. She sends missionaries as if she herself could give them a mission. . . . Religious arrogance permits itself simply everything. . . . [But] at the moment when religion becomes conscious of religion . . . it falls away from its inner character, from its truth, to idols. . . . Jesus had nothing to do with religion. The significance of his life lies in its possessing an actuality which no religion possesses—the actuality of the unapproachable, incomprehensible, inconceivable—the realization of that possibility which passes human consideration.

In developing his own theology, Barth sought to steer a middle course that would be neither modernist nor fundamentalist. He began by stating that God is "wholly other: 'That which is born of the spirit is spirit.' There are no transitions, intermixings, or intermediate stages." God is "not the continuation, the result, the consequence, the next step after the next to last . . . but, on the contrary, is forever a radical break with everything [we know] next to the last." Man is completely isolated from God and thus walks "upon a ridge between time and eternity that is narrower than a knife-edge" and that ends "before the closed wall of death." "Within the sphere of their own abilities and possibilities . . . people are tolerably well adjusted," but they know that only "eternal life can . . . be called and really be 'life.'" Moreover, they live in the fear that "the unrighteous will which . . . persecutes and tortures [them] may be the only, the profoundest, will in life. And the [idea] suggests itself—make peace with it! Surrender yourself to the thought that the world is a hell, and conform! There seems nothing else to do." Despite this temptation, man thinks that "there must still be a way from there [the divine supernatural world] to here [the finite, empirical, scientific world]." "And with this 'must'" he discovers "the miracle of the revelation of God" through Christ. In Christ, there is a truly "new element in the midst of the old, a truth in the midst of error and lies, a righteousness in the midst of a sea of unrighteousness, a spirituality within all our crass materialistic tendencies, a formative life-energy within all our weak, tottering movements of thought, a unity in a time which is out of joint. . . . The resurrection of Jesus . . . from the dead is the power which moves both the world and us, because it is the appearance in our [flesh] of a 'wholly and utterly other.' The many miracles of the Bible "are only illustrations of this, the miracle. . . . *It is beside the point even to ask whether they are historical and possible. They make no claim to being either. They signalize the unhistorical, the impossible,* the new time that is coming."

To approach this transcendent "new time" and "new life," it is not necessary, according to Barth, to subscribe to any one dogma or reading of the Bible. All human beliefs and human documents are, by definition, suffused with error. It is necessary, however, to deflate ourselves, to become genuinely humble. We must stop "flinging out accusations which . . . [have] not [been] first applied in their full weight to our own selves." We must see the Apostles and God's chosen ones in their true light as "distraught, humanly unsatisfactory figures, uncertain of their souls and of their practical success, the direct opposite of heroes, their life stories unconcluded, their life work unfinished . . . unable to found . . . any [lasting] institutions, the criteria of the historical worth of things." We must avoid all the usual religious pitfalls of "fanaticism," "conceit," "Pharisaism," and "Titanism." We must learn to be simple and silent. If we do all these things, an innermost voice will tell us that "God is righteous" and that we should believe. We will put away our fears and doubts, be reborn in hope, and experience a "childlike peace and joy."

Although Barth is not a dogmatist, he emphasizes the absolute necessity of belief ("One can only believe . . . or not believe. . . . There is no third way") and defends the Apostles' Creed, despite "its hardness," for its underlying "truth" and "depth." In no sense is he a modern relativist ("Shall we take the position that fundamentally we are all [equally] right? Shall we dip our hands into that from which the spirit of the Bible silently turns away, the dish of tolerance which is more and more being proclaimed. . . . Or may we all, jointly and severally, with our various views and various forms of worship, be wrong? The fact is that we must seek our answer in this direction—'Yea, let God be true, but every man a liar' "). Nor is he modernist or liberal on moral matters ("The Law keeps its place beside the Gospel as another, a second reality, equally true and commanding and necessary") or timid about Christian "witnessing" ("[One must not] whisper and mumble . . . [or] hint . . . [or] leave Him somewhere in the background, but [rather] disregard the universal method of science and place Him in the foreground").

Has Barth achieved his ultimate purpose? Has he formulated a Bible-based Christianity in the tradition of Jeremiah, St. Paul, Luther, and Calvin, which is neither fundamentalist nor modernist? It might seem so. Christian fundamentalists attack Barth as a modernist who has removed all real authority, whether church or biblical, from Christian life, substituting in its place a paltry and unreliable inner intuition. Christian modernists dismiss him as a conservative, a supernaturalist, a believer in ghosts and hobgoblins and miracles. Yet perhaps because of the singularity of his vision, Barth remains an isolated figure: No one church embraces him; his works, though prestigious, lie mostly unread; and his unique message of "humility" and "hope" commands neither numerous adherents nor organized support.

The Neo-Buddhism of Albert Einstein
(Combines intuition and sense experience)

A contemporary scientific writer, Boyce Rensberger, states that "modern biology confirms the view that all the phenomena that together constitute life can be understood in the purely materialistic terms of physics and chemistry." Albert Einstein, on the other hand, the preeminent physicist of our age, rejected the notion that physics was purely materialistic, at least in intent. As he wrote:

The cosmic religious feeling is the strongest and noblest motive for research [into physics]. . . . Those whose acquaintance with [physics] research is derived chiefly from its practical results easily develop a completely false notion of the mentality of the men who, surrounded by a skeptical world, have shown the way to kindred spirits scattered through the world and the centuries. . . . In this materialist cage of ours . . . serious workers [in physics] are . . . profoundly religious people.

That Einstein himself was profoundly religious is beyond dispute. But of what was his religion made? The answer, somewhat surprisingly, is that he was a kind of neo-Buddhist, and to probe his thinking, one must leave Einstein for a moment and delve deeply in time, to the very roots of Buddhism.

Original Buddhism (Sixth Century B.C.)

The early life of Gotama, the founder of Buddhism, provides a classic illustration of the workings of human intuition. Born into a princely Indian family, at age twenty-nine he abandoned wife and newly born son, along with what G. K. Chesterton called the "luxury and pomp" of an oriental court, to become a wandering beggar and religious seeker. At first, he tried to find a guru, but after living with one and then another without finding satisfaction, he continued his journey, stopping occasionally to listen to the reasoning and debates of various religious teachers, eventually throwing himself into a life of such complete fasting and self-mortification that he almost starved to death. When at last he concluded that austerity was useless as a path to spiritual enlightenment, he arose from the forest bed where he was lying, bathed, put on fresh clothes, began to eat normal meals, and rested. At this very moment, when he had put his obsessive spiritual quest out of mind, at least temporarily, his powers of intuition were rekindled, he fell into a deep trance and, on awakening, finally possessed the truth that he was seeking.

And what was this truth? Put simply, it was that all traditional religions of authority, whether God centered or guru centered, all traditional conceptions of God, all techniques and religions of logic were equally empty and worthless. To be reliable, religion must be based on direct observation and experience, not experience in its everyday, chaotic and confusing form, but experience that has been focused and filtered by the highest powers of intuition. Nor should experience be of the simple-minded, reductionist, so-called realistic type, which holds that God does not exist simply because we cannot see, hear, or touch him. Many issues simply cannot be addressed by experience, and should be left alone. Religion should, instead, concentrate on questions of human relations and psychology, down-to-earth questions that are within our powers and whose solution will make a difference in our lives.

Such a message is so modern, so Western in tone that we must immediately ask ourselves—did the Buddha really say this? Is it possible that he formulated this philosophy over twenty-five hundred years ago, half a millennium before Christ, at a time when Europeans were painting their naked bodies blue and dancing around fires? A close reading of the Pali Canon—the earliest recorded teachings of Gotama—suggests that he did teach thus. But the Pali Canon is short; its words are ambiguous; they were not recorded for four hundred years after they were allegedly spoken. Moreover, over the course of the years, Buddhism has developed into dozens, even hundreds, of different religions, many of which emphasize authority or logic. Under the circumstances, any reconstruction of original Buddhism must be speculative, but even so the Pali Canon seems to be teaching something remarkably similar to philosopher David Hume's eighteenth-century Scottish skepticism.

As this summary suggests, the Buddha's most startling contribution was his philosophical method. But his actual doctrine— the fruit of his method—was equally original for its time or any time, and may be summarized as follows:

• The main, perhaps the sole, lesson of experience is that we cause most of our own unhappiness by endlessly agitating ourselves with cravings for this and that, endlessly creating wants and trying to satisfy these wants, endlessly imagining problems and creating solutions for these problems, when the only real solution, the only hope for happiness and relief, is simply to shut off the mind's clamor, to stop wanting so much, if possible to stop wanting anything at all *for ourselves*.

• The problem is not that life is hard, that most of our desires will never be fulfilled. Even if all our immediate desires were fulfilled, they would just be succeeded by others. As Thomas Merton has written: "The truth that many people never understand, until it is too late, is that the more you try to [gain security], the more you suffer, because smaller and more insignificant things begin to torture you. . . . The one who does most to avoid suffering is, in the end, the one who suffers most: and his suffering comes to him from things so little and so trivial that . . . it is no longer objective at all." Or as a Los Angeles Hatha yogi says about his clients: "Three billion people in the world wondering what to eat, and for them, they get a couple of little ruts in the road in front of their house and it's a big disaster." The Greek philosopher Epictetus summed it up approximately five hundred years after the Buddha: "Man is not disturbed about things, but by his opinion about things."

Gotama thought that the identification of personal desire with suffering was self-evident, something that, once stated, would be apparent to everyone. On the other hand, this "self-evident" truth runs contrary to several thousand years of popular Western tradition, beginning with Callicles' statement in Plato's *Gorgias* that "he who would truly live ought to allow his desires to wax to the uttermost [and] when they have grown to their greatest . . . have the courage and intelligence to minister to them and satisfy his longings"; or as Aristotle's contemporary disciple Mortimer Adler puts it in *Philosophical Mistakes*, albeit in a very different and much more moderate vein: "Contentment . . . cannot signify anything other than the psychological state that exists when the desires of the moment are satisfied. The more they are satisfied at a given moment, the more we regard that moment as approaching supreme contentment. . . . Happiness [as opposed to mere psychological contentment] can then be defined as a whole life enriched by the cumulative possession of all the real goods that every human being needs and by the satisfaction of those individual wants that result in obtaining apparent goods that are innocuous." In other words, personal and selfish desires are just fine so long as they are rational, do not go too far, and do not harm others.

• If, according to the Buddha, personal and selfish desires are actually and always a source of misery, how can they be avoided? First, by following the advice of one of the founders of American psychology, William James: "Refuse to express an emotion, and it dies. . . . We feel sorry because we cry, angry because we strike, afraid because we tremble, and not that we cry, strike or tremble because we are sorry, angry or fearful. . . . If we wish to conquer undesirable emotional tendencies, we must assiduously go through the outward movements of those contrary dispositions that we prefer to cultivate. The reward of persistency will infallibly come!" Stated differently, it is not enough to try to avoid personal and selfish desires. Because "nature abhors a vacuum," personal desires must be replaced with impersonal desires, such as for the welfare of others, of humanity, or of other creatures. And to assist in this endeavor, the Buddha left "three" aids behind: his order of monks, which visitors were encouraged to visit for periods of spiritual refreshment; his eightfold path, a series of social, physical, and mental disciplines (*dharma*) similar to the yogic eightfold path laid out in chapter 7 of this book; and last (least in his own eyes), his own spiritual example.

• The emotions are a great obstacle to a life of impersonal and unselfish desire, but the greatest obstacle of all, paradoxically, is our conscious mind, the instrument that reigns so imperiously over all our actions. The mind is both clever and treacherous. It persuades us that it is trying to control our emotions and work for our security and welfare when it is really only creating problems to have the pleasure and prestige of "solving" them. It sinks us into endless argument and conflict; convinces us that the immediate world we see around us, which is mostly a product of our own imagination, is the only true reality, and a most solid and permanent reality at that—while everything is actually in a state of total impermanence, constantly changing and passing away before our very eyes. It is not surprising that we mistake our conscious mind for our very soul, our inner selfhood. But whatever the conscious mind is, it is not to be mistaken for the self.

• If the conscious mind is not the self, what is? Here the Buddha becomes Sakya Muni, the Silent Sage, the teacher who refuses to teach what he does not and (in his opinion) cannot know. Stripped of body and mind, the human self would appear to be a void, *anatta*, nothing. If so, one should not worry about it. Nor should one try to answer any of the following "unanswerable" questions, each of which were posed to Gotama, and each of which he silently turned away as being "not tending to edification"—that is, beyond either intuition or experience— despite the curiosity of his followers, all of whom would have eagerly accepted the Master's word as law on any subject:

Is there a God?

Is the universe eternal?

Is the universe finite (in size)?

Can life exist without a body?

Does a Buddha (an enlightened one) exist after death?

The Buddha particularly refused to discuss or dispute these matters, or indeed any matters, with other religious teachers. Nor was he impressed by reputed miraculous powers or siddhis associated with other faiths. When informed that one of his own followers had just levitated, he gently replied, "This will not help convert the unconverted or aid the converted," then returned to his prior conversation.

Western critics, even after studying the Pali Canon rather than contemporary Buddhism, have often concluded that the Buddha's doctrines were grim, pessimistic, completely passive, based on a notion of life as a kind of hell and a desire to anesthetize oneself. Though it is always possible that this is a correct interpretation—that Buddhism represents the teaching of a disappointed and recessive personality—there is no evidence to support it. It seems more likely that the Buddha was the complete Type B personality, one who wanted his disciples to be active in life (even if following his own monastic way of poverty and chastity); who wanted them to have a will to live and a purpose to live for, albeit a disinterested and unselfish will and purpose; who thought that human beings could be motivated, not by teaching drive, ambition, and desire, but rather by removing the blockages of anxiety, fear, depression, and anger that hold everyone in bondage; who hoped (unsuccessfully, as it turned out) to avoid founding another religion of authority, but rather to point out a path for all people, Brahmins and lowly untouchables alike, that would emphasize realism, modest expectations, self-reliance, and service.

Einstein's personal religion

Whether Einstein ever read the Pali Canon of early Buddhism is unknown, but seems likely. Although he was attracted to the logical religion of Spinoza (chapter 4), his own religion, as formulated in his later years, clearly followed the tenets of early Buddhism. This was manifested, first, in a rejection of personal desire ("I am happy because I want nothing from anyone. I do not care for money. Decorations, titles, or distinctions mean nothing to me. I do not crave praise"); second, in an espousal of disinterested desire ("A person who is religiously enlightened appears to me to be one who has, to the best of his ability, liberated himself from the fetters of his selfish desires and is preoccupied with thoughts, feelings, and aspirations to which he clings because of their superpersonal value"); third, in a rejection of both logic and simple experience ("This . . . aristocratic illusion concerning the unlimited penetrative power of [logical] thought has as its counterpart the plebian illusion of naive realism, according to which things 'are' as they are perceived to us through our senses. . . . But the real nature of things, that we shall never know, never"); and fourth, in the power of intuition to provide religious and moral answers to guide everyday life ("One must not attempt to justify [religious truths] but rather to sense their nature simply and clearly").

The "Detached Action" of Mohandas Gandhi (Combines intuition with emotion)

At first glance, a value system that combines intuition and emotion as primary, coequal factors might seem to be paradoxical, even impossible. Although it is a largely unconscious mode of thinking, intuition is highly cerebral and requires a certain distance from the world. All the exercises designed to evoke it (e.g., the yogic eightfold path) emphasize detachment. How, then, can intuition get mixed up with emotion, the mental mode in which we are least cerebral and detached, in which we are moved by dark and powerful drives, drives for survival (along with its second derivative, personal power); drives for reproduction; more subtle but no less compelling drives for identity, stimulation, and security (all of which are realized through participation in a tribe or community, either a blood community such as family or nation, or a community based on certain shared ideas such as liberalism or revolutionary communism)? Yet the *Bhagavad-Gita*, perhaps the central text in the Indian religious tradition, written between A.D. 200 and 500, says that intuition may be combined with emotion, that it is possible to maintain complete detachment and freedom from selfish desires while actively serving your family or nation, even, to take the Gita's somewhat gory example, while killing your nation's enemies on the battlefield. It is not only possible to do this: It is our *dharma* or duty. From time to time we may leave the world and retreat to a monastery or mountaintop. But most of the time we must live in the world and find a way to reconcile our emotions, the wellsprings of motivation, drive, and action, with a higher spiritual way of detachment and disinterested service.

The *Bhagavad-Gita* directly inspired Mohandas Gandhi, the father of Indian independence, and this one man best illustrates the possibilities of a religion of intuition-emotion, of "detached action." Gandhi was himself a welter of personal contradictions. He was married with children, yet at age thirty-six decided to practice chastity. Later, he turned his back on material possessions (although one of his wealthy supporters joked that it cost a fortune to keep him in poverty). Even as he withdrew from the "world", he kept agitating, through his unique nonviolent method, first for minority rights in South Africa and then, after his return to India at age forty-five, for Indian independence. He was clearly a holy man, a man who practiced severe self-restraint (including some very odd self-restraints such as sleeping naked with his teenage grandniece to "test" his chastity) together with love and tolerance, but he was also, in his own words, a *banya*, a crafty trader who was always ready to bargain, to make a deal. The aristocratic Indians who paid for Gandhi's crusades (people like Motilal, Jawaharlal Nehru's father and the founder of India's current political dynasty, a thoroughly Europeanized Indian who shipped his shirts to Paris to be laundered) thought they could easily control such a saintly revolutionary, but it was the backers who were controlled. The British underestimated Gandhi for the same reason—his incomprehensibility, his contradictory mix of sainthood and slyness—and he made use of their puzzlement at every turn. To maintain detachment, Gandhi practiced meditation. When this was not possible, when he was surrounded by surging humanity or being presented to the King of England, he relied on the next best thing, humor. An Englishman protested that wearing a loincloth to Buckingham Palace in 1931 was disrespectful. "The King," he replied, "was wearing quite enough for us both."

In the Indian tradition, Karma yoga, the life of selfless action, of intuition *and* emotion, is usually considered a lower yoga, suitable for spiritual beginners rather than adepts. Yet the Karma yoga of Gandhi, combining revolution with nonviolence, intense nationalism with an equal regard for the moral development and happiness of one's adversaries, is so difficult that its habitual practice would seem to be a very high attainment indeed. Even Gandhi by his own admission fell short of the ultimate ideal of this kind of yoga, in particular by neglecting the needs of his wife, who was barely consulted about the decision to undertake a life of chastity, and of his children, who saw little of their father.

The Judaism of Golda Meir
(Combines lesser elements of authority and logic with a dominant strain of emotion)

Historically, Judaism has been a religion of authority, especially the authority of Scripture. For some ultra-Orthodox rabbis such as Israeli Shalom Rabin, Scripture is simply everything: "When God gave us the Torah to run our lives by, he gave us everything we need to know." Despite this point of view, Judaism has also been a religion of logic, equally famous for the logical mastery of the great medieval Jewish philosopher Maimonides and for disputatious rabbis who may argue for hours on a street corner about whether it is logically consistent with Scripture for them to share a cab ride home. Yet to many Jews, neither authority nor logic lie at the heart of Judaism. For these Jews, Scripture, theological fine points, dietary and other rules of conduct, traditional holidays, rites, rituals, and symbols are all secondary if not irrelevant, mere means to an end: an end of simply feeling Jewish, of participating in a basically emotional fellowship, of joining a close-knit and lifelong community that simultaneously embraces, protects, nurtures, stimulates, and inspires its individual members.

Golda Meir (prime minister of Israel 1969–1974) exemplifies this essentially secular Judaism. It was not that she was overtly atheistic or nonobservant. She kept her beliefs about God mostly to herself (although she successfully fought to strike the words "our Redeemer" from the initial proclamation of the state of Israel), and was at least minimally observant. For example, she wanted a civil marriage (in Milwaukee, when she was still an American citizen), but reluctantly acceded to her mother's pleading for a traditional *chuppah* (bridal canopy and ceremony). Years later in 1946, when she was publicly fasting to protest the British refusal to permit full-scale Jewish immigration into what would become Israel, the Chief Rabbi suddenly proclaimed that all Jews must end their fast to observe Passover with a proper Seder and she again acquiesced, but only to the extent of eating a single piece of matzo (bread) "no larger than an olive." Meir's solution to the problem posed by the Chief Rabbi was typical: she was a woman of strong emotional drives who was nevertheless intensely practical. As she wrote in her memoirs: "Nothing in life just happens. It isn't enough to believe in something; you have to have the stamina to meet obstacles and overcome them, to struggle." This emphasis on believing in something, on joining together with others in pursuit of a common goal, on sacrificing and struggling for the group with little or no concern for one's own welfare or wishes, both underlay and defined Meir's particular style of "Jewishness."

Throughout her life, Meir embraced and served a wide variety of groups and causes. In addition to her core identity as a Jew, she was also a Jewish mother (to her two children, five grandchildren, and, it sometimes seemed, everybody else), a Jewish American (even after giving up her American citizenship, she remained in close contact with the United States), a Jewish socialist, a Jewish feminist, a Zionist, a member of a kibbutz, and, of course, a founder of Israel. Of all these myriad roles, membership in a kibbutz seems to have provided the most unalloyed happiness despite an unpromising beginning, in which her husband's and her application for a place in the Kibbutz Merhavia was rejected by the admissions committee on the grounds that American Jews were too "soft" for the harsh rigors of pioneering life in the early 1920s. After this initial hurdle was overcome, Meir joined a settlement of seven women and thirty men located in a mosquito-ridden and pestilential swamp in the Jezreel plain where "there were no orchards, no meadows, no flowers," communal privies and showers, clothes made of rough cloth with holes cut for head and arms, "dreadful" meals, incessant ideological and quasi-ideological debates (for example, over whether oatmeal for breakfast or cookies twice a week were too profligate for kibbutz life), no funds whatever to buy anything (only one fork *or* spoon per person and at one point only three table glasses to be shared by all), recurrent plagues of dysentery or malaria, hard physical chores from before dawn to late at night, and chronic threats from nearby Arabs. All these rigors notwithstanding, there was also a uniquely satisfying experience of community, of belonging, of intimate friends who shared "almost everything—problems, rewards, responsibilities and satisfactions."

What Meir liked best of all at Merhavia was "sharing a midnight snack with the boys coming back from guard duty and staying on in the kitchen for hours to hear their stories." Later, throughout a career that brought some supremely exhilarating moments (watching sixteen- and seventeen-year-old Jewish boys and girls jumping into the waves to greet the boats carrying survivors of Hitler's death camps immediately after World War II and carrying the older people ashore on their strong, young shoulders, the military victories against the Arabs, the capture of old Jerusalem), her thoughts always returned to the kibbutz, and to the uniquely communal life that could be lived there: "One of my great disappointments has been that I [could not return]."

11. Why Values Get So Complicated

As the preceding chapters should illustrate, values are a slippery subject, perhaps the most slippery subject we know of. In addition to the confusion represented by so many different levels of moral discourse (six types of value systems, multidimensional composites as complex as Karl Barth's Christianity, Albert Einstein's neo-Buddhism, Gandhi's "detached action," or Golda Meir's Judaism, there are other confusions as well, confusions introduced by the tendency of human beings to hide their true beliefs, form makeshift moral alliances, or change their beliefs (sometimes as dramatically as Saul/St. Paul).

The "Hiddenness" of Values

One thinks of the story of Jean Meslier, a priest leading an obscure life tending the souls of two small rural parishes in early eighteenth-century France, rising each day to comfort the sick, counsel the troubled, teach the faith, perform masses, christen and marry the young, bury the dead. Even this exemplary life did not satisfy everyone. The church was said to lack a proper confession box; keeping a pretty young cousin of twenty-three as a housemaid was causing gossip; commoners were sometimes seated in nobles' stalls. But these few lapses, regrettable as they were, could not be considered characteristic of the man. The *curé* was a pious religious who almost never left his little flock in the country. On a rare visit to Paris, he confronted a wayward young man at a friend's house and vigorously tried to restore him to the Catholic fold.

Back in the privacy of his home, however, surrounded by

books and solitude, quite another *curé* emerged. Deep into the night, he poured his hatred, his seething, rancorous scorn, his bitter contempt for Christianity into a book that was to be published after his death. The notion that God had a son was "indecent and ridiculous," the doctrine of the holy spirit "pious jumble," the resurrection of the flesh an "absurdity." Studying the Bible revealed a host of contradictions, prophets who were "liars and impostors," and above all an "unjust, cruel, and merciless" God, a fantastic wizard who performs trivial miracles for a chosen few while the mass of mankind is perpetually mired in suffering, evil, and oppression. "If God were capable of all this . . . such a God would deserve to be hated, despised, and cursed. . . . He would be crueler than the cruelest tyrants who ever existed or whom one could imagine existing."

In defense of such "childish" doctrines, Christianity had committed every conceivable "atrocity": "Wherever one looks, [Christians] persecute each other with fire and blood to defend their ridiculous beliefs. . . . There is no evil or wickedness that they have not practised against one another." The pious *curé* concluded, deep in his secret book, that theology had only three branches: "prejudice, ignorance, and fanaticism"; the Church was the root cause of virtually all the injustice and misery of the world; and humanity could only be saved by "hanging and strangling with the bowels of the priests all the nobles and rulers of the earth."

Makeshift Moral Alliances

Even when people openly reveal their beliefs, some strange alliances may be formed:

Example: Is Russian novelist and moral philosopher Alexander Solzhenitsyn a Western liberal or a fascist? *Answer:* Because he is allied with Western liberals against Soviet repression, he appears to be a liberal, but he actually favors authoritarianism (so-called Christian, not Marxist authoritarianism) and condemns democracy.

Example: Are teachers of science and teachers of the humanities (history, English, and so forth) (1) natural rivals, or (2) natural allies? *Answer:* It all depends. For much of the twentieth century, the two were locked in a battle for control of the school curriculum (*vide* C. P. Snow's 1959 book about the "two cultures" and the unbridgeable gap between them). More recently, teachers of science and the humanities have banded together against a resurgent threat to both of them: fundamentalist Christianity, especially the fundamentalist teaching of "creationism." At the Institute for Advanced Studies in Princeton, New Jersey, some of the most distinguished professors of science and the humanities in the United States raised a storm of protest against the appointment of a sociologist of religion (it was bad enough that he was a sociologist, a soft, perhaps even a pseudoscientific field, but a sociologist of religion!).

Example: On what subject did Francis Bacon, the founder of modern science, and St. Francis, the most complete Christian since Christ, entirely agree? *Answer:* On the horrors of a religion based on deductive logic. Francis: "Logic is satanic." Bacon: "The [logical] mind cannot be trusted." Yet if any two men would have found each other incomprehensible, it would be the selfless Francis and the schemingly corrupt Bacon.

Example: Religions of sense experience are often bitterly opposed to religions of deductive logic. Why, then, do popular textbooks lump together these two opposites in speaking about an alleged eighteenth-century Age of Reason? *Answer:* Because the two were making common cause, temporarily, and only temporarily, against the immediate threat of a hostile Christianity.

Example: Religions of either sense experience or of intuition tend to dismiss religions of emotion because the latter fill the mind with fervors and passions rather than calm and detachment. But if asked why this calm and detachment is desirable, what do religions of sense experience and intuition reply? So that the unimpassioned wisdom of the conscious mind may be heard, say religions of sense experience. So that you can escape the wiles, lies, and addictive games of the conscious mind, say religions of intuition.

Migration of Values/Conversions

Whether hidden or revealed, standing alone or in strange alliances, human values always migrate. In Western history, some popular migrations may be identified in the following vastly oversimplified scheme:

Period	*Themes*
Premodern	*Authority* (e.g., Christianity)
17th–19th century	*Deductive logic* (We have to find a post-Christian way to save morals, put them on a firm footing, or chaos will engulf us)
18th–20th century	*Sense experience* (Logic is a failure, but experience will show us how to cope)
19th, especially early 20th century	*Emotion* (Experience is a disappointment, but we can find refuge in a series of secular Christianities: faiths like socialism that are supposed to create a "heaven" right here on earth)
20th century, especially 1960s and 1970s	*Intuition* (Faiths like socialism have proved stressful and disillusioning; we need to retreat from the world of raging emotion to find inner peace and bliss)
19th, 20th centuries, especially 1980s	*"Science"* (Meditating for 16 hours at a time is boring; I need to become more realistic, get an advanced legal,

business, or scientific education, earn enough money to
take care of myself and my
family and to pay all the
other experts I'll need to
consult in the process)

1980s, 1990s?   *Authority* (e.g., Christianity,
Judaism)

In this context, the personal story of Pat Robertson, the Christian evangelist, entrepreneur, and presidential candidate, is
especially relevant. Raised in rural Virginia, with its bedrock
Christian fundamentalism, he was nevertheless son of a U.S.
senator, graduate of Yale Law School, an acquaintance of the
young senator John Kennedy and the "dizzy-looking brunette"
who became Kennedy's wife, an habitué of sophisticated New
York nightclubs. As a well-connected and personable expert in
the legal field, he could expect to attain whatever he sought
(value system based on "science"). When that was not enough,
he tried to find larger purpose and meaning in law (emotive
legalism), but found no "noble cause," only "emptiness." Finally,
he accepted Jesus Christ as his savior and enrolled in New York
Theological Seminary. While his Ivy League friends forged
ahead in the world, he learned "to kneel on the floor with others
and weep, to speak in tongues, to pray for cures." At the urging
of an inner voice, and somewhat against his wife's better judgment, he sold all their possessions and moved into a rectory in
the New York slums.

In the end, of course, Robertson did not entirely abandon all
worldly accomplishment and success. He simply turned it inside
out by founding the Christian Broadcasting Network (with a
weekly television audience that eventually reached 28 million
and annual revenues of $200 million) before deciding to run for
president in 1987. "God sent me," he said, "that's how . . . it got
done."

Robertson, as much as anybody, represents the complexity, confusion, misalliances, and changeability of human values. For every choice that is made, many more must be denied. For every door that closes, many more open up. No matter what is lost through circumstance or poor judgment, new possibilities always arise. It is a fascinating and truly inexhaustible process.

Part Four

USING THE
FRAMEWORK

12. A Moral Detective Story

Contemporary Americans are literally engulfed by would-be moral leaders and teachers, moral influences, and value systems, some of which seem to be alike, some antagonistic, some alike in certain respects and antagonistic in other respects. It is no wonder that everything begins to blur, that we lose our bearings and alternately cling to old values or throw them out indiscriminately. Under these confused circumstances, what we need is a way to clear the mental clutter, decide what the basic moral alternatives are and how each thinker or would-be prophet that we meet, either directly or through books and film, relates to these basic alternatives.

Allan Bloom

Consider, for example, Allan Bloom, the nonexercising, tobacco-loving, fine-food-and-drink–loving moral philosopher from the University of Chicago, the relentless critic of moral relativism, of squishy softness, of the "I-feel-good-about-myself" and "I-feel-comfortable-with-such-and-such" school, of the "nuance"-less diatribes of feminism, especially of the "barbarism" of rock music. Bloom's best-known work, *The Closing of the American Mind*, became an unexpected bestseller in the summer of 1987. Whether it will survive to be read by future generations is unknown; very, very few books last more than a few years, and the prognosis for any one book, this one included, is always doubtful. But survivability is not the point. Whether *The Closing of the American Mind* endures or not, it provides an ideal test case, an ideal opportunity to apply the framework of the six types of value systems and their innumerable variations. It offers an ideal test case because it is full of interesting ideas and passionate convictions, but it is not entirely clear what these ideas and convictions really mean—in particular, how the different pieces of Bloom's philosophy, with its numerous likes and dislikes, fit together (can one accept some elements and reject others, such as the hatred of rock music and other manifestations of popular culture, or is it a seamless web that must be accepted or rejected as a whole?). Above all, it is unclear how one might actually live Bloom's philosophy, apply it to one's own life.

Reading Bloom in isolation, we might never be able to answer these questions. With the six types of value systems and their innumerable variations in the back of our mind, however, we can look at *The Closing of the American Mind* with a fresh eye, try to get a clearer focus on a hard-to-pin-down moral thinker. In effect, we can engage in some detective work, turning Bloom's pages in search for clues that will link his thought to the framework that we have developed. If we cannot place Bloom within this framework, our approach is defective and ought to be discarded. If we can place Bloom within this framework, we will both validate the framework and get a firm "fix" on what he is saying, both in particular and as a whole.

Assuming for a moment that Bloom can be understood within the framework of six basic types of value systems, there are at least two possibilities: (1) that he exemplifies one of the six types, or (2) that he represents an amalgam of several or even all of them. If we were to guess about this, we would surely guess that he represented an amalgam: The professor's argument is too complicated and multifaceted to exemplify just one of the six. Yet, surprisingly, this guess would be wrong: Bloom does indeed carry the banner of just one of our six types of value systems, as evidenced by his fierce opposition to the other five. To reach this conclusion, however, is to jump ahead of our story; we are still at the stage of evaluating clues and are not yet ready for a conclusion. Instead of beginning at the end, let's begin at the beginning by seeing what, if anything, Bloom has to say about authority, logic, experience, emotion, intuition, and "science," and whether he demonstrates a particular allegiance to any of these modes of moral thinking.

Of the six, authority is the easiest to dismiss. People who subject themselves to external moral authorities like a church or Bible or even a know-it-all professor are described as "passive, disconsolate, indifferent [to] . . . the best of . . . thought." A "true liberal education requires that . . . no previous attachment be immune to examination and hence re-evaluation." In poking fun at a taxi driver who said he had straightened out his life through Gestalt psychology, Bloom says, "A generation earlier he would have found God and learned to despise himself as a sinner." So much for both God and Gestalt! In another passage, Christianity is described as a "superstition," although, as is often the case in *The Closing of The American Mind*, it is not absolutely clear if this is Bloom's voice or that of other individuals or schools. Similarly, in dismissing the Marxist view of human history as a kind of march to a promised land, the statement is made that "one might as well be a Christian if one is so naive," but this may be the German philosopher Friedrich Nietzsche speaking rather than Bloom. In any case, it is clearly Bloom who says that "the good life is the pleasant life and . . . the best life is the most pleasant life," a doctrine that would make both Pope John Paul II and Jerry Falwell shudder.

With authority crossed off our list, we are left with five other possibilities. What about logic? Does the professor propose to deduce a moral philosophy for the youth of our country? Evidently not. Bloom does wish to clarify language and draw sharp moral distinctions such as good versus evil, body versus soul, self versus other (drawing distinctions is an attribute of logic, although it is also typical of Christianity, as in God versus the devil). Moreover, he repeatedly exposes common logical fallacies—for example, the idea that a society can enjoy complete freedom and complete equality (to enjoy either freedom or equality fully, one must limit the other) or the Freudian fallacy that all human beings are motivated by sex and power, but one human being, Freud himself, is motivated by a love of scientific truth (even one exception invalidates the rule). In all these ways, Bloom demonstrates a love of order and consistency that is highly logical, yet his book completely pans the idea that deductive logic provides a royal road to moral truth. "The real sensation of [Machiavelli's] Florence is worth all the formulas of [logical philosophy] ten times over," he says. "[Logic] responds to none of the permanent philosophic questions."

Turning from value systems based on logic to value systems based on emotion, Bloom is once again ambivalent. As a human being, he recognizes the instinctive need for emotional community. If students love and value their families, their friends, their country, and thereby gain personal security, identity, and stimulation, these natural affections should not be tampered with unless professors really have something better to offer and are willing to give of themselves as they guide their charges through the difficult and painful/joyful process of discovery. In American society in general, people have been facilely and thoughtlessly ripped away from their roots, abandoned to a process of emotional "groundlessness" and "decomposition." The family, in particular, which used to be the "only unbreakable bond, for better or for worse," has long since been broken and thrown away. Such dislocations are dangerous as well as painful. If the dislocated individual is not regrounded, he or she may suddenly lash out in a passionately violent quest for community. The Athenian mob murdered Socrates in a desperate and ultimately futile attempt to restore the Athenian family and state. Students in the 1960s trashed the universities in a vain search for "connectedness," the feeling of being "together" in a common enterprise. Such longings, says Bloom, become particularly poisonous when transmogrified into complex and highly abstract ideologies such as feminism. Bloom is strident, and ultra-ambivalent, in his opposition to feminism. "I am not arguing . . . that the old family arrangements were good or that we should or could go back to them." But feminism is "grim, unerotic," a perversion of nature foisted on us by "Dustin Hoffman and Meryl Streep types [who] invade the schools, popular psychology, TV and the movies. . . .

Why should a man risk his life protecting a karate champion who knows just what part of the male anatomy to go after in defending herself? What substitute is there for the forms of relatedness that are dismantled in the name of the new justice?"

If logic is deficient and emotion only a lower mode of moral reasoning, can we perhaps turn to intuition, to a mode of moral reasoning that rejects both emotion and the conscious mind (the conscious mind is viewed as even more deceitful and misleading than our passions), that looks for wisdom from a state of nonemotive, unconscious cognition achieved through meditation? Bloom emphatically says no. He agrees that human beings should promote mental relaxation and calm, but only to refresh the conscious mind, not to reject or transcend it. "Necessity, tension, and conflict," the baggage of the conscious mind, are part of the soul's "eternal travail," a very necessary and useful part, not something to try to escape. Yoga for Bloom is not a "serious . . . life choice."

Value systems based on intuition are just a nuisance, a gnat for Bloom to brush away with a few dismissive sentences. What truly concentrates his ire is the mode of moral reasoning that copies the natural sciences' combination of experience, intuition, and logic with only the most limited fidelity but then confidently wraps itself in the scientific mantle, earnestly proclaiming before the huddled masses that life is just a series of problems to be overcome; that these problems can be overcome through the application of the right kind of technical knowledge; that such technical knowledge will usually be new, just discovered, hard to get without the right credentials; that one moral belief is as good as another as long as it is relevant, that is, helps us function and succeed; that anything less than complete moral relativism and tolerance make progress, both our own and that of society, utterly impossible. Bloom accurately points out that this so-called turning away from values, this obligatory relativism, actually represents the fostering of yet another set of values, yet another moral dogmatism, all the more arbitrary and tyrannical for being hidden. Human beings will always hold moral beliefs, and if they think they can escape into a technical world where such beliefs no longer matter, they are just exhibiting the most unscientific sort of naivete.

So much for five of the six modes of moral reasoning: authority, logic, emotion, intuition, and "science." By process of elimination, the professor must either be an apostle of experience or our framework is a failure. Fortunately, there can be no doubt: He is indeed a descendant of Montaigne, a believer in day-to-day experience as both humanity's highest teacher and as an end in itself, albeit an end that can only be grasped through the most strenuous personal self-discipline and through a continuous process of self-education. This self-discipline and self-education are really the heart of the matter: We must always choose, choose carefully, not merely gulp down the experiences that are most readily at hand in our family, our neighborhood, our entertainment media, our society, our era; ultimately, we must search out and rely on a treasure trove of the highest standards and heroic examples handed down from the past to illuminate the best possibilities and protect us from all the numerous wrong choices that humanity habitually makes. In this respect, the worst doctrine of all is prodigal experience, experience shorn of saving self-discipline and self-education through history.

Even though Bloom does not use the same terms, he views what we have called "science" and prodigality, taken together, as the twin-headed monster of the modern era, descended on one side from the ideas of the great English philosopher John Locke, now reduced to yuppie get-aheadism and everyone-out-for-selfism, on the other side from the ideas of the Swiss and German philosophers Jean-Jacques Rousseau and Friedrich Nietzsche, now reduced to sex, drugs, and self-destruction. *The Closing of the American Mind* argues that both as a society and as individuals, we are presently oscillating between these two equally evil poles, or combining them in ever more evil combinations. For example, the psychoanalyst is a "scientist" par excellence, but his or her prescriptions are commonly used to defend and excuse prodigality: It isn't my fault; it's the fault of my parents; it's the fault of a repressive society; if I am not allowed to have free sex, I will be neurotic; without complete freedom, I cannot find and express myself, and so on.

Tom Hanks and Faye Dunaway

The framework that we have presented (six modes of thinking → six modes of thinking about values → six dominant values → six types of value systems) is helpful in sorting out a complex thinker like Allan Bloom. It helps us to identify the thrust of what he is saying (in this case, that we should obtain our values through a refined form of sense experience), and also to relate his work to what others are saying or have said in the past. At the same time, almost any novel, play, or film in which human beings are portrayed can be analyzed within this framework. To choose an example from film, Tom Hanks is a well-known comic actor who seems to specialize in playing confused young men. In *Nothing in Common*, he plays an advertising executive and dedicated proponent of "scientific" values who opens himself up to emotional values by discovering that he wants to care for his newly divorced parents. In *Volunteers*, he plays an entertaining young prodigal (card shark, partygoer) who is transformed into a more reliable apostle of "science." To choose a quite different example, *Barfly* (starring Faye Dunaway and Mickey Rourke) depicts a large cast of down-and-out prodigals living in an alcoholic haze—until a beautiful upscale publisher (representing "scientific" values) appears from nowhere and attempts to "reform" the brilliant but lost character played by Rourke. The point of these movies is comedy or satiric melodrama or just entertainment, not analysis. But without an underlying moral "bite," they would not be nearly as funny or as melodramatic.

Our own lives

Quite apart from books, plays, or films, one can also use the framework of the six types of value systems and their innumerable variations to understand the drama of one's own personal life with its intimate cast of family and friends. A forty-two-year-old suburban Marylander writes in the *Washington Post* letters column: "I was married to a professional woman and on our dual incomes we Club Med'ed, sports-car raced, [and] alpine skied . . . our 14-year marriage into oblivion." [So far, we can perceive the combination of "scientific" and prodigal sense experience values which Allan Bloom so despises.] "I'm now remarried to a woman who gave up her 'professional' career to provide full-time care for our 1- and 5-year-old daughters. . . . Vacations are taken in our nine-year-old used pop-up camper, and dining out means 'Hooray! Daddy's bringing home a pizza from Piazamos.' We've just started into the second round of what will be 100 readings of 'Pat-the-Bunny' for our 1-year-old. Happiness is my wife and two restless kids picking me up at [the airport] after a three-day business trip. We all cry, because we are so happy to be together again." [Now the focus has completely shifted to emotive values based on a close family life, a change that has obviously made the writer much happier.]

If the preceding examples—Bloom, Hanks, and Dunaway, the suburban businessman—seem a bit oversimplified, it is because they are briefly summarized. Actual human life, whether real or fictional, in your own home or in a book or on screen, is almost never simple. The purpose of using a framework, in this case the framework of six types of value systems and their innumerable variations, is not to circumscribe, to reduce, or to caricature. It is rather to provide a guide, a readily available and easily consulted guide, a kind of catalogue for the library of life, so that people can quickly see where they are going, where others would like to lead them, and where they can choose to go if they wish. If nothing else, the framework should give us some bearings and save us some time: In a world of too much information, too many options, too many would-be prophets and teachers tugging us this way and that, it is helpful to be able to establish our bearings, on our own, as quickly and confidently as possible.

13. Values in the Classroom

The framework of six types of value systems and their innumerable variations can be used not only to shed light on moral thinkers like Bloom, or on novels, plays and films, or on your own values or those of others. It can also be used to sort through a variety of social issues—for example, the way in which values should or should not be taught in the classroom, the general problem of moral education in American schools. Although this entire issue, taken as a whole, would require another book to treat, we might usefully focus on just a few key questions, all of them perennially in the news:

Should elementary and secondary school teaching be "value-neutral"?

On one side of this issue we have Gary Bauer, former undersecretary of education under President Reagan, who wrathfully condemns the experimentation with a "value-neutral" curriculum that began in the 1970s or even earlier, and who says that "our schools must drop the ridiculous notion that it is possible to teach without teaching values." On the other side of this issue, we have Richard Cohen of the *Washington Post*:

Will . . . the teaching of values in the schools . . . remedy much of what ails the nation? My school-day recollections say otherwise. I was taught values. The day began with a prayer. We pledged allegiance to the flag and sang "My Country 'Tis of Thee," including the more religious of the verses. Once a week we had . . . singing of patriotic songs. The boys wore ties, the girls white blouses and blue skirts, and we were segregated by sex to be taught shop or cooking. We were given no classes in sex education [and] . . . told to eschew drugs. . . . We had a class called "civics" in which we learned . . . about the communist menace and the wonders of our own democracy. . . . We were taught, as I said, values . . . and yet we were the generation that first turned to drugs in a big way . . . that secured abortion as a right . . . that lived together without benefit of marriage and that now provides those awful statistics on divorce and extra-marital sex. . . .

Ours should be called the Placebo Generation. To fight everything from drugs to premarital pregnancies, we choose antiquated weapons and battle on a field of nostalgia. . . . Drugs are a problem, but for the addict not the only one. So is helplessness, despair, poverty—a bleak future in which the instant gratification of drugs (or a child) may amount to the only gratification. . . . Our appalling divorce rate (the world's highest) was not produced because we, of all the world's peoples, lack values, but by economic and social circumstances that rendered them less relevant.

It is certainly not difficult to see what is going on here. Cohen is yet another exponent of contemporary "science" in our sense of the term, the idea that life is a series of problems, including drugs and fatherless welfare children, that are situational, social or economic, that are not responsive to "antiquated" appeals to values, but that can and must be resolved with the right technical tools. What Cohen and other "scientists" of this sort fail to see or acknowledge is that their "value-free" world represents just another set of values, a set of values that are, as Allan Bloom said, all the more powerful and all encompassing for being hidden. What is really transpiring between Gary Bauer and Richard Cohen is not an argument over education with values versus education without values, but rather an argument over the kind of values to be taught. Bauer, in the words of his former boss, William Bennett, secretary of education under Reagan, wants to teach "the Judeo-Christian tradition . . . patriotism, self-discipline, thrift, honesty, respect for elders . . . that there is a moral difference between the United States and the Soviet Union." Cohen may not actually disagree with these values as stated, but he regards them as easily manipulated by fanatics; masking other, more objectionable values; trivialized by teaching in a civics class; or in any case not representative of his particular ethos and view of the world, which is "scientific" to the core. Once it is clear that we are dealing with two contending sets of values, that values of one kind or another always have been and always will be taught in the schools, either directly or suffused through the general curriculum, we can then get on with the real issue, which is forming a political consensus, imperfect as this consensus always is, on what should be taught in public schools.

Are primary and secondary schools teaching "Godless" humanism?

This question takes several forms: Are our schools teaching an organized religion called secular humanism? Are our schools teaching values inimical to Christianity? Is the teaching of evolution incompatible with the Genesis account of creation? Let us deal with each in turn.

Are our schools teaching an organized religion called secular humanism?

Margo Szews, writing in the *Washington Post* letters column, makes the case as follows:

Barbara Parker of the People for the American Way reportedly said that trying to define [secular humanism] is like trying to nail Jell-O to a tree. [Your] readers deserve more honest and accurate information. The objective ideology of contemporary secular humanism is clearly outlined in the "Humanist Manifesto II," which was printed in the September/October 1973 issue of the *Humanist* magazine, the publishing arm of the American Humanist Association. This creed, an update of the 1933 manifesto, provides a formal statement of beliefs and goals.

In the preface, magazine editor Paul Kurtz states that traditional theism, especially faith in the prayer-hearing God, assumed to love and care for persons, to hear and understand their prayers and to be able to do something about them, is an unproven and outmoded faith. The document further states that promises of immortal salvation or fear of eternal damnation are both illusory and harmful.

The secular humanist's rejection of God invalidates Christian absolutes and dictates moral relativism in the areas of ethics and sexual morality. The Humanist Manifesto II specifically states that Ethics is autonomous and situational, needing no theological or ideological sanction.

Although it is true that very few teachers, administrators and school board members are secular humanists, it must be remembered that books and curriculums used in the classroom come from publishing houses that are greatly influenced by the "progressive education" philosophy put forth by John Dewey and his present-day advocates. It is highly significant that atheist John Dewey was one of the 34 signers of the 1933 Humanist Manifesto I.

Informed Christian parents, knowing that the Humanist Manifesto II promotes moral relativism, complete sexual freedom and the "individual's . . . right to suicide" have to wonder. Are the recent increases in teen pregnancy and teen suicide a mere coincidence, or are we simply reaping the rewards of this "new faith" being taught in our public schools?

A student, John J. Dunphy, further fuels the battle between the old and "new" faith by writing a much-quoted 1983 essay for the *Humanist* stating: "I am convinced that the battle for humankind's future must be waged and won in the public school classroom by teachers who correctly view their role as the proselytizers of a new faith." The article continues: "The classroom must and will become an arena of conflict between the old and the new—the rotting corpse of Christianity, together with all its adjacent evils and misery, and the new faith of humanism." The magazine later prints a disclaimer that the young author's views are "extreme and irresponsible."

So is there a new faith called "secular humanism" and is it being foisted on America's young? The framework of the six types of value systems argues strongly against such an assertion. When one ventures beyond the boundaries of Christianity, there is not just one opposing viewpoint; there are *at least* five other basic viewpoints, and really an endless multiplicity of viewpoints. Moreover, in contemporary America, no Christian, not even fundamentalist Jerry Falwell, is just a Christian. Almost everyone incorporates and expresses some elements of "science" because it is so much part of the air we breath, and surely no one is immune to the group loyalties and feelings—for family, friends, or country—associated with emotion.

Are primary and secondary schools teaching values inimical to Christianity?

Clearly, yes. In a pluralistic world of so many values, this is inescapable. Moreover, from a Christian perspective, it is not completely undesirable: Christian values cannot be formed in isolation from the world, the flesh, and the devil, but only in opposition to these traditional temptations. A student who does not know the world may appear to have convictions but has not yet been tested, has not yet forged his or her convictions in the fire of conflict.

These advantages of plurality notwithstanding, Christian parents do have a valid complaint. Anti-Christian teaching has increased in the public schools, increased significantly in recent years, while Christianity has more and more been shut out. The first trend can be traced to the 1960s and 1970s, when "social studies" began to displace the traditional humanistic subjects of history, geography, and literature. So-called "issues" courses covering such topics as modern urban ethnics, women and social change, revolution, social justice, and economic systems proliferated while factual courses about the great names, dates, events, and thoughts of the past lost ground. A typical suggested essay question from a new American history text asked not, "What do you know about Benjamin Franklin?" but, "Do you like Benjamin Franklin—why or why not?" Behind this trend, and thoroughly mingled with it, were the same "scientific" values that we have already identified in so-called value-free education. For example, how did Dr. Ronald Smith, past president of the National Council for the Social Sciences, defend the new courses as long ago as 1975? He insisted that "what we are concerned with is [technical] problem-solving," without the slightest acknowledgment that this phrase defines and reflects a particular ethical point of view, a point of view that is often at odds with Christianity.

Even when "social science" courses strove hardest to encourage discussion without propagating values, they almost always failed: A home economics textbook cited in a court case, written by a self-described Christian of grandmotherly age and mien, advised about judgmental matters such as lying or drinking that "the best approach is to try to combine family and peer influences as you shape your personality and establish your identity." Unfortunately, court proceedings did not try to answer the most interesting questions about this advice, including: What does social science jargon like "establishing your identity" actually mean? Why are so-called ethical matters being treated in a home economics course, the sort of course where the girls used to learn how to cook and where both sexes today would presumably learn to budget or balance a checkbook or choose insurance policies? And why, above all, are the social sciences, with their private languages, hidden values, and very high level of abstraction, more suitable for young students than history, literature, or geography?

This major trend, the spread of a watered-down and unnourishing form of social science which is nonetheless replete with "scientific" values, was, in turn, accompanied by another, equally persistent trend: the overinterpretation of the Constitution's First Amendment forbidding government support for organized religion, presumably meaning direct financial or legally coercive support. By interpreting the First Amendment to mean that all references to Christianity or God must be stricken from public school textbooks, we have come to the absurdity of discussing the Pilgrims without mentioning their religion, or passing over the role of the churches in abolishing slavery. Timothy L. Smith, historian of American religion at Johns Hopkins University in Maryland, reports that when he looked over the state's eleventh-grade history texts, he was "profoundly shocked" by the total excision of any religious reference. Psychologist Paul Vitz of New York University, studying primary school texts for the National Institute of Education, found that the words "Thank God" in an Isaac Bashevis Singer story for sixth graders had been changed to "Thank Goodness." Harvard psychiatrist Robert Coles states that "what you find in these texts is the exaltation of looking at the world through psychological theories, especially of the self and its needs. There's no reference to the self as subject to something else." If schools really could teach in a value-free way, there might be a theoretical justification for the total exclusion of organized religion from the classroom. But in the real world, in which values overlie all things human, it is hard to defend.

Is the teaching of evolution in secondary schools incompatible with the Genesis account of creation?

What is most remarkable about Genesis and evolutionary theory is how closely they agree. In both accounts, the earth is created first, animals second, humans last. Genesis speaks of a creator; evolutionary theory, as pure science, neither propounds nor disagrees with the idea of a creator. The only apparent discrepancy relates to time: Genesis speaks of creation being accomplished in seven "days." But since the earth was created on the third "day" and the sun on the fourth "day," the period of time referred to could not be our 24-hour day, which is calibrated in terms of the earth's rotation in relation to the sun. Even William Jennings Bryan, the legendary defender of Christian fundamentalism, agreed that the "days" of Genesis must refer to periods of unknown duration, God's "days" rather than human "days." Science and Genesis are not really incompatible, and there is no need for intellectually dishonest substitutes for the teaching of evolution such as "creation science," the repackaging of Genesis with the spurious authority of nature, the laboratory, and the test tube rather than its own innate biblical authority.

If colleges and universities want to teach about values, how should they go about it?

All schools transmit values, which are omnipresent in human subjects, whether or not they choose to "teach" about values per se. Over the past decade, however, most colleges and universities, including the most illustrious, have made a conscious decision to teach about values, or rather, how to think about values, since there is no intention to indoctrinate students, but rather to show them how to arrive at reasonable and moral solutions on their own. In effect, American higher education, after the traumas of the 1960s, has come to agree with critic Cleanth Brooks that "it's always taken for granted . . . that any fool knows what 'the good life' is. I think that is the great lie that has been foisted on all of us, that you can leave values and the purposes of life to take care of themselves." Or as Henry Rosovsky, former dean of arts and sciences at Harvard, said in formulating a new core curriculum for the college in 1976: "An educated person [must] have some understanding of, and experience in, thinking about moral and ethical . . . choices."

The number of college and university courses on "moral reasoning" has doubled and redoubled and redoubled again—to as many as 15,000 by one reckoning. From one perspective, this is an extraordinary achievement, the virtual redirection of American higher education; from another perspective, it is not quite satisfactory: The effort is certainly there, but the élan and self-confidence are largely missing. Irksome questions remain: What exactly is being taught? Using what methods? Are students learning to make better moral choices?

To answer the first question, we might look at a Harvard course catalogue detailing the new core curriculum. Under the heading moral reasoning, we find the following:

Course Type	Number Offered
Deductive [logical] ethical theory	1
Philosophy of law	2
Applied deductive ethical reasoning	2
Political philosophy	2
Specific examples of deductive ethical theories	2

In other words, Harvard, determined to teach moral reasoning rather than specific moral precepts, chose to concentrate on three subjects — moral logic, legal logic, and political logic — all of which are characterized by an emphasis on the logical, deductive method. The intention was clear enough: to be objective, to avoid the mistake of offering up a specific religion. But, as we saw in chapter 2, modes of moral reasoning such as deductive logic are not completely objective, cannot be completely objective, inevitably carry a freightload of values with them. There is indeed an irony here: Both the logician and the social scientist want to be objective. Within their own frames of reference, within the rules developed by their own disciplines, they may achieve a remarkable degree of objectivity. But just relying on logic or social "science" involves a bias, an unwillingness to consider the rival and very different claims of authority, emotion, and intuition. To teach logic to students is commendable and useful, in morals and in every other department of life. But the model of the six modes of moral reasoning suggests that logic alone is not enough — we should teach, or at least familiarize students with, all six ways of thinking, so that for the first time they can get a true overview — not an entirely objective overview perhaps, because true objectivity is beyond human capacities, but something more all encompassing than what they have received to date.

In an ideal world of higher education, the study of values would constitute its own department, perhaps a department of "axiology" (the Greek root, *axios*, refers to values).* The starting point would not be values per se but rather how we think, our various modes of asking and knowing. Even this kind of broad-gauged epistemology (not the narrow epistemology of the logicians) might be dry; but leavened with specific examples of human values, as seen in both thought and action, it could be

---

* Would "axiology" be taught as a humanities offering or as a social science? It would make little difference, because the distinction between these two fields has always been questionable. Both cover the same human ground, one from a more factual perspective, one from a more theoretical perspective. In practice, the factual and theoretical/systematic views of human affairs are difficult to separate, as they would be in "axiology."

one of the most vibrant departments of the university. It would be the one place where students could unashamedly ask the "big questions," as Allan Bloom and most students agree they would like to do; where they could spend the passion that used to send them to the philosophy department, only, in many cases, to recoil with disillusion from whatever logical technique they were forced to master; where they could address large human subjects with intellectual rigor, without being mocked and without being subjected to any single professor's *Weltanschauung*.

A department of "axiology" would be devoted to openness and tolerance, those same virtues that Allan Bloom feels have been stripped of their real meaning by contemporary academic society. For example, in exploring different modes of human knowledge, it would seek to avoid the more dogmatic versions of contemporary "reflective judgment," a doctrinal movement that has many adherents in academe. "Reflective judgment" insists, just as we have insisted, that students need to learn to think, that different modes of thinking need to be understood and mastered. But "reflective judgment" was developed by psychologists and reflects their "scientific" biases: Authority and emotion are acknowledged as legitimate modes of thinking, but lower, less well-developed, inferior modes. Ways of thinking in this system form a hierarchy and, not surprisingly, the way of the social scientist sits at the top of the heap. This too is useful, if it makes a student recognize the different ways that his or her mind can proceed. But even a half-serious attempt at objectivity, an almost unexamined goal among universities in that most professors automatically profess it, requires that the six modes of moral reasoning presented in our framework be taught on equal terms, or as a whole, not as a hierarchy constructed to please some one teacher or group of teachers. By following this method, colleges and universities can finally achieve their often-repeated end: to teach how to think about values without propagating any specific religions, whether organized religions like Christianity, quieter, less assertive religions like those based on sense experience, or hidden religions like those based on "science."

14. A Personal Note

A few of my friends were kind enough to review a draft of this book. The almost invariable response was: all right as far as it goes, but please conclude with a statement of your own personal values, your own point of view. As one friend said: "There is so much confusion today. Which options should we choose?" Another reminded me that Nietzsche had said: "The world revolves around the inventors of new values"—not the reciters of old values, even if presented in a new framework.

Another friend drew his own conclusion about what I was saying: "What you are really saying is that the richness and complexity of values is good in itself. Values merge and separate, separate and merge, not in a Newtonian structure of six boxes, but in an Einsteinian continuum, with everything always overlapping, interfusing, interacting in complex and fascinating ways. What we really need to fight is people like the fundamentalists who do not like this fascinating world and want to put us back in just one box, where in effect we are imprisoned and suffocate." I told this friend that I liked his Einsteinian analogy, but that he was expressing values associated with the third type of value system, sense experience, and was in effect suggesting that I was promoting this type of value system. He admitted that perhaps this was not the conclusion of my book, just a statement of his own personal religion.

Other readers thought that I was clearly a Christian, or clearly not a Christian, that I was "really saying" (a much repeated phrase) that there was a hierarchy of ways to choose values, with authority at the bottom and "science" at the top (I responded that this was what the philosophy of "reflective judgment" sometimes argued and that I had rejected this approach in chapter 13.) Another reader said that the six modes of moral thinking are all very well, but it really just boiled down to two, left- versus right-brained thinking, which could be associated with reason on the one hand and emotion on the other. I know that neuropsychologists no longer put much credence in this kind of left-right brain distinction, but I pointed out that the brain has at least three parts, including the lower brain or hypothalamus, and that emotion is usually identified with that area, whereas intuition (rational but unconscious cognition) is more often identified with the right brain. In any case, moral arguments based on natural science analogies are rarely worth much, because the science keeps changing (a famous economist once spent years developing a perfect coincidence between sunspots and economic cycles, only to have the scientists change their sunspot cycles).

My friends were kind to share their thoughts, and their collective reaction shows how much we glorify and demand conclusions, commitments, solutions. This is not only a dominant feature of value systems based on "science"; it characterizes authority, logic, and emotion as well. Not every friend, to be sure, shared this desire for a forceful, charismatic conclusion. One condemned the whole enterprise of writing this book as pointless: "You can't think about values; you have to live them. All these boxes are terrible: a pattern is not living" (the writer Anais Nin said the same thing, "A pattern is not living," another example of the third type of value system). But I, quite obviously, have a different viewpoint. I do not think that classifying and trying to understand values kills the joy of living them. Indeed, I think that almost all human creativity, whether in music or dance or politics or business or thought, is based on "pattern." Nor do I think that a forceful conclusion, a "Here's what it all means," is always appropriate. There are so many answers already available in this world. This multiplication of answers, of options, is the central feature of our age: In the past, only a few people had the means or the desire, in effect the luxury of adopting their own personal values. Now even the masses, at least in the United States, have this luxury. The tendency, however, is not to formulate one's own values. It is, instead, to pick up this ready-made "religion" or that one, then another one. There is something addictive about this process, like shooting heroin, in that ready-made "religions," philosophies of the moment, always need to be at hand, and we are not too choosy about where we get them or which one we pick up. We turn on the television in the early morning, someone "famous" is telling us how to live, summarizing his book or life's thought in one or two sentences, and we get a temporary "rush" or "fix" from what he says.

In discussing this, I am reminded of the Greek philosopher Socrates as he is presented in the early Platonic dialogues. What is most irritating about Socrates is that he keeps asking questions, drawing out the opinions of others, without ever giving away what he himself thinks. The conversation moves this way or that, you think that Socrates' interlocutors have cornered him, that he will finally have to reveal what he thinks, but he just asks another question and continually evades his pursuers. Socrates realizes that you cannot be a little Socratic; if your purpose is to make others think, to come to their own conclusions after the most exhaustive (and hopefully playful) thought, you cannot begin by expressing your own beliefs. Once you express your own beliefs, other people will either be swept along in agreement or immediately put up their defenses, and either way they do not learn to think. If you express even one belief before you have heard from your listeners, you become an advocate, not—for want of a better word—a guide. I have been an advocate, and I will want to be an advocate again, but in this book I want to be a guide, a humble guide, offering critiques from alternative perspectives, with no blanket condemnation of any one approach.

Returning to Socrates, we find inescapable parallels between his time and ours. Although values are never fixed, they had seemed fixed in pre-Socratic Athens. Suddenly, value choices proliferated; the challenge, in the jargon of our own era, was "postmodern": not to create more and more new values, but rather to make sense of the explosion in values (explosion in both senses of the word). Whatever my intentions, I know that I have not played at being Socrates very well; I have revealed all kinds of prejudices and beliefs. Besides, the search for objectivity can only be carried so far; just by writing this book, I have endorsed a series of important values. In particular, I have sharply disagreed with the Scottish philosopher Adam Smith, who said that "though you despise that picture, or that poem, or even that system of philosophy which I admire, there is little danger of our quarreling on that account. Neither of us can reasonably be much interested about them." I agree instead with Irving Kristol that "it is ideas which rule the world." I also agree, fundamentally, with Bertrand Russell, that ideas should be expressed clearly or not at all. Russell said: "I suggest to young professors that their first work should be written in a jargon only to be understood by the erudite few. With that behind them, they can ever after say what they have to say in a language understanded of the people." I also reject the notion, prevalent in most discussion of values, that they should be logical or emotional or "scientific" or whatever. I think values can and will be all these things, often at the same time, which is all to the good. And finally, in a refusal to preach, I am saying that people need to think about their own values, think hard about them, think for themselves (Socrates did say that the unexamined life is not worth living, which is an exaggeration, but not too much of an exaggeration), and that there are ways to think about and teach values to students that are perfectly acceptable, and all the more desperately needed, in a pluralistic society like the United States.

Values in the Classroom Continued

Students in contemporary colleges and universities are directly exposed to personal values in at least three areas: political philosophy courses, commonly taught by members of political science departments; moral philosophy courses, commonly taught by members of philosophy departments; and humanities courses, commonly taught by members of English, foreign language, history, or art departments. In the three sections that follow, we will briefly review some of the specific value systems that are either explicitly taught, reflected, or alluded to in such college courses, and we will show how such value systems can be fitted and reinterpreted within the framework presented in this book.

Value systems such as political liberalism, conservatism, or Marxism that are currently taught, reflected, or alluded to, directly or indirectly, in college *political philosophy/political science* courses (such value systems generally combine emotion with additional elements of logic, sense experience, and "science")

During the 1930s especially, but in all periods of American history, some of the most powerful and influential value systems have been social, political, and economic ideologies such as classical liberalism, conservatism, or communism. Such ideologies are almost always hybrid value systems with a variety of sources.

Of the six primary ways of forming values, sense experience certainly plays a role (we all assess ideas like liberalism or conservatism in terms of our own personal experience in the world). "Science" is at least marginally involved, as in our sometimes desperate attempts to "prove" the superiority of one ideology over another, attempts that are rarely successful in changing anyone's mind. Emotion is always a dominant factor, usually *the* dominant factor. As we have already seen in chapter 6, people just naturally come together around an idea or cause, thereby creating an essentially tribal religion that provides a high degree of fellowship and emotional support. Although the inspiriting idea may be as basic as the desire to advance one's family or country, it may be as highly abstract and intellectual as Marxist-Leninism. Either way, once we have embraced a cause, joined together with others in a tribal compact, we will strongly, even passionately, defend it, sometimes as passionately as if we were defending our own life.

Some Composite Value Systems Based on Political Ideas (Emotion plus . . .)

Classical liberalism

Defined as an evangelical and crusading belief in human freedom, as a pure religion of liberty, classical liberalism has been the most powerful and paradoxical ideology of the past four hundred years, powerful because it has literally swept the world, paradoxical because the very idea of individual liberty and autonomy would seem to be the antithesis of tribal community. In practice, however, liberals do form a tribe, a tightly knit tribe committed to the eradication of tyranny and intolerance, and ever watchful against illiberal and "controlling" institutions such as the church, the state, the army, and the family.

Historically, the battle against the church was first and most vehement. The eighteenth-century French liberal Denis Diderot boasted that he was "raining bombs in the house of the Lord" and that the "great prostitute of Babylon" [the church] would soon give way to the "reign of Anti-Christ." By the nineteenth century liberal opposition to "controlling" institutions was concentrated on the state, and by the twentieth century liberal salvoes were being fired at the family as well, with family life characterized, according to an outraged Senator Daniel Moynihan, as "dreary, repressive, conducive to the sickness rather than the health of husbands and wives, parents and children alike." Moynihan subtly misrepresents classical liberalism by arguing that "the two primary institutions which affect the way we behave as individuals are . . . the family and . . . the state. If you weaken the one, you strengthen the other. Surely liberalism began as a movement to curb the power of the state. . . . Just as surely, then, the strength of the liberal tradition in government is bound up with the family." This statement sounds plausible enough, but it is historically inaccurate. The true classical liberal attitude is equally wary of family, church, or state, and is summed up by Moynihan's political ally from New York, U.S. vice presidential candidate Geraldine Ferraro: "You know what I learned [in convent school]? Those three [church, state, and family] are the biggest oppressors of women that will ever come along."

Although the struggle between church and classical liberalism reached its zenith several hundred years ago and is now relatively restrained, it lies just beneath the surface of American society and is symbolized by the tension between liberal Catholic politicians and their archbishops over abortion. In part, Christians and classical liberals fight so much because they are so alike. They are not just two opposing tribes: They share a belief in history, in a progression to a better life, either a life of freedom and toleration here on earth, or an unearthly paradise after death. Very often, lapsed Christians explore a religion of logic, then of experience, before settling on classical liberalism as their primary creed. If they retain the disciplines of logic and high experience, their devotion to freedom is both anti-Christian *and* austerely moral, the opposite of a wild and profligate freedom. They agree with philosopher Bertrand Russell that "[liberalism] does not consist simply in saying to grown-up people or adolescents: 'follow your impulses and do as you [please]'"; with Judith Shklar of Harvard University that liberalism should not be equated with "selfishness," that the "very refusal to use public coercion to impose creedal uniformity and uniform standards of behavior demands an enormous degree of self-control"; and with diplomat and political philosopher George Kennan that if you "tell me what framework of discipline you are prepared to accept . . . I will . . . tell you what freedom might mean for you." In other words, they are like the Englishman described by historian Crane Brinton who "can do as he likes because he couldn't possibly do anything dangerous to society."

Provided that the classical liberal is of this type, shorn of self-indulgence, at peace with himself and his passions, intent on his mission of cleansing the world of what liberal critic and historian Lytton Strachey called "this atrocious fog of superstition that hangs over us and compresses our breathing and poisons our lives," he is almost always happy, even intensely happy. It is only when the fog lifts a bit, when neither church nor state nor family is particularly oppressive, when freedom and tolerance seem generally to prevail, that the classical liberal becomes a bit nervous and fidgety. The bond that unites him with his fellow classical liberals falls away, the tribe dissolves, all that remains is autonomy, isolation, loneliness, a fertile ground for violent dissensions and the rebirth of intolerance. We see this phenomenon occasionally in academic settings. As Daniel Boorstin, Librarian of Congress and celebrated historian, has noted: "We think of universities as places where people are very tolerant, places of free speech. But individual academic people are inclined to be dogmatic." Fortunately for classical liberalism as a religion, the entire world has not yet become as free and tolerant as an American institution of higher learning; there are still multitudes of oppressive dragons yet to be slain; and, so long as threats to freedom exist, classical liberals can have it all, both an ideology of personal liberty and individualism *and* the comradeship and security of membership in a tribe of freedom fighters.

Jacobinism (utopian liberalism or Rousseauism)

Classical liberals want men to be free, not because they believe that men are naturally good, but rather because, like Christians, they believe the opposite: that men are naturally evil or at least naturally weak. By limiting the coercive power of institutions such as church, state, and family, they hope to thwart the worst evil of all, which is the concentration of power in criminal hands. Under this doctrine, men such as Hitler will from time to time grasp the reins of state—it cannot be prevented—but their power will be limited because the state itself will always be limited. Moreover, the same cautionary principle applies to church and family. In a free society, evil or foolish or weak individuals will mostly just harm themselves; they will lack the authority to terrorize fellow citizens or children.

Jacobinism, on the other hand, turns classical liberalism on its head by claiming that human beings are naturally good; that evil men are an aberration; that human institutions such as state, church, and family need not be feared, no matter how powerful and all commanding they may be, *once* they are purged of evildoers and thoroughly controlled by the "people." In addition, these cleansed institutions can and should be used to promote a variety of social goals, not just liberty (for example social justice and equality), and in the process create a more perfect social environment. Among contemporary American leaders, George McGovern, Ted Kennedy, and Barbara Mikulski epitomize this kind of social and political utopianism. McGovern's defeat in the 1972 presidential election was more than just a setback for the Democratic party and a nostalgic New Deal style of politics. It was, as Walter Lippmann described it in the *Washington Post*, a complete "repudiation" of "the 18th-century Jacobin or Rousseauistic . . . belief that man [and his social] environment . . . can be made perfect. . . . Modern society won't accept that philosophy and it is usually repudiated. . . . [It is] philosophically and morally untrue. Man is not naturally good, nor is his nature perfectible. . . . No government can bring people up. They have to achieve it themselves. The [idea] that the government can do it is one of the great illusions of our time."

Lippmann notwithstanding, the idea that human beings are good (or evil) cannot be proven one way or the other. It is an emotional rather than a factual statement, and emotions are not subject to logical or empirical demonstration. At the same time, other Jacobin beliefs are closer to factual statements, and they do not seem to be very logical. Can liberty really be advanced by concentrating power in coercive institutions such as government? Can government be big, strong, highly paternalistic, yet completely controlled by the "people"? Can the dream embodied in the French Jacobin slogan "liberty–equality–fraternity," the dream that pure liberty and pure equality are equally attainable in a just society governed by powerful liberal institutions, ever be realized? The bald truth, readily observable in life, is that maximum equality of individuals can only be achieved by curbing liberty and vice versa. A completely free society permits and encourages people to better themselves relative to their neighbors. A completely egalitarian society must have a means of enforcing its rules, either a vast controlling bureaucracy or a police state, and neither is compatible with liberty. Viewed in this light, Jacobin views are not just metaphysical, like a belief in human goodness, something to be accepted or rejected according to one's emotional preferences. They are also statements of fact and logic, which turn out to be at least partly unfactual and illogical.

Jacobin utilitarianism

This faith, which swept the United States during the 1970s in the persons of Ralph Nader, Governor Jerry Brown, and President Jimmy Carter and lingered in the unsuccessful 1988 presidential campaign of Michael Dukakis, begins by reaffirming the basic Jacobin goals of liberty, equality, and progress through government. At the same time, there is a sense that these goals, however worthy, have lead to unrealizable expectations, that related government programs have been poorly designed and managed, that inefficiency and corruption, but especially inefficiency, have become rampant in American society in general, and that all the old assumptions and techniques, especially the technique of taxing and spending to improve the social environment, must be reexamined, lest people turn away from Jacobinism entirely.

During his years as governor of California, Jerry Brown (elected in 1974 at age thirty-seven), pioneered the dramatic change in approach. He denied that he had a mission ("What do you mean mission? That's so cosmic. I just want to reduce the sum of human misery") and promised little ("There's no free lunch . . . you don't get something for nothing"), thus leaving the impression that he was not a Jacobin at all, since Jacobins always have missions and are always full of promises. By contrast, Brown was downright bleak and pessimistic ("Things are going to get a lot worse than they are now"), skeptical and critical, the inquisitor-general of government programs with an obsessive concern for detail as well as for efficiency ("Only an efficient system can be just and vice-versa"), an enthusiast of 18-hour workdays, and a nondelegator of authority. The governor's central idea and mood (what might be characterized as Jacobinism dressed up in a severe black suit, the millennarianism of the efficiency experts) was reinforced by a variety of symbols: the vetoing of a bill that would have officially redesignated garbage dumps as sanitary landfills; reducing staff salaries; cutting out funds to buy briefcases for state officials; living in a small apartment with a mattress on the floor rather than the new governor's mansion built by the previous governor, Ronald Reagan; driving an old Plymouth rather than being chauffeured in a limousine; flying tourist class after sale of the governor's jet. Behind this plenitude of symbols, which projected both populism and realism ("Public officials [should] act like servants of the people, not like kings"), were—more symbols: "People ask me, 'What's your program?' What the hell does that mean? . . . [These] words have no meaning in my head. . . . I'll provide leadership. . . . [I'll] confront the confusion and hypocrisy of government."

Jerry Brown was, himself, a singular symbol of the new and deflated Jacobinism, but he was not alone. President Jimmy

Carter and presidential candidate Michael Dukakis, despite different cultural backgrounds and languages, mirrored many of his thoughts and techniques. Consumer activist Ralph Nader also demonstrated how a purely private citizen could devote his life to "millennarian efficiency." He lived alone in a boarding house, wore old army surplus clothes, worked constantly in a small, cluttered basement office, and inspected used Corvairs with exactly the same attitude that Jerry Brown, Jimmy Carter, and Michael Dukakis brought to government. In the end, of course, Brown, Carter, and Dukakis were defeated at the polls, and Nader's political power steadily declined in Washington.

The problem for all four of these figures lay in the contradictions, both the old, unresolved contradictions of traditional Jacobinism (trying to reconcile populism and big government, freedom and equality) and the new contradictions of a "deflated" and "efficient" Jacobinism. First, Brown, Carter, Dukakis, and Nader kept stressing honesty without saying exactly what they thought or stood for, presumably because what they stood for was keeping their options open. Second, they spoke about commitment, motivation, sacrifice, and, in Carter's famous "malaise" speech, the "longing for meaning," then turned their own and their followers' attention to the dangers of ladies' high-heeled shoes, the need to put health warnings on salt labels, energy quotas, synthetic fuels, zero-based budgeting, and similar topics. The alternation between earnest exhortation and dry-as-dust engineering was not only confusing, it was disturbing. Such an approach might reform Jacobinism, but it could not save it, because it stripped away the emotional core, the ability to bring people together into a passionately shared community. Once the passion was lost, the process had to be efficient—there was nothing else to recommend it. In the end, weighed down by so many contradictions, both old and new, the process could not even be efficient, and so, over a period of years, the support for this kind of political philosophy declined, presumably (like other emotional religions, which never die completely) destined to be revived again and again in some indeterminate future.

Violent revolutionism

Religions of emotion are often contradictory and paradoxical to a degree. They are religions of emotion, after all, not religions of logic, and people's emotions are paradoxical. On the other hand, most Americans want their emotional religions to be reasonably logical, at least not overtly illogical. They are therefore not much tempted by one of the most contradictory and paradoxical movements of all, violent revolutionism, although it has played such a major role during the last two centuries: the capture of the Tuilleries and the fall of the Bastille in France; the storming of the Winter Palace and the Forbidden City in Russia and China, respectively; the fall of the shah of Iran in 1979.

Because of these momentous successes and failures, violent revolutionism has been extensively studied and is well understood. For example, most revolutionists insist that they are fighting for change.* But on a purely emotional level they are often rebeling *against* change, against the dismal dissolution and anxiety and isolation brought on by the weakening of the old order, whether triggered by discrete events, such as economic or military setbacks, political changes, or even by economic successes that come faster than people and institutions can absorb them. It may be cynical to observe that revolutions never occur in truly static, unchanging societies, only in societies already undergoing rapid change and social disturbance (cynical because this observation can and will be used by reactionaries opposed to every possible reform), but this phenomenon is confirmed by the historical record.† Once people are involuntarily expelled from the warm womb of the old order (warm and familiar even if thor-

---

* The original American revolutionists were notable exceptions. They argued that they were fighting to protect an old order against a new, more repressive order being imposed from outside.

† On the other hand, rapid change and social disturbance does not *necessarily* lead to violent revolution. For example, massive social, political, and economic changes occurring in the late 1980s in Eastern Europe did not necessarily mean that violent revolution would follow, only that the historical risk of violent revolution was very high.

oughly rotten), they may become desperate to regain a sense of community and fellowship. Frequently they are so desperate that they will trade their very lives for a moment of intense comradeship, as described by a Viet Cong guerrilla fighter: "I always liked going into battle because the atmosphere was so good. Everybody knew that they were going to die. They had no food, and nothing to drink for days. If a man had something to eat, he would share it with you, and if you had nothing to give in return, you would show him the letter you had just got from your wife. Everybody loved each other because they all knew they were going to die." And if these sentiments sound too foreign—too remote from the American experience—one need only think of those Harvard students who stormed and occupied University Hall, the local analogue of the Tuilleries and the Winter Palace, in the fall of 1969. As one of them wrote in the *Crimson* (the student newspaper): "What was most euphoric, however, was us and what we were to each other. For those few hours we were brothers and sisters. . . . You had to realize, whatever your politics and whatever your tactics, that we were very beautiful in University Hall, we were very human, and we were very together."

It is paradoxical that revolutionists should find such intense community in the very act of destroying the traditional social fabric. It is even more paradoxical that the craving for this supreme emotional "high" tends to become uncontrollable and to consume all the stated objectives of the revolution. After a time, the emphasis on "wider community" over "law and order" leads to a backlash, to fascism, to the imposition of order through fear and intimidation, and, at least temporarily, to the loss of any genuine human community at all. It is not surprising that the Harvard student just quoted, a brilliant and sensitive individual who published his first novel while still in school and who wrote in the same student newspaper article that "emotions are our guts; without them we are but thinking machines, and the destruction of which such machines (Bundy, Kissinger) are capable has left its scars on all of us"—should have committed suicide a few years after the 1969 "revolution."

Classical conservatism

Confronted with classical liberalism, Jacobinism, or violent revolutionism, classical conservatives just shake their heads as if to say: what a muddle. You all say that you want liberty or equality or a root-and-branch remaking of society, but you really want what everybody wants, you really want a loving community, and you are going about it in a completely backward way by glorifying individualism. It should be perfectly obvious that, to build true community, you have to subordinate the individual to the group. Not an ersatz group, like an enclave of classical liberals joined together only by their struggle against the alleged oppressions of church, state, or family, or a cadre of revolutionists, passionately united for a brief moment in an orgy of destruction, but a truly durable group, one built over long periods of time with patience, skill, and discipline, a permanent and organic institution—in other words, the very same church, state, or family that the classical liberals loathe.

Accepting and subordinating oneself to church, state, and family along with the entire web of traditions, customs, and obligations that come with them is not only good for society, classical conservatism holds, it is good for the individual as well. Living outside such groups is a sterile hell of isolation, a condition that magnifies all the weakness, laziness, folly, stupidity, and ignorance that is our natural condition. Within church, state, and family is the possibility, though only the possibility, of civilization, defined not as money or power, the inflaming and satisfaction of appetites, but as a spiritual search.

The British conservative prime minister Harold Macmillan once said, "If people want a sense of purpose, they can get it from their archbishops." True conservatives disagree: Serving institutions, governments and families, as well as churches, suffuses all of life with a quiet spiritual purpose. Alexander Solzhenitsyn, the Russian exile and Nobel Prize winner, captured this sentiment in a Harvard University commencement address: "If [Jacobinism] were right in declaring that man is born to be happy, he would not be born to die. Since his body is doomed to die, his task on earth evidently must be of a more spiritual nature. It cannot be unrestrained enjoyment of everyday life. It cannot be the search for the best ways to obtain material goods and then cheerfully get the most out of them. It has to be the fulfillment of a permanent, earnest *duty* so that one's life journey may become an experience of moral growth, in that one may leave life a better human being than one started it."

To pursue this spiritual quest through group service, social order is a must. Excessive personal liberty imperils this order, and so does social and economic equality. The first two statements are intuitively obvious (order ≠ liberty), but why the third? Why the ban against even trying to build a classless society? If one is meant to subordinate oneself to the group, why not divest oneself of personal wealth like a candidate for the Catholic priesthood? The conservative's answer is that equality is unnatural, contrary to human nature and gifts, impractical and unrealistic. People are born unequal so that they may play different roles, make their own unique contribution to the group. Moreover, society needs the spur of inequality to realize its full potential. In both spiritual and physical spheres, people must always be pushed to exert themselves, either by the hope of advancement or by the fear of the lash, and hope is by far the more effective method. The conservative social agenda therefore calls for a clear division of labor and rewards within the group, along with a commitment to individual and corporate excellence, no matter how much inequality or "elitism" results.

Such emphasis on the organic, institutionalized group, equally committed to spiritual experience and worldly excellence, tolerant of inequality and elitism, intolerant of individualism and social deviance, is the keynote for classical conservatism. The most consistent (perhaps the only consistent) classical conservative in American public life today is the newspaper and television commentator George Will, an individual who defies the traditional conservative reputation for being inarticulate, wary of words and abstractions. Like Burke and Disraeli before him, Will offers a colorful and reasoned defense of classical conservativism, with a redemptive call for more social control and for less emphasis on money and capitalism, for "soulcraft" rather than statecraft, but even he might have difficulty answering the following four questions posed by liberal critics:

1. *How can you tell when there is enough institutional (church, state, family) control over the individual? At what point does this control tip over into fascism?* (Presumably at the point that "impostor" conservatives such as Senator Joe McCarthy seize power, but this can be hard to know in advance or to correct after the fact.)

2. *Why are so many confirmed classic conservatives and defenders of the status quo already rich?* (It is true that many poor people, especially poor whites in America, are also conservative, at least on social issues.)

3. *If human nature is so sinful, why concentrate it in powerful and coercive institutions? Why not spread the power widely as classic liberals suggest?* (Presumably because scattered institutions won't be powerful enough to practice "soulcraft," to shape human souls, whether they want to be "shaped" or not.)

4. *Is classical conservatism consistent with democracy (a liberal invention) and vice versa?* (Alexander Solzhenitsyn exemplifies this problem. He is a passionate conservative who regards Marxist-Leninism as "a dark un-Russian whirlwind that descended on us from the West." He hates cities ["cancerous tumors"], industrialism, polluting internal combustion engines, and other examples of "liberal modernism." He wants an organic, religious, nationalistic society that will release all the captive non-Russian nationalities in the Soviet Union, isolate itself from the West, sanctify manual labor and country living, and develop Siberia for the Russian people. How to get there? Certainly

not by violent revolution, but especially not by democratic change: "Russia is authoritarian; let it remain so and let us no longer try to change that." It is no wonder that the Republican Party platform in 1976 called Solzhenitsyn a "great beacon of human courage and morality" while an aide to Henry Kissinger said in private, "Let's face it; he's just about a fascist." It is difficult to know what to make of this kind of conservatism, for in the end, in its insistence that conservatism and democracy do not mix, in its preference for authoritarian institutions that, in Solzhenitsyn's words, will "be based on genuine concern and love on the part of the rulers, not only for themselves and those around them, but also for their people, and all neighboring peoples, too," it seems to slip away from the old conservative realism, the old belief in a sinful human nature, and into a utopian and almost Jacobin fantasy about redeeming the world through big government.)

Contemporary conservatism and liberalism

What is called conservatism in America today is of course quite different from classical conservatism, just as liberalism is no longer classical liberalism. To put this in perspective, Ronald Reagan is a contemporary conservative, but this means he is a classical liberal in his economic policy (as much free enterprise as possible) and a classical conservative in his social policy (more government control over pornography, abortion, contraception, school prayer, etc.). Reagan's most emotionally charged rhetoric reflects this split: Freedom (classical liberalism) is mixed with heroism, self-sacrifice, duty, and service (classical conservatism), although the latter is more personal, less abstract, and thus more moving, as when heroic and little-known Americans are presented during State of the Union addresses. Contemporary liberals, on the other hand, including many Democrats, mix classical motifs in a nearly opposite fashion. Regardless of whether they are economic Jacobins (pro equality), economic neo-Jacobins (equality *and* efficiency), or economic classical conservatives (strengthening the cooperative social compact to guarantee jobs), they want more government control of the economy, while on the social side they tend to be classical liberals favoring less control (pro civil liberty). Complicating this picture further, the term *liberal* has fallen into such disrepute (it was a badge of honor for many people as recently as twenty years ago) that it is rapidly being abandoned. In future political discourse, we shall probably have to replace it with some suitable euphemism that will be generally understood to mean more economic and less social control.

Secular puritanism (nonreligious fundamentalism)

A variant of contemporary conservatism is secular puritanism, a movement represented by Margaret Thatcher in England and by some American conservative political activists such as Paul Weyrich. As Weyrich defines the concept, which he calls "cultural conservatism,"

It stands . . . apart from the Reagan [or Bush] administration—not because the administration is too moderate, but because it is, on the whole, often trivial. . . . Many key White House advisors appear to be utterly unaware of our cultural and national breakdown. At the same time, cultural conservatism stands apart from other Reagan [or Bush] critics on the right—such as the New Right. . . . To be blunt—and I speak as one of the founders and leaders of the New Right—it has no issues, in most people's minds, beyond school prayer and abortion. . . . Even if its positions on abortion and school prayer were adopted as national policy tomorrow, it would be no cure. The disease is the acceptance by the culture of immediate gratification. Abortion, drug abuse, alcoholism, street- and white-collar crime and casual sex are all simply symptoms. . . . Cultural conservatism also rejects the argument that the free market is the only answer to most problems . . . and unlike the Religious Right, it does not ask anyone to believe that traditional values are absolutely true, only that these values succeed in providing for citizens in our culture. . . . The Religious Right can be comfortable with cultural conservatism, especially its tenet that human nature is a constant, but it must accept the fact that some cultural conservatives may not be religious.*

Cultural conservatism, unlike the New Right, has not yet committed itself to the Republican Party. Although its fundamentalism and evangelism appeal to some Republicans, its populism and skepticism about free enterprise appeal to some Democrats. William S. Lind, whom Weyrich calls the "theoretician of cultural conservatism," worked for Democrats and even coauthored a book with Democratic presidential candidate Gary Hart, an individual who, rightly or wrongly, became identified with nontraditional values. As Weyrich explains this puzzling phenomenon:

The Democratic Party's elite is dominated by the remnants of the liberation movement of the 1970s, [but] its rank and file is more conservative culturally than the typical upwardly mobile Republican. In particular, the blue-collar voters the Democrats lost so disastrously in 1980 and 1984 [and 1988] have strong cultural-conservative instincts. It would be risky for a Democratic candidate to try to reach around the elite to the party's broad membership and to cultural conservatives who think of themselves as Republicans, but the success of one who did so might be dramatic.

Mandarinism

Another, very different, variant of contemporary conservatism, mandarinism, is reflected in the person of former national security advisor and secretary of state Henry Kissinger. Here we have the basic conservative vision—service to institutions and transmission of values—but rendered in a highly elitist and tragically pessimistic form. As with the old mandarinate of ancient China, in which the most promising students were carefully groomed to compete for the highest bureaucratic positions, primarily in gov-

---

* For example, British journalist Henry Fairlee (*The Spoiled Child of the Western World*, *The Seven Deadly Sins*) calls himself a "reluctant unbeliever" who consequently has a "hole" in his life, but who thinks that modern Westerners are in trouble because they have thrown away their Bible, knowingly transgressed the moral law, and willfully indulged in sin and indiscipline.

ernment but also in state religion, or in the army, there are a series of interlocking "great games" to be played. One game is for the leaders of our own established institutions—corporations, military services, governments, professional organizations, churches—to search out and cultivate the best and brightest of the next generation, and for these young "stars," usually the graduates of elite educational institutions, to cultivate their powerful elders in turn. The second "great game" is for the "stars" to compete with one another for a limited number of places at the top by working sixty-hour work weeks and otherwise proving their devotion and dedication. The third "great game" is for the leaders of institutions, finally crowned after decades of simultaneously serving and maneuvering, to compete against other institutions as the president of IBM eventually gets to compete against Burroughs (now called Unisys) or Kissinger eventually got to compete against the Soviets.

Described thus baldly, mandarinism seems to be about power, not religious values. Looked at more closely and gently, however, it is extremely rich in values, especially emotional values. For bright young people to devote themselves, their youth, their lives—their every waking hour, in many cases—to old and often troubled institutions, forsaking either a life of leisure and liberty *or* the chance to become entrepreneurs and build new and bold ventures, is obviously an important moral choice, one fraught with implications for society as well as for each individual. Britain's traditional devotion to mandarinism, especially a mandarinism that downgraded business and almost totally excluded entrepreneurship, was a significant factor in her decline from a world power accounting for almost 50 percent of the world's economic production during the mid-nineteenth century to one accounting for approximately 5 percent today.

For those who choose the mandarin life, either by conscious choice or out of simple conformity, swept along from one good school to another and then one prestigious job after another, there is often a sense of exhilaration, especially if they are winning the great game and their advancement is rapid. Also, after a time, comes the sober realization, so well expressed by Kissinger, that the institution one has captured and now represents is perpetually in jeopardy, beset by indiscipline and decay, utterly resistant to even the boldest efforts to lead and renew. In other words, the service of institutions, but especially of "great" institutions, is a grinding, thankless, Sisyphean task that in the end makes all the world's cleverness and all the world's victories turn to dust. The only realistic aim for a true conservative is consequently not to triumph, in the sense of redeeming the institution he or she serves, but only to achieve a certain equilibrium, to maintain order, and thus to postpone, for a little while longer, like a faithful Chinese civil servant in the waning days of an imperial dynasty, the decline or demise that is eventually sure to come.

Entrepreneurialism

The opposite of mandarinism is entrepreneurialism—the burning desire to build the new rather than preserve the old. Henry Kissinger, by serving Harvard and then the U.S. government, chose to be a mandarin; his younger brother Walter, by building a private company, chose to be an entrepreneur. While still a professor, Henry sometimes looked wistfully at what might have been if he had followed Walter's career: Entrepreneurship seemed so much freer, so much less fettered by the dead hand of the past and of bureaucracy, so much more "American," and, not incidentally, so much more rewarding financially. Later, it was perhaps Walter's turn to be wistful about his brother's career.

Although mandarinism and entrepreneurialism seem to be polar opposites, they actually share some elements in common. At first glance, entrepreneurship seems to be a form of classical liberalism rather than classical conservatism. Individuals who do not "fit in," who insist on being their own boss, who want freedom and "financial independence" from existing groups and institutions set out to build a company (or, if financial independence is less critical, set out to build a nonprofit institution). In reality, however, entrepreneurs are not free. They sacrifice themselves totally to achieve their dream, and even if they make millions in the process, they will usually have little time to enjoy their money. For one who finally "succeeds" and passes the leadership of the new institution on to others, both leisure and money quickly lose their allure. Before long, the retiree is pining for another entrepreneurial challenge, for a new sense of commitment, for the classical conservative joys of being part of a group again, especially a group that is united in the struggle to give birth to a new company or institution. So, in the end, entrepreneurship and mandarinism, for all the differences in what they hope to accomplish, for all the unbridled optimism of the one and Kissingerian pessimism of the other, ultimately boil down to something not totally dissimilar: a very practical mixture of ambition and self-sacrifice, together with a willingness to devote all one's time and energy—and then a little more—in the service of an institutional cause.

Legalism (the religion of law)

Legalism, like entrepreneurialism, is a compromise between classical liberalism and classical conservatism. It is liberal in that freedom can be guaranteed by written laws; conservative in that, once the laws are written, everyone must conform to them. Whether pursued from the liberal or conservative side, the legal life has always been much more than a profession in America. Every father wants his son to be a lawyer and, increasingly, every mother wants her daughter to be a lawyer as well. Once students have passed the bar examination, they become members of a large priesthood, one that is maintained in considerable comfort and finds its apotheosis in the single most prestigious American institution, the Supreme Court.

Within American society, the worldly religion of law mingles with and reinforces the unworldly religion of Christianity in unexpected ways. Both the legal community and the church have been forces for discipline united in their disapproval of "dropping out" and sexual freedom, though lawyers are rather more in favor of hard work and may wink at sexual escapades provided that they do not interfere with 18-hour days at the law library whereas preachers may reverse the emphasis. Lawyers have also been, until quite recently, remarkable guardians of financial probity. Whatever individuals may have done, bar associations have maintained the strictest rules against financial conflict of interest, self-promotion, and self-aggrandizement. Only during the 1980s were these constraints finally thrown off: Lawyers advertised; they clogged the courts with nuisance suits; they stopped working by the hour whenever they could get a flat fee or a percent of a financial "deal"; they began to go into business for themselves, operating as investment bankers, real estate operators, and a host of other roles while still supposedly practicing law.

Did all this mean the end of law as a religion—as more than a profession and much more than a business? Not likely, because law is such an integral part of the American emotional fabric. But if lawyers keep up their current level of financial promiscuity, they may eventually represent a debased and discredited religion, a powerful secular force that has been largely stripped of its inner emotional meaning.

Social Darwinism (the religion of selfishness, winning, and power)

All the social ideologies treated up to this point have had—at their heart—a high degree of unselfishness. Even the ones that seemed at first glance to promote selfishness—classical liberalism or entrepreneurialism, for example, have in fact promoted a great deal of selflessness as well. Social Darwinism, by contrast, is a religion of pure selfishness: Life is about survival; survival is accomplished through power and dominance; the purpose of life is therefore to gain control of others through whatever means are available, however brutal or coercive, because might is always right. The character Raskolnikov in Dostoevsky's *Crime and Punishment* defines Social Darwinism in its most extreme form: "Extraordinary men have a right to commit any crime and to transgress the law in any way, just because they are extraordinary." In everyday American life, a mild and socially acceptable form of Social Darwinism is exemplified by Pete Rose of the Cincinnati Reds or the man whose record Rose pursued over the years, Ty Cobb, who once said:

The man who stood between me and victory was my enemy. Baseball is a red-blooded game for red-blooded men . . . a game of merciless competition . . . and mollycoddles better stay out. . . . Clubs fight desperately to win. Players fight desperately for their jobs. It's survival of the fittest, a struggle for supremacy. It expresses more nearly than any other game the aggressive American fighting spirit, the determination to succeed. If thin-skinned young fellows don't like that type of play, why don't they take up ping-pong?

Cobb's doctrine is loaded with paradoxes. It is bold and assertive, yet its underlying emotional tone is one of fear. It is selfish and premised on "getting mine" yet also highly disciplined and puritanical. Even while glorifying "survival of the fittest," it constantly emphasizes duty, as in Cobb's assertion that he has a "duty" to be a man, which is to say, to try his hardest to win. It also extols team spirit. Even the nastiest, most selfish and egotistical Social Darwinist is rarely solitary. Like a Mafia chieftain, he tries to enlist a group of followers by promising them a share, however small, in the communal spoils. In the case of Hitler, he unites an entire nation in the pursuit of raw power. Those who sign up under the leader's banner of shared greed and aggrandizement are ironically expected to be model soldiers within the group: Mafiosi engage in elaborate blood oaths of brotherhood; Himmler listed the virtues of the Nazi SS as "loyalty, honesty, obedience, hardness, decency, poverty, and bravery." Moreover, the new recruits are encouraged to think of themselves as "supermen", epitomes of fitness and power, but are then forced into rigid bureaucratic structures and often made to abase themselves in the most degrading manner before their "superior" officers.

If we look around the world today for examples of Social Darwinism—persons who are out for themselves and only themselves, who embrace a group or wider cause only because they think it will further their ends, of social systems that combine bold assertion with craven fear, "getting mine" with puritanism, viciousness with a rigid code of personal loyalty, individualism with bureaucracy—we would have to choose the post–World War II Soviet Union first, not the Soviet Union of official communist ideology, but the real Soviet Union of Leonid Brezhnev,* the Soviet Union that Gorbachev proposes to reform. Ironically, we might next choose our own Wall Street. Although the comparison seems absurd, both the Kremlin of Brezhnev and contemporary Wall Street share a similar outlook—it is just that the *apparatchiks* measure their power and success in titles, fancy apartments, cars, and country dachas, whereas the investment bankers measure theirs directly in dollars. Otherwise, it is much the same: not just the encouragement but the intense glorification of personal and group greed, of macho competition within and without the group, of being the fittest, in the dual sense of strongest "producer" *and* wiliest bureaucratic manipulator, of being a "winner", no matter what the cost to self or society.

Some Composite Value Systems Based on Economic Ideas (Emotion plus . . .)

Capitalism

The unifying idea behind a social ideology (such as classical liberalism), the idea that unites people behind a common cause and against common enemies, concerns the organization of society. The unifying idea behind an economic ideology (such as capitalism), on the other hand, concerns the organization of economic production. These two kinds of ideologies tend to get mixed up in the public mind. For example, some people think that classical liberalism, the religion of freedom, is indistinguish-

---

* It is an interesting observation that revolutionaries, whether Russian or French or Chinese or other, often become Social Darwinists once they are in power. For as Theodore White has written about Mao Tse Tung's willingness to see old revolutionary comrades murdered: "Suffering is a bond, but power is a drug."

able from capitalism, the religion of private property, free enterprise, and limitless individual opportunity. But if this were true, how can one explain countries such as Singapore and South Korea, thriving capitalist economies that are socially authoritarian? Or President Ronald Reagan, who was very conservative on social issues but totally committed to "free enterprise"? In reality, it is a fantasy to suppose that the Soviet Union, if only it adopted capitalism, would by that fact eventually emerge as a liberal and democratic state. And it is equally wrong to believe, as many Jacobins have, that the elimination of capitalism will automatically produce a just society based on a fair sharing of resources.

If capitalism is neither the font of liberty nor the source of all the injustice in the world, what exactly is it? First, it is a recognition of the extraordinary power of *compound interest*, a power that has remained undiscovered and unused for most of human history. For example, if you invest $100 at 10 percent interest per year, at the end of a century you will have $1.4 million; at the end of two centuries, $19.0 billion; and at the end of five centuries, a sum vastly greater than the world's current gross national product (5 followed by twenty-two zeros). The principle of compound interest guarantees that any society can eventually get rich. Second, capitalism is about *moral qualities*, specifically hard work, discipline, and patience. To make compound interest pay off, you must be willing to save and work for your grandchildren. It is precisely because most people find it impossible to do this, to subordinate their interests to those of future generations, that human societies throughout history have been so mired in poverty. Even today, Britain and the United States, which together invented the principle of compound interest, have increasingly turned away from its disciplines and are suffering competitive reverses.

Third, capitalism is about the diffusion of knowledge and money, which means *the diffusion of economic power*. So-called moral slackness is actually only one reason that societies have failed to realize the fruits of compound interest. The other reason is that governments have monopolized power, and governments, unlike parents with children, invariably spend all their resources today without much thought for the morrow. Why did imperial China, so rich in culture, remain economically poor for thousands of years? Because the privileged class, the mandarins, worked only for the government. Even when they accumulated vast personal fortunes, they could not pass it on to future generations. Why did the great Arab cultures of the Middle Ages suffer the same fate? Because, as the French historian Fernand Braudel pointed out, the rich merchants "were rarely able to maintain their positions for more than a generation; they were devoured by political society." In postwar Russia, the state wasted most of society's substance on armaments. In the advanced democracies, government not only taxes and spends; it also inflicts hidden taxes such as inflation and deficit financing, both of which undermine the saving and investment process.

Fourth, capitalism is about *inequality*. Within its own logic, this is not viewed as a defect but as a virtue. Inequality is needed for motivation. It is hard enough to save for one's children and grandchildren, but impossible if everyone's children will have the same. Moreover, the rich, even the most profligate and undeserving rich, play a vital economic role. If all the wealth of all the richest families were redistributed throughout society, it would add only a few dollars to the average household's income, a few dollars that would almost certainly be spent. Only by piling up wealth in individual hands, so much wealth that even the most determined profligate could not spend it all, will society be sure of keeping most of its savings intact, and therefore available for productive investment. In this peculiar sense, the rich, whatever their personal qualities, are stewards and trustees of society's future.

Finally, capitalism is about *success*, the ethic of success. Hard work, discipline, patience, and similar moral qualities are lauded, but they are not enough to earn a reward. The capitalist must also be efficient and successful in order to enrich himself. As Friedrich Hayek, an economist who was perhaps the most inveterate champion of capitalism in this century, has written: "In a [capitalist] society it is neither desirable nor practicable that material rewards should be made generally to correspond to what men recognize as merit." It is not duty performed but end results that count.

Having thus stripped capitalism to its bare essentials (compound interest; savings ethic; diffusion of knowledge, money, and power; economic inequality; and success ethic), what do we see? To its defenders, we see a paragon of human artifice, especially in the third element, the diffusion of power. In a capitalist society, Nobel prize winning economist Milton Friedman points out, even the richest individual has only a tiny fraction of the power of a party leader in Russia; conversely, even the lowliest worker has enough power to secure some rights, and these rights tend to expand along with the economic pie. Moreover, he adds, the range for constructive social action is exceptionally broad: "Say I'm in a collectivist society and I want to save an endangered species; I want to save the heron. I have to persuade people in charge of the government to give me money to do it. I have only one place I can go; and with all the bureaucratic red tape that would envelop me, the heron would be dead long before I ever saw a dollar, if I ever did. In a free-enterprise capitalist society, all I have to do is find one crazy millionaire who's willing to put up some dough and, by God, I can save the heron."

Critics of capitalism, on the other hand, even friendly critics, see a different picture. The Swiss theologian Karl Barth, who accepted much of capitalism as an economic necessity, thought that the capitalist religion was an "atrocity"—on the same order as "war . . . militarism . . . prostitution [and] . . . alcoholism." Economist John Maynard Keynes, writing in the wake of the Great Depression, deplored both the "appeal to the money-making and money-loving instincts of individuals" and the banal glorification of success, but nevertheless warned that the time to abandon the less attractive aspects of the capitalist creed was "not yet. For at least another hundred years we must pretend to ourselves and to every one that fair is foul and foul is fair; for foul is useful and fair is not. Avarice and usury and precaution must be our gods for a little longer still. For only they can lead us out of the tunnel of economic necessity into daylight." Keynes's biographer Roy Harrod expressed the same ambivalence: Capitalism, properly managed, would underwrite the good life for all, but only if it was clearly understood that the term *good* was defined by art and intellect, not by money:

After so many generations of toil and drudgery, the people, through the rising standard of education and . . . the rising standard of living made possible by [science and capitalism], were coming within sight of the Promised Land. . . . There, on the bank of [a] slowly flowing river, new generations would . . . discuss books, philosophy, the nature of the good life, and the characters of their friends. There they would learn to be critical and to entertain those crisp and bold ideas that each new age needed. . . . There, too, in those happy surroundings, a love of the beautiful and of the gracious arts of life would be fostered. . . . It was a sacred trust. If art failed and intellect declined, the people would find that, after all their struggles, the promised inheritance had become a desert.

Utopian communism

Utopian communism, the doctrine of total economic equality preached by Lenin, Mao Tse Tung, and the Cambodian Pol Pot, still exists as a theoretical alternative to capitalism, from which it sprang, but as a religion in our sense of the term it is nearly dead throughout the world, and in America it is stone dead. To recapture some of the old appeal, before the tides of blood washed up from the Soviet purges, the Chinese Cultural Revolution, and the Cambodian massacres, before all the embarrassing economic failures, it is necessary to look backward, to the 1920s, when Keynes provided his usually shrewd if somewhat naive appraisal, an appraisal that capitalists need to study and think about all the harder as they see communism collapsing around them.

Leninism [like capitalism] is a combination of two things . . . religion and business. We are shocked because the religion is new, and contemptuous because the business, being subordinated to the religion instead of the other way round, is highly inefficient. . . . If we want to frighten ourselves in our capitalist easy-chairs, we can picture the Communists of Russia as though the early Christians led by Attila were using the equipment of the Holy Inquisition . . . to enforce the literal economics of the New Testament. . . .

Like other new religions, [Leninism] seems to take the colour and gaiety and freedom out of everyday life and to offer a drab substitute in the square wooden faces of its devotees. Like other new religions, it persecutes without justice or pity those who actively resist it. Like other new religions, it is unscrupulous. Like other new religions, it is filled with missionary ardour and oecumenical ambitions. . . . For me, brought up in a free air undarkened by the horrors of religion, with nothing to be afraid of, Red Russia holds too much which is detestable. . . .

Yet we shall miss the essence of the new religion if we stop at this point. The Communist may justly reply that all these things belong not to his ultimate Faith but to the tactics of Revolution. . . . The Revolution is to be a supreme example of the means justified by the end. The soldier of the Revolution must crucify his own human nature, becoming unscrupulous and ruthless, and suffering himself a life without security or joy—but as the means to his purpose and not its end.

What, then, is the essence of the new religion as a New Order upon earth? . . . In one respect Communism but follows other famous religions. It exalts the common man and makes him everything. Here there is nothing new. But there is another factor in it which also is not new but which may, nevertheless, in a changed form and a new setting, contribute something to the true religion of the future, if there be any true religion. *Leninism is absolutely, defiantly non-supernatural, and its emotional and ethical essence centres about the individual's and the community's attitude towards the Love of Money.* . . .

To me it seems clearer every day that the moral problem of our age is concerned with the love of money, with the habitual appeal to the money motive in nine-tenths of the activities of life, with the universal striving after individual economic security as the prime object of endeavour, with the social approbation of money as the measure of constructive success, and with the social appeal to the hoarding instinct as the foundation of the necessary provision for the family and for the future. The decaying religions around us, which have less and less interest for most people unless it be as an agreeable form of magical ceremonial or of social observance, have lost their moral significance just because—unlike some of their earlier versions—they do not touch in the least degree on these essential matters. A revolution in our ways of thinking and feeling about money may become the growing purpose of contemporary embodiments of the ideal. Perhaps, therefore, Russian Communism does represent the first confused stirrings of a great religion. . . . Beneath the cruelty and stupidity of New Russia some speck of the ideal may lie hid.

Democratic socialism

As a youth, Michael Harrington participated in Dorothy Day's Catholic Worker Movement. After abandoning Christianity and embracing Karl Marx, he wrote a book, *The Other America*, which helped persuade John Kennedy and Lyndon Johnson to undertake their War on Poverty social programs. Thereafter, he became increasingly uneasy with his own fame and success until he nearly fainted during a speaking engagement and had to retreat to his hotel room with such piercing chest pains that he thought he was having a heart attack:

The itinerant radical agitator, the writer of articles with long titles for magazines of small circulation, the practitioner of a comfortable poverty on the margin of the affluent society, could not recognize the middle-aging participant in the discussions with men of power, who was married and received middle-class fees for giving anticapitalist speeches. . . . By accepting every invitation to give a talk, by being casual and open to every demand, just like in the good old undemanding days, I could pretend to myself that I was still that other Michael Harrington. . . . Eventually that masquerade, and the furious pace it required, could not go on any longer. I came unstuck.

Having learned to pace himself, Harrington became until his death in 1989 the leading democratic socialist in the United States. His socialism was comprised of one part anti-Christianity, one part anti-communism, and one part anticapitalism. Harrington condemned Christianity because he thought the church was an integral part of the unjust economic order and in any case "God is dead"; communism because it is full of desperate and vicious doctrines such as violent revolution, class warfare, the end justifying the means, the puniness of individual human life beside the forces of history, the expendability of democratic methods; capitalism because it eliminates the one ideal that might replace the vanished Christian faith: the ideal of economic equality and of a loving community built on such equality. According to this view, Americans ought not to accept inequality, which is interpreted as a conspiracy of the rich against the poor. No matter how much the system tries to bribe us with efficiency and consumerism, we should demand a better economic order, beginning with much more taxation of the rich, many more goods and services provided "free" for all, the abolition of large monopolistic private companies with their deceptive advertising, and the development of people's bureaucracies that will be open to democratic participation and encourage face-to-face encounters with their constituencies.

Opponents of Harrington voiced several criticisms: that democratic socialism is oxymoronic, that is, no nation on earth is simultaneously democratic and socialist, presumably because economic equality requires enforcement and large-scale enforcement requires authoritarian methods; that the American democracy, as consulted by various polls, seems to prefer a system of inequality, probably because its citizens are incurably optimistic and like to think that their ship or at least their children's ship will soon come in; that a participative or face-to-face bureaucracy is yet another contradiction in terms; that confiscatory taxation of the rich eliminates much of society's savings, its economic seed corn, in addition to reducing incentives.

For all these reasons, among others, democratic socialism has steadily lost ground in American society since its heyday in the 1960s and early 1970s, when the chairman of the President's Council of Economic Advisors (Arthur Okun) stated, "I would prefer . . . complete [economic] equality" and a candidate for president (George McGovern) added that "citadels of [private] economic privilege [make it] foolish to expect that any fiscal or monetary policy will work, whether the adversary is inflation or recession or both." The nadir for democratic socialists occurred in the 1980s, when some conservative analysts charged, fairly or unfairly, that virtually all of statistically defined hard-core poverty in the United

States (as opposed to people who are only temporarily poor) could be identified with fatherless welfare households and that these households had been "created" by Great Society antipoverty programs of the kind espoused by Harrington.

Despite this generally low estate, democratic socialism has its strongholds, especially in universities, where a strong revival of non-communist theoretical Marxism is underway, and where what Harrington called a "common emotion" is being rekindled as well. As a professor of philosophy, Robert Paul Wolff of the University of Massachusetts at Amherst, says about his effort to become an interpreter and self-described cheerleader for contemporary Marxist economics: "Until I got involved in this stuff, I never talked to other people about my work. Now I have a sense of myself as being part of an enterprise that's larger than myself . . . of sharing it with other people, and that's tremendously rewarding . . . like being reborn."

Agrarianism

Capitalism, communism, and socialism all share one central assumption: that industrialism is a positive development, that it is already positive and will be more so in the future, that it can be managed and perpetuated in such a way as to avoid an eventual collapse, with everything crashing down in a horror of suffering and destruction. Agrarianism, on the other hand, rejects industrialism itself, not just such specific manifestations of industrialism as capitalism, communism, and socialism. Factories, chemical plants, cities, skyscrapers, sprawling "glass-and-grass" office parks and subdivisions, fast-food strips with buildings shaped like pancakes or hot dogs, expressways, temperature-controlled barbecues in automatically sprinkled backyards, suburban banks designed as Williamsburg replicas, bad air, bad water, poisoned food chains, mechanized one-crop agriculture, mass-produced junk, consumer debt, farm debt, international debt, fashion and fad, the "right" car, the "right" clothes—it is all a vast tragic mistake. To paraphrase nineteenth-century historian and moral philosopher Henry Adams on politics, the effect of industrialism "on all men is the aggravation of self, a sort of tumor that ends by killing the victim's sympathies; a diseased appetite, like a passion for drink and perverted tastes; one can scarcely use expressions too strong to describe the violence of egotism it stimulates."

Among agrarian critiques of the industrial way of life, one can distinguish at least five types: Southern (aristocratic), populist, technocratic, communitarian, and conservationist.

Southern (aristocratic) agrarianism

The Southern agrarian myth may be summarized as follows: In Europe, an old and settled and chivalric life best described by Sir Walter Scott's novels (*Ivanhoe, Waverly*) is suddenly overthrown by the malevolent forces of revolution and industrialism. A saving remnant, especially from Scotland and Wales but also from France, reaches the New World to reestablish the Old Civilization on virgin shores.

As Southern writer Frank Owsley has said:

With the environment of the New World and the traditions of the Old, the South . . . became the seat of an agrarian civilization which had strength and promise for a future greatness second to none. The life of the South was leisurely and unhurried for the planter, the yeoman, or the landless tenant. It was a way of life, not a routine of planting and reaping merely for gain. Washington, who rode daily over his farms . . . inhaled the smell of ripe corn after a rain . . . and, when in the field as a soldier or in the city as President of the United States, was homesick at the smell of fresh-plowed earth.

The Old South, proponents of this form of agrarianism will concede, labored under contradictions. In the midst of the celebrated courage and courtesy and magnanimity and loyalty and honor and integrity and generosity and leisureliness, there was pride and violence and unrestrained individualism and, of course, slavery. But, according to the myth, these flaws were belabored by men whose real motivation was to destroy the agrarian civilization and exploit it economically. The truly characteristic figure of the Old South was the white-haired "gentleman in Mississippi, a doctor . . . who [gave] most of his life to charity and [was] innocent of all money and business." Had the Confederates won the war, journalist and ascerbic essayist H. L. Mencken argued, they "would have abolished slavery by the middle 80s. They were headed that way before . . . but . . . on sound economic grounds, and not on the brum-magem moral grounds which persuaded the North. The difference here is immense. In human history a moral victory is always a disaster, for it debauches and degrades both the victor and the vanquished."

After the war, the myth continues, the ancient civilization, based equally on land, family, community, and gentility, was extinguished in both Old and New Worlds, but it was not just the South that suffered the consequences—it was the entire United States. As Southerner Andrew Lytle wrote: "[Without the South to provide restraints], an agrarian Union [was] changed into an industrial empire bent on conquest of the earth's goods. . . . This [meant] warfare, a struggle over markets . . . but [it was really] a war to the death between technology and the ordinary human functions of living." To this conclusion Mencken added:

The chief evils in the Federal Victory lay in the fact, from which we still suffer abominably, that it was a victory of what we now call Babbitts over what used to be called gentlemen. . . . Whatever the defects of the new commonwealth below the Potomac, it would have at least been a commonwealth founded upon a concept of human inequality, and with a superior minority at the helm. It might not have produced any more Washingtons, Madisons, Jeffersons, Calhouns and Randolphs of Roanoke, but it would certainly not have yielded itself to . . . raw plutocracy . . . Ku Kluxry . . . shouting Methodists . . . political ecclesiastics, nigger-baiting, and the more homicidal variety of wowserism.

Although Southern civilization died at Appomattox, Southern agrarianism as a religion refused to die. In August 1929, Allen Tate, a Southern writer, poet, critic, and "gentleman farmer" teaching at Vanderbilt University, wrote his friend Donald Davidson the following letter:

"The other day I wrote to [poet and novelist Robert Penn] Warren, and suggested the following radical program:

• The formation of a society, or an academy of Southern positive reactionaries . . . committed at first to direct agitation.

• . . . Philosophically we must go the whole hog of reaction, and base our movement less upon the actual old South than upon its prototype–the historical social and religious scheme of Europe. We must be the last Europeans–there being no Europeans in Europe at present.

• The advantages of this program are the advantages of all extreme positions. It would immediately define the muddling and *unorganized* opposition (*intellectually* unorganized) of the Progressives; they have no *philosophical* program, only an emotional acquiescence to the drift of the age, and we should force them to rationalize into absurdity an intellectually untenable position. Secondly, it would crystallize into opposition or complete allegiance the vaguely prosouthern opinions of the time.

Tate's movement, joined by critic John Crowe Ransom, Andrew Lytle, and Frank Owsley, as well as Davidson, Warren, and others, was launched with *I'll Take My Stand*, a book of essays published in 1930, whose title was drawn from the Southern national anthem. Ransom reported that it was "a group effort beyond anything I have ever taken part in. Its quality was rare and fine as a piece of cooperation. . . . It was the best days I ever had." But Northern intellectuals immediately attacked the Southern Agrarians as disguised fascists, and even novelist Sherwood Anderson, a Virginian, accused them, in Southern historian W. J. Cash's words, of wishing "to sit on cool and columned verandas, sip mint juleps, and converse exquisitely while the poor whites and the black men toiled for them in the hot, wide fields spread out against the horizon." Against such unfounded and unfair jibes, Tate offered a spirited if fatalistic defense. If America refused to listen, if even his beloved South rushed headlong to desecrate the graves of Confederate dead with factories, big cities, and shopping centers, this was only to be expected:

The older I get the more I realize that I set out about ten years ago to live a life of failure, to imitate, in my own life, the history of my people. For it was only in this fashion, considering the circumstances, that I could completely identify myself with them. We all have an instinct—if we are artists particularly—to live at the center of some way of life and to be borne up by its innermost significance. The significance of the Southern way of life, in my time, is failure. . . . What else is there for me but a complete acceptance of the idea of failure?

Populist agrarianism

As powerful as the Southern myth of aristocratic agrarianism is, there are other, equally compelling forms of agrarianism. In the nonaristocratic or populist agrarian myth, immortalized by Henry David Thoreau's *Walden Pond*, the harried urban dweller packs all his or her belongings and heads for the country, where he or she lives a life of perfect health and sanity and self-sufficiency on a small plot of ground with as few conveniences as possible.

In actual life, people do not necessarily give up all the conveniences, and perhaps keep some city ties as well, but they do emulate the Walden life, often quite successfully. For example, in the 1960s James Crawford attended Rice University on an ROTC scholarship, served with the Navy in Vietnam while simultaneously learning Russian, and then abruptly resigned from the Navy to protest the American bombing of Cambodia. Thereafter, he gave antiwar speeches, worked for Congresswoman Bella Abzug on a draft resister's amnesty bill, and attended law school at night—until the spring of 1971, when he threw it all over and removed himself and his two dogs to a life of growing and selling organic vegetables from a thirty-five-acre farm in West Virginia.

At the time, Crawford insisted that

it wasn't all negative. I didn't feel I was abandoning the movement for change or opting out on some private trip. I just felt I wanted to be useful in a more concrete way, even a small way. . . . I like the idea of earning a living by making something that is valuable to people and selling it directly to them. I like that one-to-one relationship. Sitting with a reporter by shelves of freshly "put up" tomatoes in the kitchen of his tarpaper-shingled farmhouse, he added that "the important thing was to live in the present instead of the future and not to fall prey to the consumerism that saturates American life and keeps people forever dissatisfied, seeking something bigger, costlier, faster, shinier or louder to make them feel more powerful.

Initially, of course, farming posed all sorts of problems for someone who had grown up in the suburbs of Boston: "I went to buy a plow and it was embarrassing. . . . I had to ask a lot of dumb questions. . . . In the winter, it [was] lonely and I [had] to get a regular job in the woods to [meet] . . . tractor . . . and truck payments." At times, country life seemed confining; even the nearest library was hours away. But Crawford persevered, got married, and continued selling his fine New Morning Farm organic vegetables in Washington, D.C.

Technocratic agrarianism

Most agrarians are as suspicious of science and technology as they are of industrialism: They view all three as of a piece. But at least some agrarians distinguish between technology, especially high technology, which they regard as full of hope for mankind, and industrialism, which they view as a kind of perversion of technology. Writer and inventor Buckminster Fuller, for example, thought that technology had spawned an ugly and dangerous industrialism because it was still incomplete. If we persevere, he maintained, we will eventually perfect our technical apparatus and then all the problems will disappear.

In the meantime, Fuller, who was an ardent lover of nature, thought it would be no desecration to fill the remaining wildernesses with some human structures, so long as these structures were in the "natural" shape of a tetrahedron—the famous Fuller dome. Other technocratic agrarians have pictured a day when the cities will be emptied, when most families will prefer to homestead in the country, but when electricity, air conditioning and other amenities will be supplied by solar panels and both work and entertainment will flow through high-tech telecommunications networks. This utopian vision, of "opening" the countryside without urbanizing or spoiling it, brings together all sorts of people: "New Age" dropouts, spiritual counselors, psychiatrists, computer specialists, energy experts, architects, engineers, celebrity spokespersons. One of the central figures of the movement is John Denver, the balladeer of country life, who lives in the mountains near Aspen, Colorado, who has helped fund a foundation for research into appropriate technologies for the new outdoors-oriented life, and who sometimes enhances the mood of his concerts by showing professionally produced "home movies" of himself and friends hiking through mountain glens, riding horseback through bold streams, and roasting marshmallows around roaring campfires.

Simple communitarianism

Like other agrarians, communitarians reject industrial capitalism, communism, and socialism, but for different reasons. They believe that people should live together in small, largely self-sufficient communities, sharing their hopes and activities and all their worldly resources. Whether organized as a hyperdisciplined Israeli kibbutz or a loose association of American "New Agers," what counts is not the country setting, but the subordination of individualism to the needs of the group.

Conservationism

Conservationism is a kind of agrarianism with reduced objectives. It does not seek to outlaw industrialism or make ghost towns of great cities: It merely wants to protect what is left of the countryside and, ultimately, to keep humanity from destroying the life systems on which it depends. Insofar as it defends the right to exist of a rare monkey or the rain forest habitat that supports the monkey, its aims might be characterized as esthetic or moral or both. But insofar as rain forests tie back into the world's oxygen-carbon monoxide balance, the greenhouse (warming) effect of burning too much fossil fuel, or cancer risks from ozone depletion, the esthetic or moral viewpoint becomes urgently utilitarian as well. As Kathryn Fuller, president of the World Wildlife Fund and the Conservation Foundation, has stated the case: "Environmental issues like climate change are *uniquely* global. With the exception of the proliferation of nuclear weapons, nothing has such broad ramifications. As the political divisions that drove the arms race begin to break down, we must find common ground among ourselves so that we may make peace with our environment. There is simply no alternative."

Value systems currently taught, reflected, or alluded to in college *moral philosophy* courses (such value systems generally combine logic with one or more additional modes of moral knowledge)

Logical naturalism (combines logic with elements of sense experience)

It may be recalled from chapter 4 that the father of modern religions of logic, Spinoza, sought his all-important first premise in an *a priori* (self-evident) proof of God's existence ("To be perfect, by definition, God must be; if we can imagine God, he must exist"). When this proof was later refuted by David Hume and Emmanuel Kant, philosophers sought other (not *a priori*) ways to build a constructive, not just a destructive, religion of logic, and their first thought was to find a starting premise in human experience, a purely factual premise from which a secular ethics could be deduced, an ethics that would be completely free of the idea of the supernatural.

The most important attempt in this direction was made by Jeremy Bentham (1748-1832). Bentham began by attacking all deductive systems based on God or a reality beyond this world as "nonsense on stilts" that should be swept away at a glance. The proper course was to stick to this world, not to imagine another, and the most obviously observable fact about this world was that everyone pursued pleasure and avoided pain. From this, it could be inferred that pleasure in a general sense corresponded to happiness. Selfish pleasure, on the other hand, either solitary selfish pleasure or the selfish pleasure of a small group such as a family or close circle of friends, invariably led to pain rather than happiness, either because it collided with other selfish individuals or groups or because it contradicted our natural socializing instincts. True happiness is therefore "the greatest happiness of the greatest number"—a phrase that lead Bentham to cry out "as it were in an inward ecstasy, like Archimedes on the discovery of the fundamental principle of hydrostatics, EUREKA."

To make this "greatest happiness" principle as practical as possible, Bentham invented what he called a "hedonic calculus" to measure the precise amount of pleasure that could be expected from a specific action. Among the factors to be considered were: intensity, duration, certainty (or uncertainty), nearness (or remoteness), further consequences, purity, and the number of people affected. The particular kind of action did not matter at all—for example, pushpin (a form of gambling) was just as good as poetry if it produced a commensurate amount of pleasure. Nor did motive enter into the calculus: Consequences, and only consequences, were worth considering. Believing in God, for example, was neither good nor bad in itself. But since Bentham thought it tended to produce more pain than pleasure, believing in God was by definition useless and the expenditure of scarce resources on bibles and churches was misguided at best and criminal at worst. The only proper object for human beings (and their government) was to try to increase the total sum of human pleasure in the world by feeding the hungry, sheltering the homeless, reforming the penal code, or improving public health, and if one had to be a little inhuman to get all these goals accomplished, that was all right, too. As Bentham concluded: "I would have the dearest friend I have to know that his interests, if they come in competition with those of the public, are as nothing to me. Thus I would serve my friends—thus would I be served by them."

The inventor of this remarkable doctrine, which literally stood Christianity on its head by deriving goodness and altruism from pleasure and materialism, was one of a long line of English eccentrics. A graduate of Oxford at fifteen and an obsessive toiler at dry-as-dust tracts on law, penology, economics, and public sanitation, as well as on philosophy, he was too shy to publish anything. His friends had to purloin his manuscripts and secretly publish them—with the result that the wealthy recluse unwittingly became a public figure and a hugely successful reformer. In typical fashion, he worried about making his death as useful as possible and directed that his body should be publicly dissected. Subsequently, his face was reconstructed with wax, his skeleton clothed in a respectable dark suit, and his visible remains placed on permanent display at University College, Cambridge.

The year that Bentham died, one of his chief protegés, John Stuart Mill, was only twenty-six years old. Educated by a father who thought that "life [was] a poor thing at best, after the freshness of youth and of unsatisfied curiosity had gone by," by age three he had begun to read ancient Greek; by sixteen he had coined the term *utilitarianism* to describe his own and Bentham's philosophy; by twenty-one, he had suffered a devastating nervous breakdown, a breakdown that was forever after cited by proponents of "natural" and "unstressed" child rearing. In subsequent years, Mill softened (or, as some would say, muddled) Benthamism by distinguishing between so-called higher and lower pleasures: "It is better to be a human being dissatisfied than a pig satisfied; better to be Socrates dissatisfied than a fool satisfied." He also attempted, as Bentham never had, to supply a logical proof for the proposition (deduction) that happiness can be equated with pleasure. As Bertrand Russell later described this process: "[Mill says]: Pleasure is the only thing desired; therefore pleasure is the only thing desirable. He argues that the only things visible are things seen, the only things audible are things heard, and similarly the only things desirable are things desired. He does not notice that a thing is 'visible' if it *can* be seen, but 'desirable' if it *ought* to be desired."

With this seemingly small slip, Mill stumbled into a logical fallacy highlighted by David Hume a century earlier in one of the most important passages of all moral philosophy:

In every system of morality which I have hitherto met with, I have always remarked that the author proceeds for some time in the ordinary way of reasoning, and makes observations concerning human affairs; when of a sudden I am surprised to find that instead of the usual copulations of propositions *is* and *is not*, I meet with no proposition that is not connected with an *ought* or an *ought not*. This change is imperceptible, but is, however, of the [greatest] consequence. For as this *ought* or *ought not* expresses some new relation or affirmation, it is necessary that it should be explained; and at the same time that a reason should be given for what seems altogether inconceivable, how this new relation can be a deduction from others which are entirely different from it.

These few words of Hume's (summarized as "no ought from an is") strike a death blow at Benthamite utilitarianism because they strip the philosophy of its logical grounding. As always in philosophy, nothing ever quite dies. There are contemporary American philosophers who still call themselves utilitarians and look for variants that might be logically demonstrated (for example, so-called negative utilitarianism*), but none of their efforts seem to

---

* The notion that if we cannot demonstrate logically that happiness and pleasure are synonymous, perhaps we can demonstrate that the opposite of pleasure, pain, is inconsistent with happiness, or that selfish happiness is inconsistent with true pleasure.

avail. Whatever residual appeal the religion of usefulness may hold for people—and its appeal is undeniable (indeed, as we shall see in the next chapter, economist John Maynard Keynes described it as the paradoxical source of the rampant practicality and materialism, alternating with social activism and reformist zeal, that characterize modern and especially modern American life)—it now operates primarily on an emotive rather than on a logical level.

Logical intuitionism (combines logic with elements of intuition)

A naturalistic philosopher like Bentham or Mill looks for his initial premise in the real world of sense experience. He need not, however, stir from the peace and quiet of his study; he requires only a single observation, or several observations, for a starting premise, and everything else can be deduced. If Hume is correct, however, that *no ought* can be deduced from an *is*, that a starting premise cannot be found in the real world, the world of *isness*, where else can it be found? The answer for some philosophers, such as G. E. Moore (1873–1958), is that the starting premise must simply be intuited, picked right out of our unconscious brain.

Moore was not only an intuitionist in this technical sense. He was also an ardent foe of what might be called everyday Benthamism, the idea that because pleasure constitutes the highest possible good, human energies should be directed toward useful projects that increase pleasure and alleviate misery. Somewhat confusingly, Moore is sometimes loosely described as a utilitarian because he did agree with Bentham that the consequences of actions mattered more than the motives behind them. But the main thrust of "Moorism" was violently anti-Benthamite and Moore's followers quickly abandoned all traces of Benthamism, as the following account by the economist Maynard Keynes, a student of Moore's at Cambridge, clearly reveals:

My Early Beliefs*

I went up to Cambridge at Michaelmas 1902, and Moore's *Principia Ethica* came out at the end of my first year. . . . It was exciting, exhilarating, the beginning of a renaissance, the opening of a new heaven on a new earth, we were the forerunners of a new dispensation, we were not afraid of anything. . . .

Even if the new members of the Club know what [this new] religion was . . . it will not do any of us any harm to try and recall the crude outlines. Nothing mattered except states of mind, our own and other people's of course, but chiefly our own. These states of mind were not associated with action or achievement or with consequences. They consisted in timeless, passionate states of contemplation and communion, largely unattached to "before" and "after". . . . The appropriate subjects of passionate contemplation and communion were a beloved person, beauty and truth, and one's prime objects in life were love, the creation and enjoyment of aesthetic experience and the pursuit of knowledge. Of these love came a long way first. But in the early days under Moore's influence the public treatment of this and its associated acts was, on the whole, austere and platonic. Some of us might argue that physical enjoyment could spoil and detract from the state of mind as a whole. I do not remember at what date Strachey issued his edict that certain Latin technical terms of sex were the correct words to use, that to avoid them was a grave error, and, even in mixed company, a weakness, and the use of other synonyms a vulgarity. . . .

Our religion closely followed the English puritan tradition of being chiefly concerned with the salvation of our own souls. The divine resided within a closed circle. There was not a very intimate connection between "being good" and "doing good"; and we had a feeling that there was some risk that in practice the latter might interfere with the former. . . . Perhaps it was a sufficient offset that our religion was

---

* Prepared for a "club" of intimate friends and not necessarily meant for publication, these memorable remarks (thought by many, this author included, to be the finest short essay on moral philosophy ever written) were read by Keynes as he lay draped over a favorite chaise longue in the double drawing room of his London townhouse on a September evening of 1938. The spirit of the gathering is suggested by the opening remarks: "If it will not shock the club too much, I should like in this contribution to its proceedings to introduce for once, mental or spiritual, instead of sexual, adventures, to try and recall the principal impacts on one's virgin mind and to wonder how it has all turned out."

altogether unworldly—with wealth, power, popularity or success it had no concern whatever, they were thoroughly despised.

How did we know what states of mind were good? This was a matter of direct inspection, of direct unanalysable intuition about which it was useless and impossible to argue. In that case who was right when there was a difference of opinion? There were two possible explanations. It might be that the two parties were not really talking about the same thing, that they were not bringing their intuitions to bear on precisely the same object. . . . Or it might be that some people had an acuter sense of judgment, just as some people can judge a vintage port and others cannot. On the whole, so far as I remember, this explanation prevailed. In practice, victory was with those who could speak with the greatest appearance of clear, undoubting conviction and could best use the accents of infallibility. Moore at this time was a master of this method— greeting one's remarks with a gasp of incredulity—Do you *really* think *that*, an expression of face as if to hear such a thing said reduced him to a state of wonder verging on imbecility, with his mouth wide open and wagging his head in the negative so violently that his hair shook. *Oh!* he would say, goggling at you as if either you or he must be mad; and no reply was possible. . . .

Let me give you a few examples of the sort of things we used to discuss.

If A was in love with B and believed that B reciprocated his feelings, whereas in fact B did not, but was in love with C, the state of affairs was certainly not so good as it would have been if A had been right, but was it worse or better than it would become if A discovered his mistake? If A was in love with B under a misapprehension as to B's qualities, was this better or worse than A's not being in love at all? If A was in love with B because A's spectacles were not strong enough to see B's complexion, did this altogether, or partly, destroy the value of A's state of mind? Suppose we were to live our lives backwards, having our experiences in the reverse order, would this affect the value of successive states of mind? If the states of mind enjoyed by each of us were pooled and then redistributed, would this affect their value? . . . But I have said enough by now to make it clear that the problems of mensuration, in which we had involved ourselves, were somewhat formidable. . . .

It seems to me looking back, that this religion of ours was a very good one to grow up under. . . . It is still my religion under the surface.

I read again last week Moore's famous chapter on "The Ideal". . . . The New Testament is a handbook for politicians compared with the unworldliness of [this] chapter. . . . I know no equal to it in literature since Plato. And it is better than Plato because it is quite free from *fancy*. It conveys the beauty of the literalness of Moore's mind, the pure and passionate intensity of his vision, *un*fanciful and *un*dressed-up. Moore had a nightmare once in which he could not distinguish propositions from tables. But even when he was awake, he could not distinguish love and beauty and truth from the furniture. They took on the same definition of outline, the same stable, solid, objective qualities and common-sense reality. . . .

The fundamental intuitions of *Principia Ethica* . . . brought us one big advantage. As we . . . lived entirely in present experience, since social action as an end in itself and not merely as a lugubrious duty had dropped out of our Ideal, and not only social action, but the life of action generally, power, politics, success, wealth, ambition, with the economic motive and the economic criterion less prominent in our philosophy than with St. Francis of Assisi, who at least made collections for the birds, it follows that we were amongst the first of our generation, perhaps alone amongst our generation, to escape from the Benthamite tradition. In practice, of course, at least so far as I was concerned, the outside world was not forgotten or forsworn. But I am recalling what our Ideal was in those early days when the life of passionate contemplation and communion was supposed to oust all other purposes whatever. It can be no part of this memoir for me to try to explain why it was such a big advantage for us to have escaped from the Benthamite tradition. But I do now regard that as the worm which has been gnawing at the insides of modern civilization and is responsible for its present moral decay. We used to regard the Christians as the enemy, because they appeared as the representatives of tradition, convention and hocus-pocus. In truth it was the Benthamite calculus, based on an over-valuation of the economic criterion, which was destroying the quality of the popular Ideal.

Moreover, it was this escape from Bentham, joined with the unsurpassable individualism of our philosophy, which has served to protect the whole lot of us from the final *reductio ad absurdum* of Benthamism known as Marxism. We have completely failed, indeed, to provide a substitute for these economic bogus-faiths capable of protecting or satisfying our successors. But we ourselves have remained—am I not right in saying *all* of us?—altogether immune from the virus, as safe in the citadel of our ultimate faith as the Pope of Rome in his.

Like other high priests of logical religions, G. E. Moore was quite certain that he had succeeded where others had failed, that his approach of intuiting some starting premises and then reasoning through to conclusions had at last established ethics on a firm foundation. But had he, in fact, accomplished all this? Keynes pointed out a major technical difficulty: Honest and intelligent people might disagree about initial intuitions. Another moral philosopher, H. A. Prichard (1871–1947), responded with an even more damaging assessment: Why bother at all to reason from intuited premises? Why not just intuit everything and forget about labored deductions? As Prichard wrote:

The sense that we ought to do certain things arises in our unreflective consciousness. . . . We then want to have it *proved* to us that we ought to do so. . . . If . . . by Moral Philosophy is meant the knowledge which would satisfy this demand, there is no such knowledge, and all attempts to attain it are doomed to failure because they rest on a mistake, the mistake of supposing the possibility of proving what can only be apprehended directly. . . . If we . . . doubt whether there is really an obligation to originate A in a situation B, the remedy lies not in any process of general thinking, but in getting face to face with a particular instance of the situation B, and then directly appreciating the obligation to originate A in that situation.

In suggesting this procedure, Prichard thought that he was merely simplifying and improving on Moore. Not for a moment did he imagine that he was jeopardizing the entire enterprise of establishing objective moral truth. Confronted with a doctrine of total intuitionism, even a beginning student of philosophy would immediately ask: If a few initial intuited premises lead to disagreement among honest people, what will happen if everything is intuited? And what will happen if Hitler or Stalin is doing the intuiting?

Prichard seemed unaware of these questions. Even if he had

been aware of them, he would presumably have dismissed them as theoretical and of no practical consequence. From his own cloistered perspective at Oxford, people simply did not disagree about moral intuitions. Like afternoon tea, croquet on the lawn, or freshly starched tennis whites, moral agreement was a given, a natural part of civilized life. The propositions that one should do good, avoid lying, give others pleasure, not worry too much about one's own pleasure—these were as self-evident as a mathematical relationship, as self-evident as $2 + 2 = 4$. The only remaining task for moral philosophers was to help individuals deal with conflicting goods. For example, should one shout in public to awaken a fainted man, slow one's car at a major intersection while carrying an injured passenger to a hospital, or return a borrowed book on time if its continuing possession might accomplish a useful purpose? With these outlandishly trivial issues, Prichard's logical intuitionism, already teetering on the brink, just slides off the cliff into well-deserved oblivion.

Logical subjectivism (combines logic with "science")

Prichard's most famous essay was entitled "Does Moral Philosophy Rest on a Mistake?" Although this was an arresting title, it was also quite misleading. Prichard did not really think that all moral philosophy was based on a mistake; that is, he agreed, with most of his predecessors, that the necessary task of moral philosophers was to discover an objective basis for human belief and conduct, a basis so objectively sound that no sane person would ever dispute its conclusions.

The subjectivists, on the other hand, philosophers like Ludwig Wittgenstein (1889–1951), Bertrand Russell (1872–1972), Alfred T. Ayer (1910–   ) and the American Charles Stevenson (1908–1979), really did think that moral philosophy had been based on a mistake, the mistake of desperately clinging to a facsimile of Christianity while dispensing with church and Bible. In their view, the early European and American moral philosophers, even individuals like Spinoza who had not been raised as Christians, had all tried to save God *and* Christian ethics by producing rigorous logical proofs of their necessity. When this failed, their successors, individuals like Bentham and Moore, tried to deduce Christian ethics, or something like Christian ethics, without any reference whatever to God, the nature of the universe, or any of the "great questions." This too failed, inevitably and irrevocably, because it had missed the main point: that ideas like God and ultimate reality (cosmological ideas) and ideas like free will, human nature, human ethics, beauty and justice (moral ideas) were all equally meaningless. They were neither propositions that could be tested mathematically nor facts that could be verified by observation or experiment.

David Hume, as usual, had already enunciated this position two hundred years earlier in "An Enquiry Concerning Human Understanding": "If we take in our hand any volume; of divinity or school metaphysics, for instance; let us ask, *Does it contain any abstract reasoning concerning quantity or number?* No. *Does it contain any experimental reasoning concerning matter of fact and existence?* No. Commit it then to the flames: for it can contain nothing but sophistry and illusion." But it was left to the moral subjectivists of this century to reach the final, shocking conclusion that Hume's dictum applied not just to Christian theology or "German" speculation about a metaphysical fourth dimension beyond our world. It applied just as forcefully to speculation about the very here-and-now subjects of good and bad or right and wrong.

A few of the more fire-breathing subjectivists took the rather paradoxical view that nonpropositions and nonfacts masquerading as propositions and facts were dangerous, and that both theology and moral philosophy were therefore inherently wicked. Others, such as the young A. J. Ayer, simply dismissed religion and moral philosophy as contentless, not much different than the barking of dogs. As Ayer wrote: "If a sentence makes no statement at all, there is obviously no sense in asking whether what it says is either true or false. . . . To say that God exists is to make a metaphysical utterance which cannot be either true or false. . . . As we have seen, sentences which simply express moral judgements do not say anything."

As time passed and the fury dissipated, subjectivists became more thoughtful about their position. Russell replied to a newspaper attack by stating:

What Mr. X says in criticism of my views on ethics has my entire sympathy. I find my own views argumentatively irrefutable, but nevertheless incredible. . . . [The chief ground for adopting my view] is the complete impossibility of finding any arguments to prove that this or that has intrinsic value. . . . We cannot prove, to a color-blind man, that grass is green and not red. But there are various ways of proving to him that he lacks a power of discrimination which most men possess, whereas in the case of values there are no such ways. . . . Since no way can be even imagined for deciding a difference as to values, the conclusion is forced upon us that the difference is one of taste, not one as to any objective truth.

Once he reached this position, Russell never abandoned it. But he did try to correct the more extreme and less defensible versions of subjectivism. For example, the idea that people's moral positions are totally contentless, just so much bubbala-bubbala, cannot be right. When one person speaks to another about morals, communication obviously takes place, even if it is only that, as Russell ironically put it, "ethics is the art of recommending to others what they must do to get along with ourselves." Picking up this clue, Charles Stevenson found that quite a lot was going on in moral discourse, namely, persuasion, command, grading, the adjustment of material and other interests:

People from widely separated communities have different moral attitudes. Why? To a great extent because they have been subject to different social influences. Now clearly this influence doesn't operate through sticks and stones alone; words play a great part. People praise one another, to encourage certain inclinations, and blame one another, to discourage others. Those of forceful personalities issue commands which weaker people, for complicated instinctive reasons, find it difficult to disobey, quite apart from fears of consequence. . . . Social influence is exerted, to an enormous extent, by means that have nothing to do with physical force or material reward. The ethical terms facilitate such influence. Being suited to use in suggestion, they are a means by which men's attitudes may be led this way or that.

Stevenson's linguistic analysis sounds both Freudian (nothing is what it seems or seems what it is) and Marxist (arguments about good and bad are often disguised power struggles), but his conclusions are careful, prudent, and even somewhat reassuring: "Good" cannot be defined; it is neither logically demonstrable nor scientifically verifiable. On the other hand, "this is good" means "I like this," and the statement "I like this" is neither contentless nor meaningless. So, human beings are not mere canine barkers.

Russell was also at pains to point out the limits of subjectivism. Although a major ethical argument cannot be settled by logic or experimental demonstration, most apparent ethical arguments are really something else. Imagine, for example, that someone proposed to eliminate all pollution control standards in the United States. The proposer would almost certainly try to bolster such a position both by reference to a variety of moral arguments ("Pollution controls are incompatible with personal liberties and incompatible with property rights") and by reference to a variety of alleged facts ("Pollution control is expensive and reduces productivity"). Because a variety of moral arguments and facts are used, clarity, consistency, and accuracy can all be checked. Consequently, it would be incorrect to say that one person's position on pollution control is as good as another's. One position may be either clearer, more consistent, or more factually accurate, and if so, it is the logically superior position.

Russell concludes his defense of subjectivism with what might be taken to be an *ad hominem* argument (Gula fallacy 43). Those individuals who cannot live without moral objectivity and certainty, like those who cannot live without God or God's heaven, are cowards:

Where traditional beliefs about the universe are concerned, craven fears . . . are considered praiseworthy, while intellectual courage, unlike courage in battle, is regarded as unfeeling and materialistic. . . . The universe is unjust . . . the secret of happiness is to face the fact that the world is horrible, horrible, horrible . . . you must feel it deeply and not brush it aside . . . you must feel it [in your heart] . . . and then you can start being happy again. . . . I cannot believe [that any good can come from] systems of thought which have their root in unworthy fears. . . . It is not by delusion, however exalted, that mankind can prosper, but only by unswerving courage in the pursuit of truth.

Logical subjectivism re-examined (further combinations of logic, experience, intuition, "science", and emotion)

Bertrand Russell was the last of the world-famous philosophers. His death at age ninety-eight in 1972 left no current philosopher with a comparable popular reputation.

Within universities, however, Russell, Ayer, and Stevenson's moral subjectivism was reworked, modified, or critiqued in a number of ways, some of which may be summarized as follows:

Linguistic philosophy

Even if moral opinions are entirely subjective, they can still be clarified, especially by applying a rigorous linguistic analysis. Although this idea is now sixty or more years old, it still inspires journal articles dealing with such questions as the meaning of the word *if* in the sentence: "If kangaroos had no tails, they would topple over" (a celebrated example that prompted much debate).

Philosophy as literature

This extraordinary doctrine turns philosophy on its head by apparently deemphasizing what has always been the very heart of logic: clarity, order, structure, the search for a teachable truth. Once "relaxed" in this way, philosophic works should be read for esthetic enjoyment—like poetry or a novel. As Ronald de Sousa of the University of Toronto wrote in 1985: "Good philosophy goes for subtlety, for the messy details—in short for the sort of thing we have novelists for. . . . When philosophy is . . . rich and nimble . . . it has its own esthetic rewards."

Philosophy as intermediary

In this view, espoused by Richard Rorty of Princeton, past president of the American Philosophical Association's eastern division, the questions that traditionally dominated philosophy have "dried up." A philosopher should no longer try to be a moral leader or cultural overseer but should instead act as "the informed dilettante, the Socratic intermediary between various discourses. . . . He can say something about the sciences to the humanities and say something about the humanities to the sciences — not because of any special philosophical expertise, but just because . . . [of] a general familiarity with the rest of culture." Rorty had to admit, however, that this job description left philosophers essentially indistinguishable "from the general all-purpose intellectual who writes for the *New York Review of Books*."

Intuitionism/utilitarianism

In his *Reasons and Persons* (1983), Derek Parfit of Oxford University combines elements of both attitudes in an engagingly eccentric way. He is a thoroughgoing mystic: Contrary to common sense beliefs, we are not really individuals; our selfhood, our sense of personal identity, are illusory; all of reality is one; we are elements of the whole. As Parfit comments: "The truth is very different from what we are inclined to believe. . . . Is the truth depressing? Some may find it so. But I find it liberating and consoling." Why is it consoling? Partly because "I care less about my death," but also because (and here we have a Benthamite twist) the absence of self kicks the stilts out from under selfishness. How can anyone want to be selfish when the self does not exist!?

Although Parfit thinks that he has some of the answers, there is much more work to be done: "Belief in God, or in many gods, prevented the free development of moral reasoning. Disbelief in God, openly admitted by a majority, is a very recent event, not yet completed. . . . Non-Religious Ethics has been systematically studied, by many people, only since about 1960. . . . [It] is at a very early stage. We cannot yet predict whether, as in Mathematics, we will all reach agreement. Since we cannot know how Ethics will develop, it is not irrational to have high hopes."

An example of the kind of problem that Parfit is working on:

Compare three outcomes:

a) Peace.

b) A nuclear war that kills 99 percent of the world's existing population.

c) A nuclear war that kills 100 percent.

(b) would be worse than (a), and (c) would be worse than (b). Which is the greater of these two differences?

A more vexing problem is how to justify a concern for future generations in a world where individuals do not exist. If all reality is one, why would a nuclear explosion matter? Parfit disarmingly responds: "Since I failed to find the principle to which we should appeal, I cannot explain the objection. . . . I believe that, though I have so far failed, I or others could find the needed principle: Theory X. But until this happens, [it] is . . . disturbing." Parfit then displays another Benthamite twist (moral consequences matter more than rules):

If possible [any conclusion about the immateriality of nuclear explosions] should be concealed from those who will decide whether we increase our use of nuclear energy. These people know that the Risky Policy might cause catastrophes in the further future. It would be better if these people believe, falsely, that the choice of the Risky Policy would be against the interests of the people killed by such a catastrophe. If they have this false belief, [false because "self" and "self-interest" have already been demonstrated to be non-existent], they would be more likely to reach the right decision.

Finally, in a characteristic aside, Parfit concludes that "if I or others soon solve these . . . problems, [they] will be, in a trivial way, welcome. We enjoy solving problems . . . [even though with] unsolved problems, we are further away from the Unified Theory . . . that resolves our disagreements . . . [in] truth."

Logical/emotive Jacobinism

This approach suggests, once again, that moral philosophy has rested on a mistake. Traditional moral philosophers have tended to focus on the individual, as if each individual were autonomous in his or her actions. As the ancient Greeks always emphasized, however, we are social creatures, and our moral decisions are made in a specific social and political context. Even if one accepts the philosophical idea of subjectivity, therefore, it does not mean that everyone is free to do as they please. Quite apart from the constraint of law, there is the necessity of getting along with others. In this sense, moral subjectivity is a pseudoproblem that merely clouds the real problem of social and political justice.

In one version of this argument, we construct a rational moral and political philosophy by asking ourselves what we would do if we were shipwrecked on a desert island with everyone else living on earth. What kind of "social contract" would we devise, basically starting from scratch, and not knowing the kind of society that would eventually evolve on the island? For John Rawls of Harvard, the answer is that we would start with a doctrine of "fairness," that is, that "all social values — liberty and opportunity, income and wealth, and the bases of self-respect — are to be distributed equally unless an unequal distribution of any, or all, of these values is to everyone's advantage. . . . If certain inequalities . . . would make everyone better off than in this hypothetical starting situation [for example, allowing a student more education in order to become a doctor], then they accord with the general conception."

Obviously, there are numerous artificialities about this method and conclusion. We are not necessarily rational beings, as Rawls assumes. We are not shipwrecked but rather grow up in families and communities that shape our outlook, and we do know quite a lot about the kind of society in which we will live. Even if we did not know, and had to choose, as Rawls says, under a "veil of ignorance," it is not at all clear that we would choose the "safe" alternative, a society based on complete equality, rather than the "gambling" alternative, a society based on merit and the reward of talents, or even on private property and inheritance rights. One wonders if Rawls, in choosing equality as his starting premise, is not merely extrapolating the social democratic beliefs of his own circle, rather as Prichard assumed that all the world thought like a cultivated Englishman (although, to be fair, a member of Rawls's circle, his Harvard colleague Robert Nozick, has published a strong attack on the equality principle).

Putting all these criticisms aside, however, one wonders if Rawls is not missing the larger point, that moral philosophy is not just political philosophy, not just social constraints and arrangements. Whatever social and political structure exists— even if the structure is highly repressive, as in the Soviet Union or South Africa—the individual is left with private moral choices. A philosophy that excludes such private choices as a field for discussion cannot claim to be a complete philosophy.

Logical/emotive conservatism

Like Mortimer Adler of the University of Chicago, Alastair MacIntyre of Notre Dame University is an Aristotelian who wants to return moral philosophy to its Greek roots. Like John Rawls, he believes that moral philosophy cannot be separated from a social and political context. In other respects, however, particularly his emphasis on history and tradition and his political conservatism, MacIntyre is the opposite of the other two.

MacIntyre begins by lamenting the confusion, rootlessness, and anomie, the interminable and irresolvable debates, that subjectivism has foisted on American society. This state of affairs, he says, is nothing less than "disastrous," but there is a way out, actually a way back—to ancient wisdom. Consider once again the is/ought conundrum defined by Hume. When speaking of a functional object such as an inexpensive watch, one can certainly state a fact, such as, "The watch does not work," and then derive an ought, such as, "I ought to fix the watch or throw it away." Although philosophers have usually distinguished between a watch and a human on the ground that the function of the watch is clear whereas that of a human is not, this distinction is actually quite wrong. Human purpose and function are clear: To discern what they are, one need only consult history or, as a shortcut, Aristotle's *Nichomachean Ethics*.

What, then, does Aristotle say? In MacIntyre's reading, he says that humans are social and political creatures, that their proper function and all their happiness lie in shared activity, and especially in selflessly building and serving a community. Moreover, specific virtues facilitate, but are also intrinsic to, this enterprise: honesty, fairness, reliability, consistency, obedience to law, courage, courtesy, judgment, among others. These virtues make it possible to work together; to create friendships based not solely on the shifting sands of affection but on the surer foundation of partnership and shared accomplishment. An individual human being, especially an individual obsessed with his or her own pleasure and well-being, is afunctional and miserable. But a human being as a *politikon zoon*, a member of a family and a larger political community, can achieve "merit," "honor," "harmony," and purposefulness.

MacIntyre has no illusions that we can return to the life of a Greek city-state. Nor is he a slavish follower of Aristotle. He notes that his favorite philosopher, like all philosophers, was connected to a specific time and place—one that denigrated women and permitted slavery, among other evils—and that he paradoxically contributed to the destruction of the city-state system by serving the Macedonian tyrant Philip and by teaching Philip's son, Alexander the Great. But however difficult it might be to restore the Greek ideal derived from the city-state, what MacIntyre calls "liberal individualism" must still be firmly resisted: "What matters at this stage is the construction of local forms of community within which civility and the intellectual and moral life can be sustained through the new dark ages which are already upon us."

Unlike most contemporary philosophers, MacIntyre has acquired a popular following. Perhaps this is because he has sought to deemphasize technique and return to the fundamental moral issues that trouble people. He has observed that studying "the concepts of morality merely by reflecting, Oxford armchair style, on what he or she or those around him or her say and do is barren" and has added that "the ideal of proof is . . . relatively barren" as well. Of the criticisms that have been leveled at MacIntyre's philosophy, some have been fair and some not. The charge that he is fascist cannot be supported: His concept of community specifically includes freedom and civil liberties, although perhaps not as many liberties as are taken for granted in American life today. The charge that his approach is vague, abstract, or romantic misses the point. What MacIntyre offers is a broad philosophy of history, not a road map for contemporary life and politics—a philosophy of history like that of Oswald Spengler, Arnold Toynbee, Edmund Burke, or ultimately the Jewish or Christian religion, from which all Western philosophies of history descend.

Applied ethics

Practitioners of contemporary applied ethics, preeminently Sissela Bok and Judith Shklar of Harvard University, remind us that moral disputes can be divided into at least four different categories.

1. Fundamental disputes pitting one entire value system against another opposite value system—for example, Polish Catholicism against Polish communism.
2. Disputes between parties who share a general, though perhaps ill-defined, agreement on ends, particularly family or friends.
3. Disputes between closely related parties that must be

resolved—for example, discussions of a legal bar association's canon of ethics, a hospital's approach to treating patients, or a White House internal policy dispute.

4. Legal disputes.

In the first category, moral philosophy may not provide ultimate answers. In this respect, subjectivism is correct. But answers may be logically derivable in the second category and must be derived in the third and fourth. Whatever category is involved, the moral philosopher plays a useful role in defining terms, spotting inconsistencies between multiple propositions, checking facts, clarifying consequences, grading various means to the same end, and effectively acting as a gatekeeper, bouncing "bad" arguments from the premises while allowing "good" arguments to continue to confront one another—either conclusively or inconclusively, as the case may be.

In their books and articles, applied ethicists tend to write about particular virtues or vices (*Lying*, by Bok; *Ordinary Vices*, by Shklar), grey areas between virtue and vice (*Secrets*, by Bok), specific social issues (abortion, euthanasia, animal experiments, surrogate mothers, industrial pollution, violent or obscene television, civil liberties), or a series of social issues grouped together under an important virtue or vice (such as, the issue of civil liberties in a discussion of government lying or secrecy). Such works mix anecdote with anthropology, specific people with sociological theory, colorful literary references (Lady Nijo's extramarital pregnancy in fourteenth-century Japan) with rigorous moral reasoning.

To a few friendly critics, there is a disproportion between the amount of effort required by this method and the payoff. Herbert Stein, a distinguished economist, commented about a 1983 book by Paul Menzel on medical ethics: "I repeatedly had the feeling that the only possible answers to the questions he raises [e.g., Should funds be allocated to preventative medicine or treatment? To rare killer diseases or more common, milder ones? To prolong the life of the old, or to save the young?] are 'I like it' or 'I don't like it.'" But Stein's dismissal is too easy. Applied ethics is something old that is nonetheless new and important. It is an instance of a discipline becoming larger by becoming smaller, of opening up horizons by restricting its vision. Teaching students about verbal clarity, consistency, the avoidance of logical fallacies, the application of these skills to real life—all this is potentially invaluable. To pursue this calling is not to disavow the more traditional, more grandiose modes of philosophizing, but to bring the entire philosophical enterprise back to the modesty of Socrates and thus to put it on a steadier, more sustainable course.

Value systems currently taught, reflected, or alluded to in college *humanities* courses (such value systems generally combine sense experience with emotion, logic, and "science")

The religion of high sense experience described in chapter 5 says that there are no formulas, no precise blueprints for building a life. Everyone has to find his or her way by living, traveling, reading, looking, and listening—in brief, by experiencing, but by experiencing with a necessary degree of self-discipline. The related religion of prodigal sense experience generally dispenses with the self-discipline. The contemporary academic religion of sense experience (represented especially by professors of literature, but also of history and art) clearly lines up with high sense experience—it wants the discipline in, but also deviates from high experience by borrowing ideas, concepts, and values from very different sources, notably emotion, logic, and "science." From emotion, the idea of social commitment—the notion that everything we do must somehow relate to politics and social issues—has steadily crept in. From "science," a whole series of ideas have been absorbed, beginning with an emphasis on professional specialization, professional technique, hidden knowledge available only to specialists, and extending to the notion that research and study must be "useful." From logical subjectivism (itself a cross between logic and "science") has come a pervading skepticism about the meaning and content of language, a skepticism that is most violently expressed by a form of literary criticism called deconstructionism. Whatever the "ism," we must always remember that when we observe professors arguing about how to teach history or literature or art or music, we are always, at least to a degree, watching them argue about how to live, and such quarrels can be both fierce and unrelenting. To try to make sense of all this, we will begin with some of the simpler ideas fighting it out in contemporary college and university humanities departments, then sample a few of the more recondite approaches.

Critical specialization

In practice, the idea of concentrating on a small field, emphasizing depth over breadth, produces the most sublime or the most ridiculous results. An example of the sublime, achieved at considerable self-sacrifice, is the University of Pennsylvania's Sumerian Dictionary project. As one of its authors, Erle Leichty, reports:

> To be an Assyriologist [a professional student of the Assyrians in the ancient Middle East, but also, by extension, of ancient Sumerians and other neighboring peoples] you don't have to be crazy, but it helps. . . . Not only is the path [toward a Ph.D. in Assyriology] fraught with pitfalls, traps and barriers, but there is no light at the end of the tunnel. I remember that my first teacher in Assyriology, George Cameron, told me the first day: There are no jobs in Assyriology, there never have been any jobs in Assyriology, and there never will be any jobs in Assyriology. . . . A few [Assyriologists] spend part or most of their careers in virtual slavery, working on large research projects such as the Pennsylvania Sumerian Dictionary. This . . . group is acutely aware of the meaning of 'soft money.' The next grant is all that stands between them and the unemployment line.

Assyriology is a well-defined subject requiring an arduous and disciplined intellectual preparation. By contrast, literary specialties such as "The Trickster Figure in Chicano and Black Literature," or "The Absent Father in Fact, Metaphor, and Metaphysics in the Middle Generation of American Poets"—all topics highlighted at an early 1980s Modern Language Association convention—must be defined by their practitioners. Professor W. Jackson Bate of Harvard dismisses these latter specialities as a "progressive trivialization" of "humane letters." Barbara Johnson of Yale then dismisses Bate: "[He] uses the word 'human' or 'humane' all the time," but means "anything that makes a white, dominant-class, Harvard-affiliated male feel good about himself." If some subjects are "trivial to him," the explanation is that "none of them are what he is."

Similar chaffing can be heard about what Jonathan Yardley rather harshly calls the "Faulkner factory," the concatenation of scholarship that results when a great number of people rush into the same speciality:

Within the ranks of American literary academicians, there are two great industries. One of these is the writing, photocopying and broadcasting of resumés. . . . The other is the exhumation of the literary remains of William Faulkner, America's greatest writer and these days its most exhaustively scrutinized by the drones of academe.

By now Faulkner Inc. should be a candidate for the Fortune 500. Certainly its "output"—the word is used advisedly—is proof positive that productivity in America is not dead. For a decade or more a mighty river of Faulkneriana has spewed forth from English departments, filling untold miles of library shelves with microfilm copies of deservedly unpublished doctoral dissertations; university presses lard their lists with scholarly exegeses of Faulkner's work both great and small; small presses enter the fray with facsimile editions of the great man's fugitive work. . . .

[All] these labors serve only to stifle literature, to smother it under the accumulated weight of scholarship that exists only for its own sake, to alienate the general reader who is deliberately excluded from the world of the 'professionals.' . . .

The belief is widespread within the academy that . . . a literary reputation such as Faulkner's is made 'a fact' by the endeavors of the drones of academe. . . . But the drones don't produce serious criticism; they produce makework, and the only people who read it are other drones. To imagine that the literary reputation of William Faulkner is enlarged or diminished by a thesis or dissertation grubbed out in order to meet the academy's voracious appetite for the trivial is the height of folly—or, more likely, of arrogance. The reputations that are made and broken within the academy have no effect on the real world out there.

New criticism

New critics wanted to cut through the luxuriant overgrowth of contextual scholarship and concentrate directly on the "naked" text or object. What do the words actually say? How are they used? The entire exercise of "close reading" seems modest, objective, down to earth, especially in the hands of American critics such as Robert Penn Warren and Cleanth Brooks, but the underlying motivation may be strikingly visionary. The English new critic I. A. Richards has argued that literature "is capable of saving us . . . of overcoming [the] chaos [of scientific industrialism] by supplying new unifying myths" to replace the discredited popular myth of Christianity. Richards' colleague F. R. Leavis goes further: Literature (and by extension history or art) is synonymous with the life-sustaining, creative, and civilizing force of the universe. To study this subject is not just useful, like studying law or science; it is the highest form of life imaginable.

Semiotics (semiological structuralism)

Semioticians (semiologists) are concerned with the "structure" of all human communication, which they assiduously study. As William McPherson has said about this effort: "One of the newest . . . religions . . . is the cult of the semiotician, whose field is the way we communicate with one another . . . what we mean by what we say and do. To the semiotician, everything is a form of communication and communication, naturally, is everything. Thus does the cult endure and its tribe increase. The new priestly caste, by the way, will consist of semioticians, among such other contemporary shamans as psychologists, anthropologists, and physicists."

Not every semiotician adopts the shamanistic style. Roland Barthes, perhaps the most celebrated semiotician, was a shy man ("I find it hard to bear seeing several people at a time") who lived simply in a sparsely furnished apartment near the University of Paris. He taught and also wrote elegantly crafted books extolling, among other things, "romantic" and "sentimental" love. Other semioticians are more earnest, cranking out tracts on such communication devices as traffic lights, medical symptoms, or cryptographic codes, or even consulting with government agencies on communication problems. In 1984, the Department of Energy asked Thomas A. Sebeok, a semiotician at the University of Indiana, to devise a way to "mark" nuclear waste dumps so that human beings of A.D. 12,000, who might no longer speak English, would be warned away from them. Sebeok filed a report suggesting that warnings

be launched and artificially passed on into the short-term and long-term future with the supplementary aid of folkloristic devices, in particular a combination of an artificially created and nurtured ritual-and-legend. . . . A ritual annually renewed can be foreseen, with the legend retold year-by-year. The actual 'truth' would be entrusted exclusively to—what we might call for dramatic emphasis—an 'atomic priesthood', that is, a commission . . . [that] would be charged with the added responsibility of seeing to it that our [warning], as embodied in the cumulative series of metamessages, is to be heeded—if not for legal reasons, then . . . with perhaps the veiled threat that to ignore the mandate would be tantamount to inviting some sort of supernatural retribution.

Deconstructionism

Deconstructionists* wish to overthrow, once and for all, the "great works, great men" school of literary criticism with its fixed canon of literary excellence and its fixed readings of established texts and objects. Works mean whatever you, the reader or viewer, think they mean, and meaning will vary from person to person. Deconstructionists literally shout from the rooftops: Down with elitism, down with "taste", down with tradition, down with all the "standards" and "certainties" of the aristocratic past. Nothing, or almost nothing, should be spared; every-

---

* Part of a larger group of poststructural hermeneuticists (*hermeneutics* means interpretation), also referred to as reader response theorists.

thing should be subjected to the same relentless leveling. Is Shakespeare's *Hamlet* a great work? Impossible to say, since the word *great* is an emotive—that is, a contentless and meaningless—word. What does the play *Hamlet* mean? Well, it is rife with linguistic contradictions and indeterminacies and may mean anything—or nothing.

In the hands of some critics, such a radical deconstruction of literal readings is not, itself, to be taken literally: It is ironic and meant to be fun. In the hands of others, such as the founding father of the movement, the French critic Jacques Derrida, the assault on literature and art is supposed to be the first step toward a worldwide political and social revolution—a revolution that is difficult to get off the ground because no one can understand Derrida, who writes in the following style: "Thus it has always been thought that the center, which is by definition unique, constituted that very thing within a structure which governs the structure, while escaping structurality. . . . The center is at the center of the totality, and yet, since the center does not belong to the totality (is not part of the totality), the totality has its center elsewhere." Evidently this kind of writing is highly communicable, because some American disciples have picked it up, as in the following example: "As we read him now, Homer is to us both what he is and what he is not. What he is not is the silent potential surrounding all that he is, and yet existing there, definingly, only because he is what he is in his work."

"Scientific" criticism

Of the various "scientific" modes of interpreting literature, history, and art, psychoanalysis is the most daring, because it often seeks to shock the reader. Matthew Arnold's famous line from the poem "Dover Beach," "Where ignorant armies clash by night," is actually about the sex life of his parents; T. S. Eliot's *The Waste Land* is an unwitting confession of homosexuality. The evidence for such assertions is scanty (a reviewer of the Eliot interpretation notes that the author "uses . . . speculation treated as fact to reinterpret poems, then uses his reinterpretations as evidence for the biographical 'fact'"), but slippery scholarship is concealed behind masses of jargon. Harold Bloom, one of the best-known Freudian literary critics, argues that the writing of poems represents an "Oedipal death-struggle" against the castrating power of precursor poets and then divides the struggle into six "reversionary ratios" styled "clinamen, tessera, kenosis, daemonization, askesis, and apophrades." If this seems a bit obscure, we are admonished that "no reader . . . can describe her or his relationship to a prior text without taking up a stance no less tropological than that occupied by the text itself." We are also assured that Bloom's interpretation — indeed, the interpretive act in general — is not mere criticism; it stands alone, independent of the poems or poets analyzed, a work of art in its own right. Not surprisingly, this example of hubris (to maintain the classical motif) has created an enormous notoriety in literary circles and inspired numerous symposia speakers, many of whom seem convinced that Bloom will be read and studied by future generations right alongside Milton, Wordsworth, Shelley, and Browning.

In contrast to the psychoanalytical mode of interpreting texts and art objects, the sociological mode has unquestionably opened up new vistas, especially in history: the lives of ordinary people living in huts rather than palaces; food; sex; health and medicine; marriage and death — all those subjects that add up to the "day-to-dayness" of life. When social historians and sociological literary critics focus on these neglected topics, ransacking the archives for long-forgotten and often quite illuminating facts, the effect is to liberate historiography and criticism from the stuffy, aristocratic biases of the past. Unfortunately, these same facts, painstakingly rescued by sometimes heroic feats of research, are all too often obscured by such woolly concepts as "elites" or "social class," neither of which have ever been satisfactorily defined or empirically validated, or else they are drowned in Marxism, a Marxism that is not sociology at all but a stridently ideological and emotive religion of egalitarianism. Occasionally the tension between old-fashioned critics, who want to concentrate on history and literature and art itself, and the Marxists, who look through these subjects to a hidden agenda of class conflict and capitalistic and bourgeois oppression, erupts into a violent war of words. Sidney Freedberg of Harvard laments that "the political direction of the [art] department has become notorious. Some members of the faculty have gone so far as to suggest that works of art be sold . . . almost as if they were a capitalistic self-indulgence." A Philadelphia curator agrees: "As far as art history goes at Harvard, the things in the museums might as well be a thousand miles away." The direct object of Freedberg's wrath, the "avowed Marxist" professor Tim J. Clark, responds: "I have no interest in grayness, in indiscriminate leveling. Neither, in fact, did Marx. He was a worshipper of Greek art, a fanatic for Balzac and constantly quoting Shakespeare and Goethe." An even fiercer partisan of the "leather jacket" school of art criticism excoriates old-style connoisseurship as "handmade shoes and bow ties and clothes from Savile Row," as either being rich or chasing after the rich—in short, as a decadent and snobbish aestheticism that offends "decent" as well as "proletarian" values.

Political criticism

Montaigne would have strongly disapproved of both psychoanalysis and sociology, especially the kind of psychoanalysis and sociology that really just covers for frankly emotive politicking, but he would have been even more appalled by the purely emotive and political approach to teaching and experiencing literature, history, or art. In his view, great works were to be treasured as a window on life, not distorted in the service of some tawdrily abstract political cause. He would have been equally unhappy with patriotic criticism of the type sponsored by George Gordon earlier this century at Oxford ("England is sick, and . . . English literature must save it. . . . The Churches . . . have failed, and social remedies being slow, English literature has now a triple function: still, I suppose, to delight and instruct us, but also, and above all, to save our souls and heal the State") *and* with the sourily unpatriotic contemporary criticism depicted by A. M. Eckstein of the University of Maryland:

[At] a conference on [George] Orwell and "1984" at an unnamed mid-western university . . . [the first speaker talked about] the "oppression" of psychotics in America; [the second] did not even attempt to keep to a topic related to Orwell, launching instead a direct and impassioned appeal for support for his own particular group of nuclear-freeze activists; [the third] spent his time fiercely advocating vegetarianism . . . and castigating U.S. capitalism for failing to inform people that "when they eat meat, they eat death"; [the fourth and fifth speakers continued in the same vein and the sixth launched] a bitter, hourlong attack on America—and only America—for its lies, distortions, evasions and hypocrisy.

Looking at these methods as a whole—from specialization to deconstruction to political criticism—it appears that professors of literature, history, and art are still a little unsure of how to deal with the modern world of science and mass culture. For centuries, most teachers of what we now call the humanities shared some common beliefs descended from Montaigne: that experience is both a means and an end of life; that works of literature, history, and art are supremely important as interpreters of experience; that the very greatest works, those preserved and handed down from generation to generation, provide a magic passage to a larger world; that through them, and only through them, one learns to enjoy the variety of life without being overwhelmed, to separate the gold from the dross, to acquire taste, to form personal standards, both moral and esthetic, of the very highest order. Very gradually, two new ideas have insinuated their way into this beautiful ideal of the most splendid high culture, ideas that are foreign to the original conception and that are now locked in an Oedipal death struggle (to borrow critic Harold Bloom's phrase) for survival and dominance.

The first of these ideas is that personal experience and observation, the empirical method, the concentration on fact, especially the fact of a particular work of literature or art, are no longer enough. What counts is not experience per se, but what is thought to lie beneath the surface of experience, that is, symbolic patterns or structures. This emphasis on abstraction over fact, theory over experience, defines a totally new direction, a striking reversal of the historic approach to teaching literature, history, and art.

The second new idea that is transforming college and university humanities departments is that of relevance. This notion takes so many forms it is difficult to enumerate them all: the resurgence of frankly ideological criticism; the rapid spread of what is called literacy studies as a new literary specialty, although the primary emphasis is on theory rather than on teaching people to read and write; calls for a return to an "open" and "accessible" form of literary criticism; the growing demand for interdisciplinary studies or especially the willingness of some leading literary academicians to appear in *People* magazine (Paul Fussell of the University of Pennsylvania) or to admit their fondness for daytime television "soaps" (William Pritchard of Amherst writing in *TV Guide*).

The problem, of course, with all these concepts of relevance is that, like most literary terms, they are very much in the eye of the beholder. Professor Bate of Harvard considers deconstructionism to be remote, esoteric, trivial, a form of secret and malevolent gnosticism, thus clearly "irrelevant." Opponents of Bate, on the other hand, think that his reverence for the old ideal of directly teaching "great works, great men" is so elitist that, even if it deals with the most common, everyday human concerns, it is still, by definition, remote, esoteric, irrelevant, and so on. Indeed, one of the ironies of the current warfare in the humanities departments is that these same terms of abuse (along with other favorites such as "self-absorbed," "decadent," and especially "faddish") are regularly applied by each party to its opponent much in the way that the United States during the Cold War referred to the Soviet Union as antidemocratic and the Soviets tossed back the same word, weirdly redefined, at the U.S.

Whereto these particular quarrels? No one can say. But it is fair to observe that both extreme abstractionism and extreme relevance seem to be losing some momentum. Much effort has gone into elaborate theoretical constructs like reader response theory. Will future generations want to keep them up? Should they? Even more fundamentally, will the humanities, which have always focused on and been defined by specific texts, objects, and facts, renew themselves by turning away from direct experience? It would seem doubtful. If the humanities are to thrive, to recover lost ground and lost prestige, to recapture the exhilarating achievements of the past—as when professors of literature and history battled churchmen in the eighteenth and nineteenth centuries for control of the great universities and won—it must presumably find answers that are rooted in the great works and objects themselves; in a reaffirmation of the belief that literature, history, and art are supremely important (and always relevant) because they offer what James Wolcott has called "contesting visions of what's true and what's good"; in the repetition of familiar but necessary critical tasks; in the patient transmission of important and easily lost-sight-of experience from the past; and in the continual search for experience worth preserving and passing on to future generations.

How to Read
This Book

Apart from the first chapter, this book is comprised of **three basic** building blocks:

1. Summary presentation of a particular theory, model, **or tax**-onomy of values.
2. Descriptions of each of the six types of value systems distin-guished by the theory, model, or taxonomy.
3. Examples (case studies) of specific value systems drawn from each of the six types of value systems or composites of the six types of value systems.

Depending on the reader's interests, it is possible to read the entire book as written, to concentrate on one or more of the three building blocks, or to concentrate on specific value systems of interest—for example, Christian fundamentalism or Freudian psychology, to name two that are immediately recognizable to most people. Although the index is an indispensable tool for any-one who does not wish to read the book straight through or who, having done so, wishes to consult it again, the following detailed table of contents may also be helpful:

		Pages
1.	Summary presentation of a particular	6–20
	theory, model, or taxonomy of values:	135–41
		158–63
		167–74
		175–84
		185–88

Pages

2. Descriptions of each of the six types of
   value systems distinguished by the theory,
   model, or taxonomy of values:

   • Authority   23–24

   • Logic   38–47
                                                  51–52

   • Sense experience   53
                                                  69–75
                                                  75–77
                                                  83–85
                                                  246–47
                                                  254–56

   • Emotion   86–92
                                                  93–97
                                                  189–90

   • Intuition   98–104
                                                  106–8

   • Science   109–12
                                                  131

3. Seventy-one examples (case studies) of
   specific value systems drawn from each
   of the six types of value systems or composites of them:

   • Johannine Daist Communion (an Ameri-   24–25
     can spiritual community)

   • Protestant fundamentalism   25–30

   • Roman Catholicism   30–37

   • Spinoza (seventeenth-century philoso-   47–50
     pher living in Holland)

Pages

- Mortimer Adler (American philosopher)   50–51

- Eudora Welty (American author)   53–55

- Michel de Montaigne (sixteenth-century French essayist)   55–69

- Thomas Merton (American author and Trappist monk)   76

- Lawrence Durrell (Anglo-Irish author)   77–79

- Henry Miller (American author)   79

- Harold Acton (Anglo-American author)   79–81

- Richard Nelson (creative director in advertising)   81

- Constantine Cavafy (Greek author living in Egypt)   82

- Tennessee Williams (American author)   82–83, 85

- Ronald Reagan (American president)   90, 202

- Mikhail Gorbachev (Soviet Communist General Secretary)   90–91

- Mitch Snyder and Carol Fennelly (social activists and advocates for the homeless)   92–93

- Sawan Kirpal Ruhani Mission (Indian spiritual movement)   105–6

- Freudian psychology, updated by Anna Freud and George Vaillant   112–18

- Cognitive psychology, developed by Karen Horney and Aaron T. Beck   118–20

- Psycho-neuro-immunological medicine, critiqued by Ellen Goodman   121–23

Pages

- Combination of Freudian defense theory and psycho-neuro-medicine — 123–25
- Socio-demo-anthro-eco-enviro-techno model building — 125–26
- Sociobiology — 126–29
- Behavioral psychology, especially B. F. Skinner (American psychologist) — 129–31
- The nonfundamentalist, nonmodernist Christianity of Karl Barth (Swiss, leading Protestant theologian) — 142–46
- The neo-Buddhism of Albert Einstein (preeminent physicist of twentieth century) — 146–53
- The "detached action" of Mohandas Gandhi (founder of modern India) — 153–55
- The Judaism of Golda Meir (one of the founders and prime minister of Israel) — 155–57
- Jean Meslier (eighteenth-century French priest who secretly hated Christianity) — 158–59
- Alexander Solzhenitsyn (Russian author) — 159, 201–2
- Pat Robertson (American Evangelist) — 162–63
- Allan Bloom (American political and moral philosopher) — 167–73
- Suburban Marylander — 174

(From Epilogue)
- Classical liberalism, as updated by Judith Shklar — 190–92

Pages

- Jacobinism (e.g., American senators Ted   193–94
Kennedy, George McGovern, and Barbara
Mikulski)

- Jacobin utilitarianism (e.g., American   194–96
politicians Ralph Nader, Jerry Brown,
Jimmy Carter, and Michael Dukakis)

- Violent revolutionism   197–98

- Classical conservatism   199–202

- Contemporary conservatism   202–3

- Contemporary liberalism   202–3

- Secular puritanism, also nonreligious   203–4
fundamentalism (e.g., former British
Prime Minister Margaret Thatcher)

- Mandarinism (e.g., former American   204–6
secretary of state Henry Kissinger)

- Entrepreneurialism   206–7

- Legalism (religion of law)   207–8

- Social Darwinism (e.g., American Wall   208–10
Street firms)

- Capitalism (as religion)   210–14

- Utopian communism   214–16

- Democratic socialism (e.g., American   216–18
socialists Dorothy Day and Michael
Harrington)

- Agrarianism   218–19

- Southern agrarianism   219–22

- Agrarian populism   222–23

Pages

- Technocratic agrarianism (e.g., American writer and inventor Buckminster Fuller) 223–24

- Simple communitarianism 224

- Conservationism (e.g., Kathryn Fuller) 224–25

- Logical naturalism (e.g., nineteenth-century British philosophers Jeremy Bentham and John Stuart Mill) 225–29

- Logical intuitionism (e.g., British philosophers G. E. Moore and H. A. Prichard) 229–34

- Logical subjectivism (e.g., British and American philosophers Ludwig Wittgenstein, Bertrand Russell, Alfred T. Ayer, and Charles Stevenson) 234–38

- Linguistic philosophy 238

- Philosophy as literature 238–39

- Philosophy as Intermediary 239

- Intuitionism/utilitarianism (e.g., British philosopher Derek Parfit) 239–41

- Logical/emotive Jacobinism (e.g., American philosopher John Rawls) 241–42

- Logical/emotive conservatism (e.g., American philosopher Alastair MacIntyre) 242–44

- Applied ethics (e.g., American philosophers Sissela Bok and Judith Shklar) 244–46

- Critical specialization 247–49

- New criticism 249

	Pages
• Semiotics	249–50
• Deconstructionism	250–51
• "Scientific" criticism	251–53
• Political criticism	253–54

Sources

For a complete list of sources keyed to the text, please write the author at: Route 2, Box 426, Crozet, VA 22932.

Books

Acheson, Dean. *Fragments of My Fleece*. New York: W.W. Norton, 1971.

Acton, Harold. *More Memoirs of an Esthete*. London: Methuen & Co., 1970.

Adams, Henry. *The Education of Henry Adams*. Cambridge, MA: Riverside Press, 1961.

————. *Mont St. Michel and Chartres*. Boston: Houghton Mifflin Co., 1933.

Adler, Mortimer. *Ten Philosophical Mistakes*. New York: Macmillan, 1985.

Ayer, A.J. *Language, Truth, and Logic*. New York: Dover Publications, 1952.

Barrett, William. *The Illusion of Technique*. New York: Anchor Press/Doubleday, 1978.

Barth, Karl. *The Word of God and the Word of Man*. New York: Harper & Row, 1957.

Berlin, Isaiah. *Personal Impressions*, edited by Henry Hardy. New York: Penguin Books, 1982.

Bloom, Allan. *The Closing of the American Mind*. New York: Simon & Schuster, 1987.

Brinton, Crane. *Ideas & Men*. Englewood Cliffs, NJ: Prentice-Hall, 1963.

Burns, David D. *Feeling Good*. New York: William Morrow & Company, 1980.

Cavafy, C.P. *Collected Poems*. Princeton, NJ: Princeton University Press, 1975.

Chesterson, G.K. *The Everlasting Man*. New York: Dodd, Mead & Co., 1925.

Cox, Harvey. *Religion in the Secular City: Toward a Postmodern Theology*. New York: Simon & Schuster, 1985.

Da Free John. *The Enlightenment of the Whole Body*. San Rafael, CA: Dawn Horse Press, 1980.

Durant, Will. *The Story of Philosophy*. New York: Simon & Schuster, 1926.
————, and Ariel Durant. *The Age of Louis XIV*. New York: Simon & Schuster, 1963.
————. *The Age of Napoleon*. New York: Simon & Schuster, 1975.
Durrell, Lawrence. *The Big Supposer: An Interview by Marc Alyn*. New York: Grove Press, Inc., 1974.
————. *The Black Book*. New York: E. P. Dutton, 1960.
————. *Prospero's Cell*. London: Faber & Faber, 1945.
Eagleton, Terry. *Literary Theory*. Minneapolis, MN: University of Minnesota Press, 1983.
Edwards, Paul, ed. *Encyclopedia of Philosophy*. New York: Macmillan Publishing and The Free Press, 1967.
Fracchia, Charles A. *Living Alone Together*. San Francisco: Harper & Row, 1979.
Fuller, Buckminster. *Utopia or Oblivion*. New York: Bantam, 1969.
Gay, Peter. *The Enlightenment: An Interpretation*. New York: Alfred A. Knopf, 1969.
Gerth, H. H., and C. Wright Mills, eds. *From Max Weber: Essays in Sociology*. New York: Oxford University Press, 1958.
Gula, Robert. *Nonsense: How to Overcome It*. New York: Stein & Day, 1979.
Harrod, Roy. *Life of John Maynard Keynes*. New York: Avon Books, 1951.
Havard, William C., and Walter Sullivan, eds. *A Band of Prophets: The Vanderbilt Agrarians After Fifty Years*. Baton Rouge: Louisiana University Press, 1982.
Hittleman, Richard. *Guide to Yoga Meditation*. New York: Bantam, 1969.
Holroyd, Michael. *Lytton Strachey: A Critical Biography*. New York: Holt Rinehart & Winston, 1968.
Hume, David. *An Enquiry Concerning Human Understanding*, edited by P. H. Nidditch. New York: The Liberal Arts Press, 1975.
————. *Treatise of Human Nature*. London: MacMillan Publishers, 1979.
Huxley, Aldous. *The Perennial Philosophy*. New York: Harper & Row, 1970.
Johnson, Paul. *Modern Times*. New York: Harper & Row, 1985.
Johnson, Oliver A., ed. *Ethics*. New York: Holt Rinehart & Winston, 1984.
Keynes, John Maynard. *Essays in Biography*. London: MacMillan, 1972.
————. *Essays in Persuasion*. New York: W. W. Norton, 1963.
Lippmann, Walter. *A Preface to Morals*. New York: Macmillan Publishing, 1929.
MacIntyre, Alasdair. *After Virtue*. Notre Dame, IN: University of Notre Dame Press, 1981.

Meir, Golda. *My Life*. New York: Putnam, 1975.

Mencken, H. L. *A Mencken Chrestomathy*. New York: Knopf, 1949.

Merton, Thomas. *Seven Storey Mountain*. New York: Harcourt Brace Jovanovich, 1948.

———. *The Way of Chuang-Tzu*. New York: New Directions, 1965.

Montaigne, Michel de. *Essays*, translated by J. M. Cohen. London: Penguin Books, Ltd., 1953.

———. *Montaigne's Travel Journal*. San Francisco: North Point Press, 1983.

Norman, Richard. *The Moral Philosophers: An Introduction to Ethics*. New York: Oxford University Press, 1983.

Owsley, Frank, and Andrew N. Lytle, et al. *I'll Take My Stand: The South and the Agrarian Tradition by Twelve Southerners*. New York: Harper & Row, 1930.

Parfit, Derek. *Reasons and Persons*. New York: Oxford University Press, 1985.

Rawls, John. *A Theory of Justice*. Cambridge, MA: Belknap Press of Harvard University, 1971.

Reich, Wilhelm. *The Sexual Revolution*. New York: Farrar, Straus & Giroux, 1974.

Russell, Bertrand. *A History of Western Philosophy*. New York: Simon & Schuster, 1945.

———. *The Basic Writings of Bertrand Russell*. New York: Simon & Schuster, 1956.

———. *Religion & Science*. New York: Oxford University Press, 1961.

———. *Fact and Fiction*. London: Allen & Unwin, 1961.

Schaeffer, Francis A. *Escape from Reason*. Downers Grove, IL: InterVarsity Press, 1968.

Skinner, B. F. *Beyond Freedom and Dignity*. New York: Knopf, 1971.

Somervell, David C. *English Thought in the 19th Century*. New York: David McKay Co., Inc. 1965.

Spinoza, Benedict de. "On the Improvement of the Understanding" from *The Chief Works of Benedict de Spinoza*, translated from the Latin with an introduction by R. H. Elwes. New York: Dover Publications, 1951.

Vaillant, George G. *Adaptation to Life*. Boston: Little, Brown & Co., 1977.

Welty, Eudora. *One Writer's Beginning*. Cambridge, MA: G. K. Hall, 1984.

———. *The Collected Stories of Eudora Welty*. New York: Harcourt Brace Jovanovich, 1980.

Williams, Tennessee. *Memoirs of Tennessee Williams*. New York: Doubleday, 1975.

Worthington, Vivian. *History of Yoga*. London: Routledge & Kegan Paul, 1982.

Periodicals

Business Week
Chronicle of Higher Education
Daedalus
Executive Health Report
Forbes
Fortune
Harvard Magazine
Laughing Man Magazine
Mind
New Age Journal
Newsweek

People Magazine
Playboy
Reader's Digest
Revision
Smithsonian
University of Pennsylvania
   Museum Newsletter
Vanity Fair
The Virginian
W Magazine

Newspapers

The New York Times
The Village Voice

The Wall Street Journal
The Washington Post

Television

ABC News
Billy Graham—Anaheim,
   California Crusade

McNeil/Lehrer News Hour

Index

Abortion, 191
Abstraction: humanities and, 254–55, 256; Montaigne and, 61–62
Abzug, Bella, 222
Acheson, Dean, 95
Acting out, as defense, 115, 188n
Acton, Harold, 79–81
Adams, Henry, 218–19
Adaption to Life (Vaillant), 113–14
Ad hominen argument, 237
Adler, Mortimer, 47, 50–52, 149–50, 242
Aesthete, 79–81
Africa, Catholics in, 36
Age of Reason, 160
Agrarianism, 218–25
Ajaya, Swami, 141
Alexander the Great, 243
Alger, Ferris, 98
Alsop, Joseph, 74–75
Altruism: as defense, 116, 118n; logical naturalism and, 227; sociobiology and, 127
Ambition, Montaigne and, 65–67
America: and authority, 23–24; in Cold War, 116, 255; and compound interest, 211; and democratic socialism, 217; fundamentalists' view of, 29–30, 35; revolutionists of, 197n
American Humanist Association, 177
American Philosophical Association, 239
Anarchy, social, 46
Anderson, Sherwood, 221
Anger, as emotional category, 121n

"Anthropic principle," 49
Anticipation, as defense, 116, 118n
Apostles' Creed, Barth and, 145–46
Applied ethics, 244–46
Arab cultures, economics of, 212
Aristocratic agrarianism, 219–22
Aristotle, 41, 149, 243
Arnold, Matthew, 251
Art, 253, 256. *See also* Literature
Assyriology, 247–48
Atheists, 13, 29, 178
Athens, 20, 170, 187
Authoritarianism: and equality, 217; Solzhenitsyn and, 159, 201–2
Authority, 9, 10, 12, 14, 23–37, 141, 185, 186; Adler and, 50; Barth and, 142, 146; and bias, 18; Bible as, 24, 25–26, 27–28; 86; Bloom and, 169; Buddhism and, 148; conditional, 23–24; defenses and, 117n; divine revelation as, 13; education and, 184; identifying mode of, 16; institutional, 24, 29, 30–37; Meir and, 155; migration of, 161, 162; Montaigne and, 59–61, 71; and "science," 140–41; summarized, 135; unconditional, 23, 24–30. *See also* Christianity
Aversion therapy, 129
"Axiology," in schools, 183–84
Ayer, Alfred J., 234, 235–36, 238

Bacon, Francis, 160
Banting, Frederick Grant, 98
Banya, 154
Barfly, 173

Barth, Karl, 142–46, 213
Barthes, Roland, 249–50
Bastille, fall of, 197
Bate, W. Jackson, 248, 255
Bauer, Gary, 175, 176
Beck, Aaron T., 119, 120
Behavioral psychology, 129–31
Beliefs: values as, 7, 8, 9. *See also*
Values
Bennett, William, 176
Benson, Herbert, 103
Bentham, Jeremy, 226–27, 229, 235;
Hume and, 228, 229; logical intui-
tionism and, 229, 232; Parfit and,
239, 240
Bhagavad-Gita, 153–54
Bias, 17–19
Bible: as authority, 24, 25–26, 27–28,
86; Barth and, 146; "historical-
critical" method with, 27; inerrancy
of, 27–28; and logic, 44
Biological determinism, 127, 128
Birth control, 32
Blood values, 88–91. *See also* Family;
Nationalism
Bloom, Allan, 167–73, 174, 176, 184
Bloom, Harold, 252, 254
Bok, Sissela, 244
Bolingbroke, Lord, 74
Boorstin, Daniel, 192
Braudel, Fernand, 212
Breckinridge, Mary, 97
Brezhnev, Leonid, 91, 210
Brideshead Revisited (Waugh), 85
Brinton, Crane, 192
Britain: and compound interest, 211;
and Gandhi, 154–55; and man-
darinism, 205; Thatcher in, 203
Brooks, Cleanth, 182, 249
Brown, Jerry, 194, 195, 196
Bryan, William Jennings, 181
Buddha, 40, 147–49, 151–52
Buddhism: Einstein and, 146, 147,
152–53; and intuition, 107, 146–48,
153; and logic, 44; Neo-, 147,
152–53; original, 147–52

Burke, Edmund, 201, 244
Burns, David D., 119
Bush, George, 90, 203

Callicles, 149
Calvin, John, 26
Cameron, George, 247
Capitalism, 210–14, 218; classical
conservatism and, 201; fundamen-
talists and, 29, 30, 32–35; Harring-
ton and, 217
Carter, Jimmy, 194, 195–96
Cash, W. J., 221
Castrillón, Hoyos Dario, 36
Cataloguing: common fallacies,
41–43; and Montaigne, 69–71
Catholic Bishops' Synod, 32
Catholic Church: authority of, 24,
30–37; Barth and, 143; classical
liberalism and, 191; Merton and,
76; Meslier and, 159; Montaigne
and, 71, 75; and political action,
33–34, 36–37; women and, 36
Catholic Worker Movement, 216
Cavafy, Constantine, 82
Celibacy, religious, 8, 32
Changeability: "science" and, 131; six
modes and, 15
Character disorders, 114–15, 116
Chesterton, G. K., 37, 147
China: economics in, 212; Forbidden
City, 197; mandarinate of, 204–5, 212
"Chosen" people, tribe and, 87
Christian Broadcasting Network, 162
Christianity, 12, 18, 185; Adler and,
50; and Age of Reason, 160; Barth
and, 142, 143–46; Bloom and, 169;
classical liberalism and, 191; and
emotive value system, 94, 96; Harrington and, 216; legalism and,
207–8; and logic, 44, 49, 50, 51; logical intuitionism and, 232; logical
naturalism and, 227; logical subjectivism and, 234–35; MacIntyre and,
244; Meslier and, 159; Montaigne
and, 59–61, 63, 67, 75; new criti-

cism and, 249; Robertson and, 162; schools and, 179–81; secular humanism and, 178, 179–81; and Spinoza, 49. *See also* Church; Protestants; Roman Catholics

Church: classical conservatism and, 199; classical liberalism and, 190–91, 193; and slavery, 180. *See also* Catholic Church

Churchill, Winston, 96

Clark, Tim J., 253

Class: emotive value systems based on, 91; Montaigne and, 64–65

Classical conservatism, 199–202, 203, 207

Classical liberalism, 189–93, 202, 203, 206, 207, 208, 210–11

Classroom. *See* Education

Closing of the American Mind (Bloom), 167–73

Cobb, Ty, 209

Cocteau, Jean, 82n

Cognitive psychology, 52, 118–20

Cohen, Richard, 175–77

Cold War, 116, 255

Coles, Robert, 180–81

Comforts, fundamentalists and, 29

Common fallacies, 41–43

Common sense, defined, 62

Communism, 189–90, 218; Harrington and, 216–17; utopian, 214–16. *See also* Leninism; Marxism

Communitarianism, simple, 224

Community: Bloom and, 170; classical conservatism and, 199, 207; and Jacobinism, 196; logical/emotive conservatism and, 243–44; revolutionists and, 197–98; vs. tribe, 88n

Community for Creative Non-Violence, 92–93

Compound interest, capitalism and, 211

Conditioning, 129–30

Confucianism, and logic, 44

Conscious mind: Bloom and, 171; Buddhism and, 150–51

Conservationism, 224–25

Conservatism: classical, 199–202, 203, 207; contemporary, 202–6; cultural, 203–4; logical/emotive, 242–44; political, 189–90, 199–206, 242

Constitution, U.S., 180

Control, 9; "science" and, 131. *See also* Self-discipline; Social control

Conversions, 161–63

Cosmological argument, for existence of God, 49

Countersyllogism, 42

Cox, Harvey, 141

Crane, Florence, 80–81

Crawford, James, 222–23

Creationism, 160, 181

Credentials, 18, 131, 171

Crime and Punishment (Dostoevsky), 208

Crimson, 198

Critical specialization, 247–49

Criticism: biblical, 27; literary, 247–49, 250–54, 255

Cubans, in Grenada, 90

"Cults," 24–25

Da Free John (Franklin Jones), 24–25

Darshan Singh, 105–6

Darwinism, Social, 208–10

Davidson, Donald, 221

Day, Dorothy, 216

Decadence, 81–82

Deception, six modes and, 15

Deconstructionism, 247, 250–51, 255

Deduction. *See* Logic (deductive)

Defenses, 113–18, 123–25; immature, 114–15; mature, 116; neurotic, 115–16; physical, 121; psychotic, 114

Delusional projection, as defense, 114, 118n

Democracy: church, 32; classical conservatism and, 201–2; and inequality, 217; political, 32, 159, 201–2, 216–18, 242; social, 216–18, 242

Democratic Party, 204

Denial, as defense, 114, 118, 124

Denver, John, 224

Depression, 119, 121n

Derrida, Jacques, 251

Desensitization techniques, 129

Desire, 149–50; Einstein and, 152–53

de Sousa, Ronald, 238–39

Detachment: and intuition, 103, 153–54, 160; sense experience and, 67, 160

Determinism: biological, 127, 128; environmental/cultural, 129–30

Dewey, John, 178

Dharma, 154

Dialectic, 40

Diderot, Denis, 58, 190–91

Different Drum (Peck), 88n

Discipline. *See* Self-discipline

Discoveries, recent, "science" and, 131, 171

Dishonesty, Montaigne and, 64–65

Displacement, as defense, 115–16; 118n

Disraeli, Benjamin, 201

Dissociation, as defense, 115, 118n

Distortion, as defense, 114, 118n

Divine revelation, mode of, 13

Divorce, fundamentalists and, 32

"Does Moral Philosophy Rest on a Mistake?" (Prichard), 234

Dostoevsky, Fyodor, 208

"Dover Beach" (Arnold), 251

Dukakis, Michael, 194, 196

Dunphy, John J., 178

Dunaway, Faye, 173, 174

Durrell, Lawrence, 77–79, 82

Eccentricity, Montaigne and, 65

Eckstein, A. M., 254

Economics, 210–25; classical conservatism and, 201, 203; fundamentalists and, 29, 30, 32–35; Jacobinism and, 202–3, 211; liberalism in, 202; mandarinism and, 205

Education: college and university, 160, 181–84, 189–256; elementary school, 175–81; secondary school, 175–81; values in, 159–60, 175–84, 188, 189–256

Efficiency, Jacobinism and, 194–95, 196, 203

Egoism, Montaigne and, 71–72

Einstein, Albert, 49, 146–53, 185

Eliot, T. S., 251

Elitism: conservatism and, 200, 204; and deconstructionism, 255; of Montaigne, 72–73

Emotion, 10, 12, 14–15, 86–97, 141, 174, 186; authority and, 140–41; Barth and, 142; Bloom and, 170–71; Buddhism and, 150–51; conservatism and, 205, 242–44, 246; criticisms of religion of, 93–97; defenses and, 117n; education and, 179, 184, 189, 190; Gandhi and, 153, 154, 155; and good/evil, 194; in humanities courses, 246; identifying mode of, 16; and intuition, 100, 101, 153–54, 160; and Jacobinism, 196, 241–42; logical subjectivism and, 238; Meir and, 155, 156; migration of, 161, 162; in political philosophy/political science courses, 189, 190; religion of, 93–97, 160, 190, 197; and revolutionism, 197–98; and sense experience, 95–96, 160, 253; summarized, 137–38; utilitarianism and, 229

Empirical reasoning: Freudian psychology and, 116; and humanities, 254–55; Montaigne and, 62–63; sociobiology and, 127, 128. *See also* Factuality

Enemy, tribe and, 87

"Enquiry Concerning Human Understanding" (Hume), 235

Entrepreneurialism, 205, 206–7, 208

Epictetus, 149

Equality: capitalism and, 212, 217; classical conservatism and, 200; Harrington and, 217; Jacobinism and, 194, 202, 241–42

Escape/Escapism, 75–85, 118, 124
Essay form, Montaigne and, 55, 70
Essays (Montaigne), 55–69
Ethics: applied, 244–46. *See also* Moral philosophy courses; Values
Evil, Jacobinism and, 193–94
Evolution vs. Genesis account, 181; genetic, 127
Experts: authority and, 23; "science" and, 131
Externalization, 118, 124
"Extroverts," 8

Factuality: in education, 183n, 254–55; humanities and, 254–55; Jacobinism and, 194; psychology and, 116, 119–20; sense experience and, 62–63
Fairlee, Henry, 204n
Faith: conditional, 23–24; in institution, 24, 30–37; unconditional, 23, 24–30. *See also* Authority; Religion
Fallacies, logical, 41–43, 119, 169–70, 228, 237
"False dilemma," 43
Falwell, Jerry, 29, 30, 169, 178
Family: blood value systems and, 88; Bloom and, 170; classical conservatism and, 199; classical liberalism and, 191, 193; fundamentalists and, 29, 32
Fantasy, 75–85
Fascism: classical conservatism and, 201, 202; MacIntyre and, 244; revolutionism and, 198; Solzhenitsyn and, 202; Southern agrarians and, 221
Fassbinder, Werner, 84
Fastidiousness, Montaigne and, 65
Faulkner, William, 248
"Faulkner factory," 248–49
Fear, as emotional category, 121n
Feeling Good (Burns), 120
Feelings, vs. emotions, 86–87
Feminism: Bloom and, 170–71; relevance and, 255

Fennelly, Carol, 93
Ferraro, Geraldine, 90, 191
Fight-or-flight response, 121
Finance: lawyers and, 208. *See also* Economics
First Amendment, 180
Forbidden City, China, 197
Formality, Montaigne and, 64–65
Forrester, Jay, 125–26
France: Bastille fall in, 197; Catholics in, 36
Francis, St., 160, 232
Freedberg, Sidney, 253
Freedom, 9; classical liberalism and, 190, 191–92; conservatism and, 200, 202; Jacobinism and, 194; legalism and, 207; logical/emotive conservatism and, 244. *See also* Liberalism
Freud, Anna, 113
Freud, Sigmund, 113, 114, 118, 120, 169–70
Freudian psychology, 112–18, 169–70, 237, 251–52
Friedman, Milton, 213
Fuller, Buckminster, 223–24
Fuller, Kathryn, 225
Fundamentalism, 185; Barth and, 142, 143–44, 146; Catholic, 30, 36; and creation, 160, 181; nonreligious, 203–4; Protestant, 24, 25–36, 63, 142, 143–44, 146
Fundamentals, 26
Fussell, Paul, 255
Fustianism, 41–42

Gandhi, Mohandas, 117, 153–55
Genes, values and, 8
Genesis, 181
Gilder, George, 29
God: arguments for existence of, 49; authority and, 24, 26; Barth and, 143–44; logical naturalism and, 226; logical subjectivism and, 234–36, 239–40; secular humanism and, 177–78; Spinoza and, 49, 225. *See also* Religion

Goethe, J. W. von, 49–50
Good: capitalism and, 214; Jacobinism and, 193–94; logical intuitionism and, 230–31; logical subjectivism and, 237
Goodman, Ellen, 122
Gorbachev, Mikhail, 90–91, 210
Gordon, George, 253–54
Gorgias (Plato), 149
Gotama, 147–49, 151–52
Gould, Stephen Jay, 127
Government: Adler and, 50; and capitalism, 211–12; Catholic church and, 33–35; classical conservatism and, 202, 203; fundamentalists and, 29
Graham, Billy, 27
"Great games," mandarinism and, 205
Greek ideal, 242–44
Grenada, 90
Guinness, Alec, 14
Gula, Robert, 41–42

Hanks, Tom, 173, 174
Hannibal, 69
Happiness: as emotional category, 121n; logical naturalism and, 226, 228
Hard work: capitalism and, 211; Montaigne and, 65–67, 71
Harrington, Michael, 216–18
Harrod, Roy, 214
Hart, Gary, 204
Harvard, 182–83, 198
Hayek, Friedrich, 212–13
Hearing, sense experience of, 53–55
"Hedonic calculus," 226
Helmholtz, Hermann von, 100–101
Henry III, 57
Henry of Navarre (Henry IV), 58
Hermeneutics, 250n
Hiddenness: of knowledge, 112, 131, 246; of values, 158–59
Himmler, Heinrich, 209
History, 256; (A.) Bloom and, 172;

emotive value systems based on, 91; logical/emotive conservatism and, 242–44; "scientific" criticims and, 252, 253
Hitler, Adolf, 45, 96, 193, 209
Hittleman, Richard, 44
Holy Office of the Inquisition, 32
Horney, Karen, 119
Humanism, 29, 177-81
Humanist, 177, 178
Humanist Manifesto, 177–78
Humanities courses: and "science," 159–60, 183n, 246; values in, 246–56
Humanity, emotive value systems based on, 91
Humans: fundamentalist view of, 28; Montaigne's view of, 67. *See also* Individual; Social order
Hume, David: Buddhism and, 148; and defense theory, 117–18; and logical naturalism, 225, 228, 229; and logical subjectivism, 235; MacIntyre and, 242–43; and Spinoza, 49, 225
Humor: as defense, 116, 118n; Gandhi and, 154–55
Huxley, Aldous, 106
Hypochondria, as defense, 114, 118n

I'll Take My Stand, 221
India, and logic, 44
Individual: Adler and, 50; logical/emotive Jacobinism and, 241, 242
Individualism: classical conservatism and, 199, 200; classical liberalism and, 192, 206; communitarianism and, 224; entrepreneurialism and, 206; logical/emotive conservatism and, 243–44; of logical intuitionism, 232; Social Darwinism and, 210
Industrialism, 218–19, 223, 224
Inequality: capitalism and, 212, 217
"Inner space," 105, 106

Instincts, vs. values, 7–8
Institutions: Christian, 24, 29, 30–37; classical conservatism and, 199, 200, 201; entrepreneurialism, and 207; Jacobinism and, 193; liberalism and, 191, 193; mandarinism and, 204, 205–6, 207. *See also* Church; Family; State
Intellectualization, as defense, 115, 117, 118n
Interdisciplinary studies, 255
Internal dialogue, 119
"Introverts," 8
Intuition, 10–11, 12, 14, 98–108, 141; Barth and, 142, 146; Bloom and, 171; brain and, 186; defenses and, 117n; divine revelation as, 13; eight steps in developing, 100–104; Einstein and, 146–47, 153; and emotion, 100, 101, 153–54, 160; Gandhi and, 153, 154, 155; Gotama and, 147–48; identifying mode of, 17; logical, 229–34; logical subjectivism, and 238, 239–41; migration of, 161; and "science," 109, 111, 140, 141; summarized, 138–39
Iran, Khomeni in, 90
Israel, Meir and, 156

Jacobinism, 193–96; classical conservatism and, 202; economic, 202–3, 211; logical/emotive, 241–42; neo-, 202–3
James, William, 150
Japan: and logic, 44; ritual suicide in, 8
Jews, 155–57; fundamentalist Protestants and, 27; Hitler and, 45; Orthodox, 24. *See also* Judaism
Johannine Daist Communion, 24–25
John Paul II, Pope, 33, 36, 169
Johnson, Barbara, 248
Johnson, Lyndon, 216
Johnson, Paul, 127
Judaism: Adler and, 50; and logic, 44, 155; MacIntyre and, 244; Meir's, 155–57

Jung, Carl, 8

Kant, Immanuel, 49, 225
Kapor, Mitch, 100
Kennan, George, 192
Kennedy, John, 216
Kennedy, Ted, 193
Keynes, John Maynard, 99–100, 213–14, 229–33
Khadafi, Colonel, 90
Khomeni, Ayatollah, 90
Kibbutz, Meir and, 156–57
King, Martin Luther, Jr., 117
Kissinger, Henry, 202, 204–6
Kissinger, Walter, 206
Knowledge: hidden, 112, 131, 246; technical, 131, 171–72, 223–24, 246
Knox, John, 26
Kristol, Irving, 188
Kurtz, Paul, 177

Language: humanities and, 247. *See also* Linguistic philosophy; Literacy studies; Literary criticism
Laughing Man magazine, 25
Law, religion of, 207–8
"Leather jacket" art criticism
Leavis, F. R., 249
Legalism, 207–8
Leichty, Eric, 247
Lenin, V. I., 214
Leninism, 190, 201, 214–15
Levine, Thelma, 43
Liberalism: classical, 189–93, 202, 203, 206, 207, 208, 210–11; contemporary, 202–3; MacIntyre and, 243–44; utopian, 193–94 (*See also* Jacobinism)
Liberty. *See* Freedom
Libya, Khadafi in, 90
License, prodigals and, 75, 83
Lincoln, Abraham, 74, 75
Lind, William S., 204
Linguistic philosophy, 238
Lippmann, Walter, 19–20, 31, 193–94
Literacy studies, 255

Literary criticism, 247–49, 250–54, 255
Literature, 256; criticism, 247–49, 250–54, 255; deconstuctionism and, 250–51; philosophy as, 238–39
Locke, John, 172
Logic (deductive), 10, 12, 14, 38–52, 141, 186; and Age of Reason, 160; Bacon and, 160; Barth and, 142; Bloom and, 169–70; Buddhism and, 148; defenses and, 117n; as dominant personal value, 43–46; in education, 182–83, 189, 225, 246; Einstein and, 152, 153; and emotion, 94–95, 197; four tools of, 39–43; Francis (St.) and, 160; in humanities courses, 246; identifying mode of, 16; and intuition, 107–8, 229–34, 238, 239–41; Jacobinism and, 194, 241–42; lapsed Christians and, 191; Meir and, 155; migration of, 161; Montaigne and, 59–61, 71; in moral philosophy courses, 225; naturalist, 225–29; negative form of, 46; in political philosophy/political science courses, 189; religion of, 46–52, 160, 225; and "science," 109, 116, 117–18, 119–20, 127–28, 140, 234, 238; subjectivist, 234–47; summarized, 136
Love, logical intuitionism and, 230
Luther, Martin, 26, 27, 31, 142–43
Lytle, Andrew, 220, 221

McCarthy, Joe, 201
McGovern, George, 193, 217
MacIntyre, Alastair, 242–44
Macmillan, Harold, 199
McPherson, William, 249
Maimonides, 155
Malula, Cardinal, 32
Management, "science" and, 131
Mandarinism, 204–6, 207, 212
Mao Tse Tung, 210n, 214
Marx, Karl, 112n, 216
Marxism: Bloom and, 169; in class-

room, 189–90, 218; logical intuitionism and, 232; logical subjectivism and, 237; "scientific" criticism and, 252; Solzhenitsyn and, 201. See also Leninism
Materialism: Einstein and, 146–47; logical naturalism and, 227
Matthiesen, Leroy, 35–36
May, John, 37
Meditation: Bloom and, 171; Gandhi and, 154; and intuition, 103–4, 105
Meiji Restoration, 44
Meir, Golda, 155–57
Memoirs (Williams), 82–83
Mencken, H. L., 220
Menzel, Paul, 245
Merhavia, Kibbutz, 157
Merton, Thomas, 31, 76, 107, 123, 149
Meslier, Jean, 158–59
Middle Ages, economics in, 212
Middle class, Montaigne and, 64–65
Migrations, of values, 161–63
Mikulski, Barbara, 193
Mill, John Stuart, 227–28, 229
Miller, Henry, 79, 100
Mind: Bloom and, 171; Buddhism and, 150–51
Miracles, Gotama and, 151–52
Modernism: Barth and, 142–43, 146; Bloom and, 172; fundamentalists and, 30, 31–32; Solzhenitsyn and, 201
Money, 213–14, 215–16. See also Finance
Montaigne, Michel de, 55–69; Bloom and, 172; and emotive value system, 95–96; and humanities, 253, 254; objections to, 69–75; and prodigality, 75, 79
Moore, G. E., 229, 230–33, 235
Moral philosophy courses, values in, 225–46
Moral qualities: of capitalism, 211. See also Values
"Moral reasoning" courses, 182–83
Mother Teresa, 27
Moynihan, Daniel, 191

Nader, Ralph, 194, 196
Naif, 79
National Conference of Catholic Bishops, 33–34
National Council for the Social Sciences, 179
National Institute of Education, 180
Nationalism: Catholic church and, 30, 35–36; emotive value system and, 88, 89–91, 96; fundamentalists and, 29, 30, 35
Naturalism, logical, 225–29
Natural selection, 127
Nazis, 209
Negative logic, 46
Negative thinking, 119–20
Nehru, Jawaharlal, 154
Nehru, Motilal, 154
Neighborhood, value systems of blood and, 88, 89
Nelson, Richard, 81
Neuromedicine, 121–25
Neuropsychologists, 186
New criticism, 249
New Right, 203, 204
Newsweek, 26, 122
Newton, Isaac, 99
Nicaragua, Sandinistas in, 90
Nichomachean Ethnics (Aristotle), 243
Nietzsche, Friedrich, 169, 172, 185
Nin, Anaïs, 186
Nisbet, Robert, 128
Nonsense (Gula), 41–42
Nothing in Common, 173
Nozick, Robert, 242

Objectivity, 17–19, 183, 188
Observation, 9, 107–8. See also Empirical reasoning
Obsessions, Montaigne and, 65–67
Okun, Arthur, 217
"One Night" (Cavafy), 82
Ontology, 49, 95–96
Other America (Harrington), 216
Oversimplification, 128
Owsley, Frank, 219, 221

Pali Canon, 148, 152
Pantheism, 49
Parfit, Derek, 239–41
Parker, Barbara, 177
Passive-aggression, as defense, 114–15, 117, 118n
Pastoral Letter on Catholic Social Teaching and the U.S. Economy, 33–34, 35
Pastoral Letter on War and Peace, 35
Pater, Walter, 75
Patience, capitalism and, 211
Patriotism, 253–54. See also Nationalism
Peck, M. Scott, 88
Peer pressure, and values, 9
Pence, Gregory, 122
Pentecostals, 36
People magazine, 255
People for the American Way, 177
Perfection, Spinoza and, 48–49
Personalities, values and, 8
Philip of Macedonia, 243
Philosophical Mistakes (Adler), 149–50
Philosophy, 18; education in, 184, 189–210, 225–46; as intermediary, 239; linguistic, 238; as literature, 238–39; moral, 225–46; political, 189–210. See also Religion; Values
Physical exercise, and intuition, 102–3
Physics, 146–47
Pilgrim Fathers, 26, 180
Plato, 20, 149, 232
Pleasure: Bloom and, 169; fundamentalists and, 29, 63; logical naturalism and, 226–28, 229; Montaigne and, 63–64
Polanski, Roman, 84
Political action, Catholic church and, 33–34, 36–37
Political criticism, 253–54
Political philosophy/political science courses, values in, 189–210
Political values, 90–91, 189–210, 242, 243. See also Conservatism; Liberalism
Pol Pot, 214

Populism: agrarian, 222–23; cultural conservatism and, 204; Jerry Brown and, 195
Postmodernism, 187
Poverty, 211–12, 216, 217–18
Power: diffusion of economic, 211–12, 213; "science" and, 131; Social Darwinism and, 208, 209, 210n
Preface to Morals (Lippmann), 19–20
Presley, Elvis, 84
Pretense, Montaigne and, 64–65
Prichard, H. A., 233–34, 242
Pride, Montaigne and, 64–65
Priests, 18
Principia Ethica (Moore), 230, 232
Pritchard, William, 255
Privacy, six modes and, 15
Problem solving, 131, 179
Prodigality, 75–85, 172, 173, 174, 246
Professionalism, humanities and, 246
Profligate, 82–83
Projection, as defense, 114, 118n
Prospero's Cell (Durrell), 77–79
Protestants, fundamentalist, 24, 25–36, 63, 142, 143–44, 146
Psychoanalysis. *See* Freudian psychology
Psychology, 141, 150; behavioral, 129–31; Bloom and, 172–73; cognitive, 52, 118–20; Freudian, 112–18, 169–70, 237, 251–52; schools and, 180–81; social, 18
Psycho-neuro-immunological medicine, 121–23
Psychotherapy East and West (Ajaya), 141
Puritanism: secular, 203–4; Social Darwinism and, 210

Quakers, 35

Rabin, Shalom, 155
Race, emotive value systems based on, 91
Ramakrishna, 104

Ramana Maharshi, 106
Ransom, John Crowe, 221
Ratzinger, Cardinal, 32
Rawls, John, 241–42
Reaction formation, as defense, 115, 118n
Reader response theorists, 250n
Reagan, Ronald, 175, 176, 195; and capitalism, 211; classical liberalism of, 202; contemporary conservatism of, 202; cultural conservatism and, 203; and emotive values, 90
Realism: Buddhism and, 148; classical conservatism and, 202; Einstein and, 153; Jerry Brown and, 195; "science" and, 131
Reasons and Persons (Parfit), 239–40
Rebellion, 75–85. *See also* Prodigality
"Reflective judgment," 184, 185
Reformation, Protestant, 26, 27, 29, 31
Reich, Wilhelm, 112–13
Relativism, 46, 171, 178
"Relaxation response," 103–4
Relevance: Bloom and, 171; fallacies and, 42; humanities and, 255, 256
Religion, 186–87; agrarianism as, 220–21; Barth and, 143–45; behavioral psychology as, 129–31; of capitalism, 213–14; classical liberalism as, 192; communism and, 214–15; of Einstein, 152–53; of emotion, 93–97, 160, 190, 197; Gotama and, 148; of intuition, 148, 160; of law, 207–8; of liberty, 190; of logic, 46–52, 160, 225; of logical intuitionism, 230–33; Montaigne and, 60; schools and, 180–81, 183, 184; and "science," 111–12, 126–31, 141, 184; "scientific," 112; of sense experience, 160, 246; of Social Darwinism, 208–10; sociobiology as, 126–29; sociologist of, 160; of usefulness, 229. *See also* Buddhism; Christianity; Judaism; Shinto; Values
Religion in the Secular City (Cox), 141

Religious Right, 203–4
Remarriage, after divorce, 32
Rensberger, Boyce, 146
Repression, as defense, 115, 118n
Reproduction, 127, 153
Republican Party, 202, 204
Research discipline: behavioral psychology as, 129; sociobiology as, 126
Revolutionism, 210n; American, 197n; violent, 197–98
Richards, I. A., 249
Rigidity, Montaigne and, 65
Robertson, Pat, 162–63
Robinson, A. E. G., 100
Roman Catholic church. See Catholic Church
Romantic escapist, 77–79
Rorty, Richard, 239
Rose, Pete, 209
Rosovsky, Henry, 182
Rourke, Mickey, 173
Rousseau, Jean-Jacques, 172
Rousseauism, 172, 193–94. See also Jacobinism
Russell, Bertrand, 45, 188; classical liberalism and, 191–92; and intuition, 98; and logical naturalism, 228; as logical subjectivist, 234, 236, 237–38; and Montaigne, 69
Russia: economics in, 212; Solzhenitsyn and, 201–2; Winter Palace storming in, 197. See also Soviet Union

Sacred Congregation for the Doctrine of the Faith, 32
Sadness, as emotional category, 121n
Saint Laurent, Yves, 81
Sakya Muni, 151
Salvation, exclusive, doctrine of, 27
Sandinistas, 90
Sankara, 107
Savings ethic: capitalism and, 211–12; democratic socialism and, 217
Sawan Kirpal Ruhani Mission, 105–6

Schaeffer, Francis, 29
Schizoid fantasy, as defense, 114, 118n
Schools. See Education
"Science," 9, 11, 12, 14, 109–31, 141, 174, 185, 186; agrarians and, 223; authority and, 140–41; Barth and, 142; Bloom and, 171–72, 174; Cohen and, 176–77; defined, 109–10; education and, 159–60, 178–81, 183, 184, 189, 190, 246; exact, 110; fundamentalists and, 32; and humanities, 159–60, 183n, 246; identifying mode of, 17; inexact, 111; logical subjectivism and, 234, 238; migration of, 161–62; in political philosophy/political science courses, 189, 190; pseudo-, 111, 129, 131; quasi-, 111; summarized, 139–40
"Scientific" criticism, 251–53
Scipio, the younger, 69
Scott, Walter, 219
Sebeok, Thomas A., 250
Secrets of nature, 131
Secular City (Cox), 141
Secular humanism, 29, 177–81
Secular puritanism, 203–4
Seeing, sense experience of, 53–55
Self: Buddhism and, 151; schools and, 181
Self-discipline: Bloom and, 172; capitalism and, 211; Christian, 28–29, 67; Gandhi and, 154; and intuition, 102, 103n; sense experience and, 67–68, 75, 82, 83, 246
Self-education, Bloom and, 172
Self-hypnosis, and intuition, 104
Self-improvement, "science" and, 131
Selfishness: liberalism and, 192; logical naturalism and, 226; of Montaigne, 71–72; Parfit and, 239; Social Darwinism and, 208, 209
Self-preservation. See Survival
Self-reliance, Montaigne and, 68, 72
Semiotics, 249–50

Sense experience, 9, 10, 12, 14, 53–85, 86, 141, 174, 185; and Age of Reason, 160; Barth and, 142; Bloom and, 172–73, 174; defenses and, 117n; described, 53; divine revelation as, 13; Einstein and, 146, 153; and emotive value system, 95–96, 160, 253; high, 55–69, 72–77, 246; and humanities courses, 246, 253, 254; identifying mode of, 16; lapsed Christians and, 191; lessons of, 62–63; logical naturalism and, 225, 229; logical subjectivism and, 238; migration of, 161; in political philosophy/political science courses, 189, 190; prodigal alternative to, 75–85, 172, 173, 174, 246; and "science," 109; six modes known through, 12n; summarized, 136–37

Seriousness of purpose, Montaigne and, 65–67

Seven Storey Mountain (Merton), 76

Sex, 8; Freudian psychology and, 112–13, 251–52; fundamentalists and, 32; legalism and, 207–8; literary criticism and, 251–52; logical intuitionism and, 230; Montaigne and, 64, 67

Shinto, and logic, 44

Shklar, Judith, 192, 244

Simeon Stylites, 29

Singapore, capitalism of, 211

Singer, Isaac Bashevis, 280

Sixty Minutes, 92

Skepticism: Buddhism and, 148; cultural conservatism and, 204; fundamentalists and, 32; humanities and, 246–47

Skinner, B. F., 130–31

Slavery, 180, 219, 220

Smith, Adam, 188

Smith, Ronald, 179

Smith, Timothy L., 180

Smithsonian Magazine, 109

Snow, C. P., 160

Snyder, Mitch, 92–93, 96

Social activism: logical intuitionism and, 232; Snyder and, 92–93, 94. *See also* Political action

Social anarchy, 46

Social commitment, humanities and, 246

Social control: behavior psychology and, 130; liberalism and, 203. *See also* Government

Social Darwinism, 208–10

Social ideologies, 90–91; 189–210. *See also* Economics; Political values; Social activism

Socialism, 218; democratic, 216–18, 242

Social order: classical conservatism and, 200, 201, 202; logical/emotive conservatism and, 243; logical/emotive Jacobinism and, 241. *See also* Community, Social control; Social ideologies; Tribe

Social pressures, and values, 9

Social psychologists, 18

Social science: identifying mode of, 17; in schools, 179–80, 183, 184. *See also* Psychology; "Science"; Sociology

Sociobiology, 126–29

Socio-demo-anthro-eco-enviro-techno model building, 125–26

Sociology: of religion, 160; "scientific" criticism by, 252–53

Socrates, 39–40, 46, 170, 187, 188, 246

Socratic questioning, 39–40, 187

Solzhenitsyn, Alexander, 159, 199–200, 201–2

"Soulcraft," 201

South America, Catholics in, 36

Southern (aristocratic) agrarianism, 219–22

South Korea, capitalism of, 211

Soviet Union: in Cold War, 116, 255; economics in, 211, 212, 214–16; Gorbachev in, 90–91, 210; Kissinger and, 205; Social Darwinism and, 210; Solzhenitsyn and, 201–2

Specialists, 18, 246

Specialization, critical, 247–49
Spengler, Oswald, 244
Spinoza, Baruch de, 47–50, 152, 225, 234–35
Stability, personal, cognitive psychology and, 120
Stanford Research Institute, 7n
"Stars," mandarinism and, 205
Star Wars, 14, 15, 87
State: classical conservatism and, 199, 201; classical liberalism and, 191, 193. *See also* Government; Nationalism
Status symbol, high sense experience as, 73–74
Stein, Herbert, 245–46
Stevenson, Charles, 234, 236–37, 238
Strachey, Lytton, 192, 230
Structuralism, semiological, 249–50
Subjectivism, logical, 234–47
Subjectivity, 17–19
Sublimation, as defense, 116, 118n
Success, capitalism and, 212–13
Suffering, Buddhism and, 149
Suicide, 198; ritual, 8; secular humanism and, 178; teen, 178
Sumerian Dictionary project, 247–48
Suppression, as defense, 116, 118n
Supreme Court, 207
Survival: emotion and, 153; instincts and, 8; Social Darwinism and, 208; sociobiology and, 127
Syllogism, 40–41, 42
Szews, Margo, 177–78

Taoism: and intuition, 107; and logic, 44
Tate, Allen, 220–22
Taxes, 212
Technical knowledge, 131, 171–72, 223–24, 246
Technocratic agrarianism, 223–24
Teleology, 49, 95–96
Thatcher, Margaret, 203
Theism, 49, 177
Thomas, St., 13
Thomas Aquinas, St., 51, 107

Thoreau, Henry David, 222
Tibet, celibacy in, 8
Tolerance: Bloom and, 171; classical liberalism and, 192; and intuition, 102; Montaigne and, 64
Torah, 155
Toynbee, Arnold, 244
Trance, and intuition, 104
Tribe, 87–97, 190; classical liberalism and, 190, 192. *See also* Community
Tropic of Cancer (Miller), 100
Tuilleries, capture of, 197
Type A, B, C behavior, 121–23, 124, 125, 152

Unconscious mind, 117, 118, 120
United States. *See* America
University Hall, Harvard students and, 198
University of Pennsylvania, 247
Updegraff, Robert, 98, 101
U.S. Bishops' Conference, 37
Utilitarianism: conservationist, 225; humanities and, 246; Jacobin, 194–96; logical naturalism and, 227, 228–29; logical subjectivism and, 239–40; Moore and, 229; negative, 228
Utopianism: classical conservatism and, 202; communist, 214–16; liberal, 193–94 (*see also* Jacobinism); in technocratic agrarianism, 224

Vaillant, George, 113–18
Value judgments, 14, 38, 61–62
Value-neutral curriculum, 175–77, 179, 181
Values, 6–20, 135–40; author's 185–88; choice of, 9–12; in classroom, 160, 175–84, 188, 189–256; combinations of, 140–57; defined, 7; economics, 210–25; hiddenness of, 158–59; humanities, 246–56; vs. instincts, 7–8; makeshift alliances among, 159–60; migrations/

conversions of, 161–63; political, 90–91, 189–210, 242, 243. *See also six individual modes*

Vitz, Paul, 180

Vivekenanda, 104

Voltaire, 63

Volunteers, 173

W, 81

Walden Pond (Thoreau), 222

Wallace, Mike, 83

Wall Street, 210

Warren, Robert Penn, 221, 249

Washington Post: on fundamentalism, 26; on Maryland businessman's values, 174; on politics, 193–94; on secular humanism, 177–78; on sense experience, 74–75; on value-neutral education, 175–76

Waste Land (Eliot), 251

Waugh, Evelyn, 85

Weakland, Archbishop, 34

Wealth: classical conservatism and, 201; fundamentalists and, 32–33; inequality in, 212

Weber, Max, 111

Welty, Eudora, 53–55, 79n

Weyrich, Paul, 203–4

White, Theodore, 210n

Will, George, 200–201

Williams, Tennessee, 77, 82–83, 85

Winning, Social Darwinism and, 208, 209

Winter Palace, Russia, 197

Wittgenstein, Ludwig, 234

Wolcott, James, 256

Wolfe, Thomas, 70

Wolff, Robert Paul, 218

Women, Catholic church and, 36

Work ethic: capitalism and, 211; Montaigne and, 65–67, 71

Work group, value systems of blood and, 88, 89

World Christian Fundamentalist Association, 28

World War I, 37

World War II, 90

Yardley, Jonathan, 248–49

Yoga: Bloom and, 171; eight steps of, 101–4, 150; Gandhi and, 155; Karma, 155

Zen Buddhism, 107

This page is a continuation of the copyright page.

Grateful acknowledgment is made for permission to reprint excerpts from the following works: *Ten Philosophical Mistakes* by Mortimer Adler. Copyright © 1985 by Mortimer J. Adler. Reprinted with permission of Macmillan Publishing Company. *Essays* by Michel de Montaigne, translated by J. M. Cohen (Penguin Classics, 1958), copyright © J. M. Cohen, 1958. Edmund Keeley and Philip Sherrard, trans. *C. P. Cavafy: Collected Poems,* ed. George Savidis, reprinted with permission of the Estate of C. P. Cavafy. Trans. copyright © 1975, by Edmund Keeley and Philip Sherrard. Excerpt pg. 55 reprinted with permission of Princeton University Press. *The Seven Storey Mountain* by Thomas Merton, copyright © 1948 by Harcourt Brace Jovanovich, Inc., and renewed 1976 by The Trustees of the Merton Legacy Trust, reprinted by permission of the publisher; British Commonwealth, © The Abbey of Our Lady of Gethsemani 1949, 1961. Reproduced by permission of Sheldon Press, London. *The Word of God and the Word of Man* by Karl Barth, translated by Douglas Horton. Copyright © 1957 by Douglas Horton; copyright © renewed 1985. Reprinted by permission of Harper & Row, Publishers, Inc. *Essays in Biography* by John Maynard Keynes, by permission of Royal Economic Society and Macmillan, London and Basingstoke, and the Subsidiary Rights Department, Cambridge University Press. *Tennessee Williams: Memoirs* by Tennessee Williams, copyright © 1972, 1975 by Tennessee Williams. Used by permission of Doubleday, a division of Bantam, Doubleday, Dell Publishing Group, Inc. *A Preface to Morals* by Walter Lippman. Copyright © 1929 by Walter Lippman; copyright renewed © 1957 by Walter Lippman. Reprinted with permission of Macmillan Publishing Co. "Students Confront Nuclear Dilemma," by Elsa Walsh; *The Washington Post,* June 10, 1985. *The Basic Writings of Bertrand Russell* by Bertrand Russell. Edited by Robert E. Egner and Lester E. Denonn, Simon & Schuster, New York, 1956, and Unwin Hyman Ltd., London. *More Memoirs of an Esthete,* by Harold Acton. Methuen & Co., London, 1970. "On the Improvement of the Understanding" from *The Chief Works of Benedict de Spinoza* by Benedict de Spinoza. Translated from the Latin with an introduction by R. H. Elwes. Dover Publications, New York, 1951. *Prospero's Cell* by Lawrence Durrell. Reprinted by permission of Faber and Faber Ltd.